Elie Wiesel and the Politics of Moral Leadership

ELIE WIESEL AND
THE POLITICS
OF MORAL LEADERSHIP

MARK CHMIEL

Temple University Press
PHILADELPHIA

Temple University Press, Philadelphia 19122
Copyright © 2001 by Temple University
All rights reserved
Published 2001
Printed in the United States of America

♾ The paper used in this publication meets the requirements of the American National Standard for Information Sciences—Permanence of Paper for Printed Library Materials, ANSI Z39.48–1984.

Library of Congress Cataloging-in-Publication Data

Chmiel, Mark, 1960–
    Elie Wiesel and the politics of moral leadership / Mark Chmiel.
        p. cm.
    Includes bibliographical references and index.
    ISBN 1-56639-857-6 (alk. paper)
    1. Wiesel, Elie, 1928– —Political and social views.   I. Title.

PQ2683.I32 Z63 2001
813'.54—dc21   00–064847

Quotations from *Against Silence* (1985) reprinted with the permission of the United States Holocaust Memorial Museum, Washington, D.C., from the book *Against Silence: The Voice and Vision of Elie Wiesel*, compiled and edited by Irving Abrahamson, originally published by the Holocaust Library.
  Quotations from *All Rivers Run to the Sea* by Elie Wiesel, Copyright © 1995 by Elie Wiesel. Reprinted by permission of Alfred A. Knopf, a Division of Random House, Inc.; and in the U.K. by permission of HarperCollins Publishers Ltd., U.K.
  Quotations from *And the Sea Is Never Full* by Elie Wiesel, Copyright © 1999 by Elie Wiesel. Reprinted by permission of Alfred A. Knopf, a Division of Random House, Inc.; and in the U.K. by permission of HarperCollins Publishers Ltd., U.K.
  Quotations from *From the Kingdom of Memory* by Elie Wiesel, Copyright © 1990 by Elirion Associates. Reprinted by permission of Georges Borchardt, Inc., for the author.
  Quotations from *A Jew Today* by Elie Wiesel, Copyright © 1978 by Elirion Associates, Inc. Reprinted by permission of Random House, Inc.
  Quotations from "The Jews of Silence," from the Spring 1967 issue of *Conservative Judaism*, reprinted by permission of the Rabbinical Assembly.
  Quotations from *Legends of Our Times*, by Elie Wiesel. Copyright © 1968 by Elie Wiesel. Reprinted by permission of Georges Borchardt, Inc., for the author.

For Pat Geier and Marc Ellis

We come immediately after a stage of history in which millions of men, women, and children were made to ash. Currently, in different parts of the earth, communities are again being incinerated, tortured, deported. There is hardly a methodology of abjection and of pain which is not being applied somewhere, at this moment, to individuals and groups of human beings. Asked why he was seeking to arouse the whole of Europe over the juridical torture of one man, Voltaire answered, in March 1762, "c'est que je suis homme." By that token, he would, today, be in constant and vain cry.

—George Steiner, *In Bluebeard's Castle: Some Notes towards the Redefinition of Culture*

Contents

Preface

ike many American Christians, my first acquaintance with the Holocaust was through the work of Elie Wiesel. As an undergraduate, I read Wiesel's memoir, *Night*,[1] in a course entitled Theology and Modern Literature with Professor George Kilcourse at Bellarmine College (Louisville, Kentucky) in the spring of 1982. My youthful sense of Christian innocence was interrogated by Wiesel's haunting recounting of the horrors inflicted on the Jewish people in "civilized" Europe. Even as I was at the same time discovering the engaged Catholic tradition of such women and men as Dorothy Day and Daniel Berrigan, I realized through Wiesel that Christianity had a tremendous amount of transformation ahead of it.

After college, through my friendship with Rev. Jim Flynn and Rev. Joe Graffis, I became involved in grassroots ministry at two Catholic parishes in Louisville, Saint William and the Church of the Epiphany. There, my friends and I became involved in a variety of church-based initiatives in solidarity with Central Americans, which led our communities into opposition with U.S. foreign policy throughout the 1980s. We offered sanctuary to El Salvadoran refugees, traveled to Nicaragua with Witness for Peace, and pledged to resist any U.S. intervention in Nicaragua. Later, I was drawn to relate this ministry and activist work to a course of study at the Maryknoll School of Theology. I worked with the young Jewish theologian Marc Ellis and considered anew the challenges posed by the Holocaust to Christianity.[2] At that time, I could appreciate the struggles of some older Christian thinkers who wrestled with the anti-Semitism of the Christian tradition and sought new ways forward. To indicate the utter centrality of the Holocaust to his own religious identity, Harry James Cargas took to describing himself as a "post-Auschwitz Catholic."[3] Protestant ethicist John Roth believed that Christians needed to learn to "become more Jewish" and become immersed in the wisdom and ethics of the tradition so long demeaned by Christianity.[4] Theologian Robert McAfee Brown argued that Christians need to pay attention to the "madmen" and prophets such as Elie Wiesel, who might sensitize us to the injustices around us.[5] I was challenged a great deal by these people who struggled to confront what Albert Camus once called "the blood-stained face history has taken on today." Studying with Dr. Ellis and continuing to read more of Wiesel's work led me to discover part of my own heritage, Jewish, in fact, on my father's side. In getting to know my great-aunt, I heard for the first time stories about the part of my father's family that left Russia early in the twentieth century.

While at Maryknoll, I was not only focusing on the agonies of the Holocaust period but also learning of progressive movements within the American Jewish community such as *Tikkun*, which, like my Catholic communities in Kentucky, were attempting to integrate spirituality, solidarity, and social analysis.[6] Through my work with Dr. Ellis and subsequent travel to the Middle East, I also came to appreciate the struggle of some Jews and Christians who were speaking out on behalf of Palestinians oppressed by the Israeli government, backed by the United States. During the intifada, I, along with other U.S. theologians, visited Palestinians in the Occupied Territories and were amazed at their courage and commitment in the struggle for independence.[7]

These particulars of my own journey—a self-critical perspective on Christianity, grassroots activism in opposition to U.S. foreign policy, Jewish affinities, an awakening to the suffering and resistance of the Palestinians—strongly influence the current work, which focuses on the crucial theme of solidarity in the work of Elie Wiesel. Wiesel has provided important challenges to me and many Christians with his testimony and criticism: The liturgy, Scriptures, and doctrines could not be viewed the same after the disturbing encounter with this Jewish "Other." In this book, I do not attend to these religious issues— addressed thoughtfully and thoroughly by many other Christian theologians in recent decades—but rather on the contemporary political challenges that we Christians, Jews, and other citizens face regarding the policies of the United States and our allies.

One Catholic theologian who has managed to make a constructive and critical bridge among Jews, Christians, and Palestinians is the American feminist Rosemary Radford Ruether. A strong critic of Christian anti-Semitism and Israeli domination of the Palestinians, Ruether urged that "[d]ialogue and solidarity between Christians and Jews today cannot be based solely on the innocent victim–guilty victimizer relation of the remembered pogroms and death camps. It must be a mutually self-critical collaboration of peoples, both of whom know that they are capable of abuse of power. Each are seeking to regain their prophetic voice toward injustice, both in their own societies and in relation to each other."[8] In this book, I take Elie Wiesel seriously by entering into a critical dialogue with his work and by seeking to regain a prophetic voice toward the injustice and abuse of power by the U.S. government in much of the third world. Many friends, acquaintances, and teachers have sometimes been unwitting collaborators in this book, by virtue of their many insights and inspiring work. Still, on many levels, writing this book has been an exacting and chastening experience. For although Elie Wiesel is the subject, the questions I pose and the issues I explore have a broader pertinence to us as intellectuals and citizens as we confront the global economy and ongoing ethnic cleansing and the consequent expendable peoples of both in the twenty-first century.

Acknowledgments

The Dominican preacher Meister Eckhart once stated, "If the only prayer you say your entire life is 'Thank you,' that would suffice." Many people helped me in the long period of producing this work and they have my great thanks.

Elie Wiesel was kind enough to meet with me when he was between lectures and meetings in St. Louis in October 1996. Harry James Cargas helped secure that meeting and he shared many hours speaking with me about remembrance and responsibility. In Palo Alto and Berkeley, Robert McAfee Brown generously discussed his own insights about and experiences with Elie Wiesel. Noam Chomsky provided stimulating reflections on ethics and intellectuals in corresponding with me on this project and other matters. As scholar-in-residence at Washington University's Catholic Student Center, John F. Kavanaugh, S.J., invited me to give a series of lectures on Elie Wiesel and Noam Chomsky in the fall of 1997. And my teacher Marc H. Ellis shared his vision of solidarity and nurtured me in many ways, up close and at a distance. His challenge and support have been indispensable to the birth of this book.

John Coleman, S.J.; Marie Giblin; Otto Maduro; Bill O'Neill, S.J.; Carol Robb; and Barry Stenger, my teachers at the Maryknoll School of Theology and the Graduate Theological Union, impressively synthesized the work of scholarship and social change. Also, my own students have shared with me their passion for learning and life, which reinvigorates my own: Cris Araighi; Robert Ard; Kevin Born; Bill Duffield; Christine Dupiche; Kevin Foy; Marlene Guth; Elizabeth Hadland; Bo Han; Michelle Hankins; Dan Horkheimer; Brian Horton; Mariah Howard; Colleen Jameson; Emily Johnson; Jamar Johnson; Chris Kaufman; Nicole Kinen; Vito Krischke; Jamie Lippert; Kara Lubischer; Jessica McMichael; Dana Naughton; Erin Nealon; Michael Onu, S.J.; Kara Picirilli; Katy Schluge; Eric Sears; Paul Spitzmueller; Tricia Stackle; and Tanya Usher-Moser. I am also grateful to my colleagues at Webster University, Saint Louis University, and the Aquinas Institute of Theology for their collegiality and support: Julie Birkenmaier; Mary Boles; Robert Goss; Julie Hanlon Rubio; Cathy Heidemann; Diane Kennedy, O.P.; Dennis Klass; Belden Lane; J.J. Mueller, S.J.; Ron Modras; Chris Parr; and Bill Shea.

Friends and colleagues who read earlier versions of this work or engaged me in wide-ranging discussions on these issues include Lilia Azevedo; Jerome Baggett; Daniel Berrigan, S.J.; John Dear, S.J.; Nina Diamond; Jim Douglass; Polly and Danny Duncan-Collum; Mary Dutcher; Hedy Epstein; Charlotte Fonrobert; Angela Graboys; Lucy Lee Helm; Dan Hoffmann; Rob Henke; Jack Jezreel; Bill Jordan; Bob Lassalle-Klein; Edward T. Linenthal; Rick "Mugsy" Malloy, S.J.; Patrick Murray; Esther Neuwirth; Sharon McMullen Orlet; Kathryn Poethig; Jim Reale; Ellen Rehg; Suzanne Renard; Lenore Salvaneschi; Jeannie Schuler; Naomi Seidman; Don Steele; Libby Wood; Richard Wood; Joao Xerri, O.P.; and K.C. Young, O.P.

Over the years, I've been fortunate to know people who have worked tirelessly in the struggle for human rights. True mensches and compañeras in the broader activist community (Louisville, Berkeley, Saint Louis, Palestine, Guatemala, and Brazil) whose work and activism have informed and challenged my own are Maria Goreth Barradas, Toinha Lima Barros, Dennis Bricking, Christy Finsel, Jim Flynn, Ivone Gebara, David Horvath, Christy Huck, Pierre LaBoussiere, Nancy LaLeau, Mary Kate MacIsaac, Christobhal Mayorga, Patrick McCarthy, Mary Ann McGivern, Bill Ramsey, Marla Schrader, Mira Tanna, Anne Tresedor, Anne Walter, and Michael Whiting. The core community of the Center for Theology and Social Analysis has welcomed me and found many creative ways to embody a more just and inclusive future now: Jean Abbott, Gwen Crim, Louise Lears, Angie O'Gorman, Mark Scheu, Joe Wright, and Mary Wuller. Dear friends in the St. Louis Karen House Catholic Worker community have energized me with their dedication and hospitality: Courtney Barrett, Teka

Childress, Colleen Etling, Rebekah Hassler, Tony Hilken, Tim Pekarek, Annjie Schiefelbein, Fernando Sorolla, Jenny Truax, and Rodney Yarnal.

Doris Braendel, Tamika Hughes, Jennifer French, and Lois Patton at Temple University Press were extremely supportive throughout this long process. Dave Updike and Jean Anderson contributed their savvy production and copy-editing skills to this project. The library staff at Saint Louis University regularly offered cheerful and efficient assistance. Peter A. Puleo, Jr., and Joe Angert gave timely and indispensable aid with computers and printers. Jenny Truax also did helpful research amid the stacks and microfilm at Saint Louis University.

Drs. Jerry and Mary Wuller provided abundant financial and moral support, which sustained me at a critical juncture. My Chmiel and Puleo families in Louisville and Saint Louis gave me vital emotional, social, and financial assistance. Steve Kelly, S.J., shared lively letters from jail during the writing of this book; his refusal to sit still is testimony to his fidelity to people who suffer from war and injustice. Sheri Hostetler has discussed these issues with me in innumerable conversations from Cambridge to Berkeley; her deep insight and compassion have often left me amazed. Pat Geier has been a trusted confidante, resourceful travel partner, gentle activist, and best friend; she has taught me the meaning of accompaniment. Joanie French, *donna gentile* extraordinaire, consistently offered me a receptive ear and a discerning eye. From our first meetings in 1988 at Maryknoll, Mev Puleo inspired me to go deeper: in writing, learning, engaging, and loving. Throughout our marriage, she lived out a deep faith and commitment, even through her acute suffering with a brain tumor from 1994 to her death in 1996. Her memory is a blessing and an invitation to ever-deeper solidarity.

ELIE WIESEL AND THE POLITICS OF MORAL LEADERSHIP

The Jewish Remembrancer
A Political Reading

If only I could recapture my father's wisdom, my mother's
serenity, my little sister's innocent grace. If only I could
recapture the rage of the resistance fighter, the suffering of the
mystic dreamer, the solitude of the orphan in a sealed cattle
car, the death of each and every one of them. If only I could
step out of myself and merge with them. If only I could hold
my memory open, drive it beyond the horizon, keep it alive
even after my death. I know it isn't possible. But what of it? In
my dreams the impossible is not a Jewish concept.

—Elie Wiesel, *All Rivers Run to the Sea: Memoirs*

The struggle of man against power is the struggle of memory
against forgetting.

—Milan Kundera, *The Book of Laughter and Forgetting*

magine two encounters. The first is of a young, diffident Jewish man, living in Paris, eking out a living as a journalist, meeting with a famous French novelist. For a story his newspaper
wants him to write, the journalist is attempting to gain access
to the French Prime Minister, for he knows that the novelist
is intimate with the powerful leader. The year is 1954, the
journalist is Elie Wiesel, and the novelist is François Mauriac,
and their meeting is charged with drama: a poor Jewish survivor of the Holocaust interviewing a renowned Catholic
writer. Elie Wiesel has written of that meeting on more than

1

one occasion and the story he recounts is how, when confronted by Mauriac's passionate devotion to Jesus, he could not suppress his own indignation at what had happened to his people under the Nazis a scant ten years earlier during World War II. He abruptly leaves Mauriac, but the startled writer pursues Wiesel and interviews him and solicits *his* story. Within a couple of years, Mauriac champions the Jewish writer's testimony about his experience in Auschwitz. Elie Wiesel's vocation as witness then begins in earnest.[1]

Now, picture another engagement, over thirty years later. At an official ceremony at the White House, President Ronald Reagan bestows upon this former journalist the Congressional Gold Medal for Lifetime Achievement. Reagan praises the now accomplished novelist and witness to the Holocaust, "Like the Prophets whose words guide us to this day, his words will teach humanity timeless lessons."[2] At this time, Reagan is involved in a controversy over an impending ceremonial visit to the Bitburg cemetery in West Germany. And on this occasion of receiving such national recognition, Elie Wiesel challenges the American President *not* to go to Bitburg, because his place should instead be with the Jewish victims, not the Nazi SS officers who are buried there.

Here, then, are two major steppingstones in Elie Wiesel's life with powerful elites, one cultural, the other political. In the former instance, Wiesel was an undistinguished journalist just looking for an inside scoop for his paper. In the latter, he had become a celebrated icon speaking up to an American president who did not quite grasp the fervor of Wiesel's commitment to Holocaust remembrance. This book deals with this amazing trajectory of Elie Wiesel, who has become the very symbol of the Holocaust tragedy in his adopted homeland of the United States. Winner of the Nobel Peace Prize in 1986, confidant of and advisor to presidents, author of forty books, Wiesel has acted as a Jewish guardian of memory and an international conscience. Even as he has expressed suspicion about politics, Wiesel has drawn on his own experience to enter the public realm as a witness to atrocity so as to awaken, sensitize, and rebuke ordinary citizens and powerful government leaders the world over.

Themes of a Life

Although Elie Wiesel had published two long volumes of memoirs in his sixties, it is true that he has been telling and retelling his life's story—

with all of its agonizing questions, hesitant responses, and modest initiatives—for more than forty years.[3] And although he has become a kind of moral hero in American culture, his existential roots are "over there" in the geography of Eastern Europe, the death camps, and the vanished world of a vibrant Judaism. In novels, essays, reportage, speeches, dialogues, cantatas, dramas, and interviews, Wiesel linked his Holocaust experience both to earlier and subsequent chapters of Jewish history. But in one of the tensions that mark Wiesel's life and work, this gravitation toward remembering the Holocaust has been matched by a desire to see Jewish history as more than just a series of unending victimizations. As a guardian of Jewish memory, Wiesel's aim has not been only that of lamentation but also that of celebration. Both modes have been joined in Wiesel's commitment to storytelling, the one done with great consternation and trepidation, the other with palpable enthusiasm and reverence.

In this section, I introduce three main themes of Wiesel's life: his childhood in a traditional Judaic culture in Eastern Europe; his traumatic experience in a Nazi death camp and his postwar trials as a survivor and refugee; and his commitment to testimony in a variety of genres.

The Judaic Tradition

In their study of American character *Habits of the Heart*, sociologist Robert Bellah and his colleagues emphasize the importance of religion and other communities of memory in fostering bonds that might resist the peculiar individualism of American culture.[4] Sociologist Edward Shils argues more generally for people in contemporary society to nurture a greater sense of tradition, which has been undermined both by modern individualism and nationalism. Shils advocates a healthy respect for "substantive traditionality," which he describes as "the appreciation of the accomplishments and wisdom of the past and of the institutions impregnated with tradition, as well as the desirability of regarding patterns from the past as valid guides."[5] Elie Wiesel's life and work have been rooted profoundly in such a substantive traditionality, namely, the Judaic community of memory.

Elie Wiesel was born on 30 September 1928 in Sighet, Transylvania, in the Carpathian mountains. The region alternately had been claimed and ruled by Romania and Hungary. Wiesel's father, Shlomo, was the owner of a grocery store and a leader in Sighet's Jewish community; he frequently was more immersed in the often-troubled daily affairs of that community than he was in his son's life. He believed it was important that his son learn modern Hebrew, one indication of the inroads that the modern world was then making into Orthodox Jewish communities.[6] His mother Sarah encouraged him to pursue a rigorous religious education and she exuded a fundamental confidence:

> The Messiah. My poor mother never ceased to demand and await his coming. He was never far from her mind. At night, as she rocked me to sleep, she would sing of her deep conviction that nothing bad would happen to her child, since the Messiah would come in time to protect him. Anti-Semites? Doomed, reduced to impotence. His merest stirring would scare them off. Military service? "Fear not, my child. There will be no more armies." My mother believed this with all her soul. The Jewish people would soon be delivered, never again sending their children to be killed for European emperors and kings.[7]

Because his father was a distant, though respected, figure, Wiesel felt closest to his mother, whom he considered "my sole ally and support. She alone understood me."[8] Along with his three sisters, Wiesel lived in the polylingual world of Romanian, Hungarian, Hebrew, and, for daily intercourse, Yiddish. Years later, Wiesel testified to his abiding affection for his mother tongue: "I love speaking that language. There are songs that can be sung only in Yiddish, prayers that only Jewish grandmothers can murmur at dusk, stories whose charm and secret, sadness and nostalgia, can be conveyed in Yiddish alone."[9]

In Sighet Wiesel grew up steeped in the Jewish religious tradition. He and his friends arose early in the morning to study the Bible and Talmud. Memorization of texts was privileged in a routine of study that went on for many hours each day. His sensibility was profoundly shaped also by the Hasidic mystical tradition inaugurated by Israel Ba'al Shem Tov in the eighteenth century. In a recent study of the Ba'al Shem Tov, Moshe Rosman contends that "[t]he historical image of the Besht has been exceptionally malleable in the service of ideology. With so little in the way of written sources, traditions could be interpreted, shaped, and rewritten to make the Besht conform to the perceived needs of contemporary reality."[10] Not surprisingly, Wiesel interprets the Hasidic movement and its founder to conform to the needs of a post-Holocaust Judaism: "Our generation resembles that of the Ba'al Shem Tov. Just as in his time, it is necessary today to build on ruins, to hold on to something—another human being, a faith. Hasidism? An antidote to resignation."[11] Wiesel's maternal grandfather Doyde Feig introduced Wiesel to the Hasidic path by

recounting the stories of the masters and their disciples: "The enchant-
ing tales of Rebbe Nahman of Bratslav, the parables of the Rebbe of
Kotzk, the sayings of the Rebbe of Rizhin, and the witticisms of the Rebbe
of Ropshitz: he knew them all, and he taught me to savor them."[12] Wiesel
also experimented audaciously with the secrets of the Jewish mystical tradition of the Kabbalah.[13] Along with his young friends, he experienced an
intense mystical yearning for salvation.[14] They met frequently with their
master, engaged in spirited incantations, and subjected themselves to
ascetic practices, such as fasting, rolling around in the snow, and maintaining strict silence. Wiesel must have appropriated his mother's love for
the Messiah, as he himself recollects, "I was convinced that every Jewish
child must either bring the Messiah or become the Messiah."[15] He was
far more attracted to sacred writings than secular subjects in school such
that his future path seemed clear: He would become a teacher in a yeshiva,
with the modest hope of writing a commentary on one of the traditional
texts. With his enthusiasm for mysticism, Wiesel paid little attention to
the political events that were then engulfing Europe: "Tragedy loomed,
but life went on. I paid little attention to the outside world. I was growing up, maturing, learning more difficult and obscure texts. Hitler's howling failed to penetrate my consciousness."[16]

Whereas other Jewish youth of his time were preoccupied with the
secular variations of messianism in Zionism and Communism, Wiesel's
own adolescent convictions were traditional and mystical, and these
continued to influence his own interpretations of contemporary social
and political events.[17] His devout love for the Jewish people was nurtured by the substantial inheritance he received in Sighet's stable community. His parents, grandfather, and teachers; the Bible, Talmud, and
Hasidism; modern and classical Hebrew and Yiddish; mysticism and
messianism—all of these contributed to the formation of Wiesel's
intensely Judaic worldview. This world of childhood has remained precious to him and often he has evaluated his adult actions by making reference to the innocent child he once was: "Sometimes I feel that the
child accompanies me, questions me, judges me."[18] In his 1995 memoir, Wiesel extended his identification with children to all those exterminated by the Nazis: "To this day I am shaken when I see a child, for
behind him I glimpse other children. Starving, terrified, drained, they
march without a backward glance toward truth and death—which are
perhaps the same."[19] Indeed, Wiesel would come to feel a lacerating
nostalgia for this world that was eradicated in the Nazis' Final Solution.

Incomparable Trauma

In his early years, Wiesel felt a special affinity for the Passover celebration. Many decades later, he wrote a commentary on the traditional ritual in which he admitted to a profound shift in his own understanding of the Seder, because Passover was the last Jewish holiday Wiesel spent with his family in Sighet before the Nazis invaded. As an adult, Wiesel recited the prayers and engaged in the rituals, but he acknowledges that "[a] lifetime separates me from the child I once was. Today I know that happiness can never be complete. The joyousness of this holiday is so tinged with melancholy that it seems more like a time of sadness."[20] After Passover 1944, Wiesel, his family, and townspeople joined millions of other European Jews in suffering the relentless cruelty of the Nazis and their accomplices.

Wiesel had been well acquainted with anti-Semitism in his hometown. Churches filled him with apprehension, and he knew that beatings of Jews were likely at Christmas and Easter. And even though Wiesel's mother maintained her fervent hope in the protective powers of the Messiah, Sighet's citizens witnessed omens of terror. As early as 1942, Wiesel's teacher, Moshe, had been deported from Sighet; he had survived a mass killing of Jews and returned to warn his people of the Nazis' murderous plans. Moshe's agitated testimony largely was ignored or dismissed by the town's Jewish population. Sighet's Jews could not believe that Hitler could eliminate Jews throughout Europe and so turned their attention to other matters, such as the hopes of diplomacy or Zionism.[21] By the spring of 1944, the Nazis began their plan to exterminate the large Jewish population of Hungary. Jews were stripped of all their rights, forced into a ghetto, and then deported to Poland. It was in the Sighet ghetto, Wiesel later marvels, that he "truly began to love the Jews of my town. Throughout the ordeal they maintained their dignity as human beings and as Jews. Imprisoned, reduced to subhuman status, they showed themselves still capable of spiritual greatness."[22]

Wiesel and his family endured the long railroad journey to a place of which they had never heard, Auschwitz. He and his father were immediately separated from his mother and three sisters. During his first night in the camp, Wiesel was shocked beyond belief to see how Jewish children were being thrown alive into burning pits. Forty years after the war ended, Wiesel gave voice to the perduring agony from that first night:

And if I bear within me a nameless grief and disillusionment, a bottomless despair, it is because that night I saw good and thoughtful Jewish children, bearers of mute words and dreams, walking into darkness before being consumed by the flames. I see them now, and I still curse the killers, their accomplices, the indifferent spectators who knew and kept silent, and Creation itself, Creation and those who perverted and distorted it. I feel like screaming, howling like a madman so that that world, the world of the murderers, might know it will never be forgiven.[23]

Wiesel worked as a slave laborer in the Auschwitz-Buna camp, often accompanied by his stoic father, whose presence was enough to keep Wiesel alive. They and the other prisoners suffered the endless affliction of beatings, meager food rations, brutal humiliations, and the ever-present specter of death in the "selections" that led to the gas chambers and crematoria. When it was clear that the Russian Army would soon overtake Auschwitz in January 1945, the Nazis forced their captives to engage in a long march through the deadly winter cold toward German soil. Countless people died from starvation, exhaustion, and beatings along the march from Auschwitz to Buchenwald, including Wiesel's father. Buchenwald finally was liberated by American troops in April 1945, and Wiesel recovered in a hospital and faced dangers even there—the U.S. soldiers did not know that to give the emaciated survivors food with fat could prove deadly.

Wiesel presumed that no one in his family had survived and the thought of returning to Sighet was more than he could bear. Upon the invitation of French General Charles de Gaulle, Wiesel and others in a contingent of young Jewish survivors accepted an offer of resettlement in France. He soon learned that his two older sisters also survived. With home now being a French orphanage, Wiesel began his life over by resuming his religious studies:

> I rededicated myself to the study of the sacred works. Spontaneously, without thinking about it, I recovered my religious fervor, perhaps as a way of closing the parentheses on my recent past. Most of all, I needed to find my way again, guided by one certainty: However much the world had changed, the Talmudic universe was still the same. No enemy could silence the disputes between Shammai and Hillel, Abbaye and Rava.[24]

He also continued his mystical quests with the itinerant genius Shushani, who was said to know thirty languages and who also taught the philosopher Emmanuel Levinas. Wiesel and his brilliant, inscrutable teacher might have spent weeks studying one page of Talmud, and it was from these exhilarating encounters in France that Wiesel admitted, "It is to him I owe my constant drive to question, my pursuit of the mystery that lies within knowledge and of a darkness hidden within light."[25] During these first years in France, he worked as a Hebrew teacher and choirmaster. In addition to maintaining this continuity with his past, Wiesel made a necessary linguistic and cultural break: He began to learn French. For Wiesel, the French language "meant a new home. The language became a haven, a new beginning, a new possibility, a new world. To start expressing myself in a new language was a defiance."[26] He studied at the Sorbonne in the late forties and discovered the postwar philosophies of Jean-Paul Sartre and Albert Camus, whose existentialist doctrines, such as humanity's inescapable decision to confer meaning in an absurd world, would later give Wiesel a resource for reckoning with the destruction of his family, hometown, and culture.[27]

It would take years before Wiesel articulated his experience of what he called the Kingdom of Night. Prior to his twentieth birthday, he had experienced being a victim intended for extermination; he had witnessed humanity's depravity and indifference; he had survived torture and hunger; he had become a refugee who could not return home because home had been destroyed; he had endured poverty as a young refugee in France; and he had faced the uncertainties and awkwardness of embracing a new language and culture. Much later, as an adult, he would affirm in no uncertain terms:

> The Holocaust was the greatest event in my life, and I think the greatest event in the life of my people, and I think the greatest event in the life of mankind. I believe that that event cannot be compared to any other, should not be compared to any other, and should not be invoked in vain. It has a special status. It is a mystery whose parallel may only be the one of Sinai when something was revealed to mankind.[28]

In this formulation, Wiesel's mystical sensibilities were joined to the experience of physical, emotional, cultural, and religious trauma. In his own study of Wiesel, Michael Berenbaum asserted, "Wiesel's fundamental experience is one of absence in a world that was once pregnant with presence. Where Wiesel formerly experienced God, he has come to encounter the void."[29] However, Wiesel claimed in his memoir, "I have never renounced my faith in God. I have risen against His justice, protested His silence and sometimes His absence, but my anger rises up within faith and not outside it."[30] Wiesel could not break with his precious patrimony and he attempted to maintain some continuity with his youthful mysticism in fidelity to his murdered family and people.[31] But in the 1950s Wiesel began to embark upon a very different world in France from the religious one that shaped him as a child and teenager.

The Duty of Testimony

With his fluency in modern Hebrew, Wiesel found employment as a Paris correspondent for an Israeli newspaper. This work afforded him many opportunities to travel, including assignments to South America, North Africa, and India. In 1954 Wiesel received an assignment to interview French Prime Minister Pierre Mendès-France. Wiesel hoped that he could gain access to the statesman through his associate, the famous novelist François Mauriac. During Wiesel's first meeting with Mauriac, the Catholic writer began to talk about his faith in Jesus. Soon, however, the normally soft-spoken Wiesel could not restrain himself. He challenged Mauriac's faith in that one Jew who had been murdered two thousand years ago and whose death still moved hundreds of millions of people worldwide, whereas, just ten years earlier, millions of Jews were murdered with scarcely a protest. Wiesel then left Mauriac, but the novelist pursued and implored Wiesel to come back and speak of his experiences. Wiesel confided that he had decided not to speak about his time in the camps until he had maintained a vow of silence for ten years after liberation; he wanted to be sure he was ready to do justice to the event. Mauriac countered, "I think that you are wrong. You are wrong not to speak. . . . Listen to the old man that I am: one must speak out."[32]

However, as Naomi Seidman pointed out in an insightful study of Wiesel's first efforts at writing-to-remember, he had already written a long manuscript in Yiddish on the events that marked the demise of his family and people.[33] Before the encounter with Mauriac, Wiesel learned that this Yiddish work had been accepted for publication in Argentina, to be published in 1956 with the title *Un di velt hot geshvign (And the World Stayed Silent)*. Eventually, Wiesel pared down his Yiddish memoir and translated it into French. Mauriac became a major advocate for the young journalist by using his own publishing contacts and authorial prestige to see that Wiesel's memoir would be published in France. Wiesel expressed gratitude:

> I owe him a lot. He was the first person to read *Night* after I reworked it from the original Yiddish. He submitted it to his own publisher, promising to write a preface for the book, to speak of it in the press, and to support it

with all the considerable means at his disposal. "No one's interested in the death camps anymore," he was told. "It won't sell."[34]

Thus, the initially disconcerting encounter with the devout French Catholic was instrumental in securing a major literary consecration for Wiesel. His memoir was published as *La Nuit* in 1958 and subsequently translated into English as *Night*. Perhaps more than any other, this volume introduced U.S. readers to the shattering effect of the death camps on a young person, his family, and faith.[35]

Throughout the 1950s, Wiesel earned his livelihood as a journalist. Often called upon to confront the great events of the day, he was frustrated with political issues, and considered himself a political naïf:

> Don't ask me how I became a journalist. I don't know. I needed to do something, so I became a reporter and managed to fool everybody. I wrote about politics but understood nothing about politics. I still don't. I wrote about anything under the sun, because I had to, without understanding what I was writing.[36]

Although Wiesel was enchanted with the new State of Israel, he did not emigrate there. Upon recovering from an accident, for which he was hospitalized in New York in 1956, he decided to begin the process of becoming a U.S. citizen. While living in New York as a UN correspondent for an Israeli paper, he also wrote for the Yiddish *Jewish Daily Forward*. In addition to this journalism, Wiesel wrote novels—*Dawn, The Accident, The Town Beyond the Wall, The Gates of the Forest*—that explored the painful realities confronting Jewish survivors of the Holocaust.[37] In 1965 Wiesel visited the Soviet Union to witness and report on the plight of the harassed Russian Jews and he worked tirelessly to mobilize the American Jewish community to take up their cause.[38] Beginning in 1966, he became a popular lecturer on the Hasidic movement (as well as the Bible, Talmud, and other Judaic themes) at the 92nd Street YMHA in New York. He eventually collected these lectures in a series of books that helped introduce this branch of Jewish mysticism to a wider American audience.[39] Although Wiesel was not immersed in the steadfast orthodoxy of the Hasidic Jews in New York, he maintained a fervent connection to the Hasidic movement, largely based on his devotion to his grandfather and his upbringing in that tradition.[40] He also began to meet weekly with the renowned scholar Saul Lieberman to study Talmud.

In the spring of 1967 the world Jewish community was shocked by

Arab threats to wipe out the Israeli Jews. That this was the second time in a generation that Jews had received a promise of impending extermination jolted the American Jewish community into giving greater public support to Israel as well as confronting the calamity of the Holocaust. When the war broke out, Wiesel traveled to Israel fearful of witnessing the final chapter of Jewish history. Instead, he was mesmerized by the swift Israeli victory and the army's capture of the Old City of Jerusalem. Because of America's enthusiasm for Israel's military prowess and the non-Jewish public's nascent recognition of the centrality of the Holocaust and Israel to Jewish life, Wiesel became an increasingly sought after speaker on cultural, religious, historical, and contemporary issues. His 1968 novel *A Beggar in Jerusalem* won the prestigious Prix Médicis, and the English translation was the first of Wiesel's novels to be reviewed widely and favorably.[41] In 1969 in Jerusalem he married Marion Rose, who became the translator of his works. In 1970 he published *One Generation After*, a collection of essays that articulated the Jewish survivor's burden of memory and the excruciating ordeal of choosing between silence—because that which was experienced in the death camps could not be expressed in speech—and testimony—at the risk of the message falling on deaf ears or being trivialized by sensation-seeking media.[42]

In the 1970s Wiesel enthusiastically identified himself with Jewish causes, especially the plight of the Jewish refuseniks in the Soviet Union. In 1972 his son was born; he decided then to work more vigorously to build a world worthy for his son to inherit, particularly by calling attention to a variety of non-Jewish issues of human suffering, from state-sponsored violence to starvation.[43] He also stopped journalistic work and embraced a new career as a professor. At City University of New York, he was Distinguished Professor of Judaic Studies from 1972 until 1976 when he became the Andrew W. Mellon Professor of the Humanities at Boston University. He maintained an arduous schedule of twelve-to-sixteen-hour workdays, in a succession of traveling, teaching, writing, and speaking. Throughout all of this productivity, Wiesel's work exemplified both a hermeneutics of suspicion and generosity.[44] Because of the enormity of Jewish suffering during the Holocaust, Wiesel maintained a suspicion toward God from within the Judaic tradition, even as he practiced a generous retrieval of that tradition, most evident in his reinterpretation of the tales of the Hasidic masters he had heard at his grandfather's side. Indeed, Wiesel's ambition was not to offer a critical perspective on these tales and teachers but rather to pay them respect and honor.[45] In the preface to *Messengers of God*, a book of commentaries on biblical figures, Wiesel affirmed his modus operandi:

> And so, faithful to his promise, the storyteller does nothing but tell the tale: he transmits what he received, he returns what was entrusted to him. His story does not begin with his own; it is fitted into the memory that is the living tradition of his people. The legends he brings are the very ones we are living today.[46]

Throughout the 1960s and 1970s, Wiesel committed himself to transmit, testify, and remember in the genres of journalism, novels, Hasidic tales, biblical narratives, and ethical commentaries. He had come full circle, trying to hold together the glories of the Jewish tradition and the ordeals of his own generation.

As Wiesel continued his propagation of remembrance in the 1970s, he extended his associations beyond fellow Jews to include Christian intellectuals. The official Catholic world had become more open to the Jewish religion after the Second Vatican Council (1962–1965) and shortly thereafter some Christians began to develop a strong critique of Christian anti-Semitism.[47] Wiesel had a profound effect on several U.S. Christian thinkers, precipitating in their lives something akin to a theological and ethical conversion. In 1978 Harry James Cargas collected testimonies from Jews and Christians as to Wiesel's import, *Responses to Elie Wiesel: Critical Essays by Major Jewish and Christian Scholars*, while Alvin Rosenfeld and Irving Greenberg added their book, *Confronting the Holocaust: The Impact of Elie Wiesel*.[48] In 1979 Christian philosopher John Roth, in his book, *A Consuming Fire: Encounters with Elie Wiesel and the Holocaust*, also testified to Wiesel's unsettling yet inspiring effect on him.[49] In 1983 Robert McAfee Brown added his study, *Elie Wiesel: Messenger to All Humanity*.[50] Thereafter, various symposia and journals were dedicated to surveying Wiesel's work and its theological, literary, and ethical implications. Sometimes seeing Wiesel as a kind of "rebbe," or Hasidic master himself, his Christian disciples played an important role in promoting his works and furthering his renown in American Christian communities.[51]

By 1978 Wiesel had become so recognized as a powerful speaker on Holocaust-related themes that President Jimmy Carter invited him to chair his Commission on the Holocaust.[52] Wiesel's charge was to lead a group of religious and civic leaders to envision an appropriate way of commemorating the European Holocaust on the national mall in Washington, DC. In this way, Wiesel's own objective of Holocaust remembrance was given powerful backing by a directive from the Executive Office. In 1979 he was appointed chairman of the U.S. Holocaust Memorial Council and thereafter played a key role in helping to establish Holocaust Remembrance Days in Washington, DC, with these annual services attracting the participation of government leaders and officials. In subsequent years, he received one award after another: the Congressional Gold Medal (1985), the Presidential Medal of Freedom (1986), and the Nobel Peace Prize (1986), all of which enhanced his fame in the United States and around the world. In these national and international distinctions, Wiesel was lauded for his pursuit of remembering the Holocaust and speaking out on behalf of contemporary victims. Such eminence gave Wiesel much greater access to media, heads of state, and the general public.

He put his Nobel Prize money to work in a Foundation for Humanity that supported various humanitarian projects. He also organized international conferences on the theme Anatomy of Hate, hoping to illumine this human penchant for domination.[53] He marched with Polish Solidarity leader Lech Walesa; conferred with Czech President Václav Havel and Soviet President Mikhail Gorbachev; and advised U.S. President Bill Clinton. He traveled to scores of universities to receive honorary doctorates and found time to continue to write novels.[54] Throughout this period, he addressed human rights issues from South Africa, Bosnia, Burma, and Tibet to Central America, Cambodia, and Vietnam. Acclaimed as a "messenger to all humanity" in McAfee Brown's honorific phrase, Wiesel achieved an unusual kind of celebrity in American culture, that of iconic witness to a twentieth-century atrocity.[55] In addition to counseling the cultural and political elite, Wiesel shared his message of morality and memory in the broader American popular culture by appearing on Oprah Winfrey's talk-show and excerpting his memoirs in the Sunday newspaper supplement *Parade Magazine*.[56]

Whether it is delivered before enthralled university audiences or the Senate Foreign Relations Committee, Elie Wiesel's public message has been rooted deeply in his own life history.[57] As a Jew, Wiesel has interpreted the world principally from his formative immersion in Judaic religiosity. As a survivor, he escaped from the Nazi attempt to make Europe *Judenrein* and he struggled to find ways to make a new life for himself in France and the United States. As a witness, he has felt compelled to challenge others to remember the Holocaust, in fidelity to the Jewish dead. In his study of how the Holocaust came to assume such a prominent place in American life, historian Peter Novick acknowledged a central place for Elie Wiesel as the emblematic survivor of the European catastrophe. Novick asked what he considered an "unanswerable question": "What would talk of the Holocaust be like in America if a skeptical rationalist like Primo Levi, rather than a religious mystic like Wiesel, had been its principal interpreter?"[58] As a venerated spokesman, Wiesel has used his acknowledged moral authority to draw attention to urgent issues of violence and suffering. In the analysis that follows, one can more fully appreciate Wiesel's strengths and limitations in his many social and political interventions by keeping in mind these biographical data of mysticism, trauma, and testimony. For, in an essay on why he writes, Wiesel noted, "I owe the dead my memory. I am duty-bound to serve as their emissary, transmitting the history of their disappearance, even if it disturbs, even if it brings pain. Not to do so would be to betray them, and thus myself."[59] It is this refusal to betray the dead that also has propelled Wiesel into social and political activism and led him to attempt to take sides with victims in opposition to their oppressors.

The Political Economy of Worthy and Unworthy Victims

Elie Wiesel's work has been examined from a variety of disciplinary viewpoints, including literary and theological studies, but there has yet to be a sustained analysis of Wiesel's mission of Holocaust remembrance and social engagement.[60] In their focus on Wiesel's challenge to Jewish or Christian theology, many writers typically read Wiesel's message and practice, its production and reception, apart from the social-political context of U.S. domestic and foreign affairs. Colin Davis came closer than many, though, in locating Wiesel politically:

> This concern with general moral issues and the attribution of universal significance to individual instances of suffering lie behind Wiesel's consistent claims to be uninterested in and ignorant about politics: "I distrust politics—moreover I don't understand anything about it"; "politics is not my field." He insists that his campaigning is ethical rather than political, and this perhaps helps to explain the uncontroversial nature of many of his interventions, at least for a Western readership. Because the position from which he speaks cannot easily be identified as, say, left- or right-wing, then both left- and right-wing readers and activists can find reason to support him: he criticizes Communist and Fascist regimes, champions the cause of

the oppressed and the rights of the individual, opposes state violence and individual acts of terrorism, and attacks Western indifference as a whole without singling out particular nations, leaders, or parties. In short, it is easy to find oneself in agreement with him.[61]

However, this study focuses on such issues as Wiesel's refusal to "single out" as well as on the political nature of many of these supposedly apolitical interventions. My aim is to analyze the stringent either/or in Wiesel's discourse, practice, and evolving social location: Either a political silence before victimization (which benefits the powerful) or a practical solidarity (which sides with the victims of power).

In their lucid study *Social Analysis: Linking Faith and Justice*, Joe Holland and Peter Henriot, S.J., identified three models of social analysis and social change: the traditional, liberal, and radical. Naturally, writers coming to Wiesel with either a liberal or conservative social analysis would make a very different interpretation and arrive at a dissimilar assessment of his work than the one offered here. The authors stressed that social analysis "never provides the complete picture. However it does offer a set of important questions that help to expose the basic contours of the reality before us."[62] The contribution of radical social analysis, these authors contended, is its systematic interrogation of the political, economic, and cultural structures of society. Such radical analysis increasingly has been used as a tool in recent religious social ethics.[63] Indeed, it has been the key, if also controversial, contribution of Latin American liberation theology to employ radical social analysis in its investigations of capitalism and third world suffering.[64] Other North American Christian theologians and ethicists have complemented their biblical, theological, and ethical tasks with radical social analysis in their studies of faith and society.[65] For example, the feminist ethicist Beverly Harrison noted in one of her essays that "the particular social theories most employed [traditionally] in religious ethics, whether informed by a neoconservative or a liberal ideology, mask the existence of the modern economy."[66]

The U.S. political analysts Noam Chomsky and Edward S. Herman have focused a great deal of their attention on the function and ethical implications of political economy in the United States.[67] Both men have been strong critics of U.S. foreign policy since the Vietnam War and have contributed their intellectual skills to popular movements organizing for social change. Chomsky has commented that such popular movements since the 1960s have helped to raise the moral level of the country by asking unprecedented critical questions about long-neglected dimensions of

U.S. history, such as the treatment of Native Americans and the persistence of U.S. intervention in the affairs of other countries.[68] In three coauthored works as well as their numerous individual studies, Herman and Chomsky have made a radical critique of what they termed the U.S. political economy of human rights and the mass media.

In a two-volume 1979 work, they described how, since World War II, the U.S. government organized under its control and protection a global system of allies and clients whose economic and military elites regularly controlled their own populations through terror.[69] These third world associates (Marcos in the Philippines, Duvalier in Haiti, and Somoza in Nicaragua immediately come to mind) were friendly to U.S.-based corporations and provided impressive incentives for them to do business in their countries. According to Chomsky and Herman, what drives U.S. foreign policy is the quest for "economic freedom— meaning freedom for U.S. business to invest, sell, and repatriate profits—and its two basic requirements, a favorable investment climate and a specific form of stability."[70] In another work, Chomsky has allowed one of the elites to speak to these issues with impressive candor. He quoted the State Department's George Kennan in the once-classified Policy Planning Study 23 from 1948:

> We have about 50% of the world's wealth, but only 6.3% of its population. . . . In this situation, we cannot fail to be the object of envy and resentment. Our real task in the coming period is to devise a pattern of relationships which will permit us to maintain this position of disparity without positive detriment to our national security. To do so, we will have to dispense with all sentimentality and day-dreaming; and our attention will have to be concentrated everywhere on our immediate national objectives. We need not deceive ourselves that we can afford today the luxury of altruism and world-benefaction. . . . We should cease to talk about vague and—for the Far East—unreal objectives such as human rights, the raising of the living standards, and democratization. The day is not far off when we are going to have to deal in straight power concepts. The less we are then hampered by idealistic slogans, the better.[71]

The kind of desired stability necessitates the elimination of disruptive elements, such as dissident students, priests and nuns organizing peasants, labor unions, and investigative journalists. Many of these U.S. allies were National Security States that employed torture against their own populations to maintain this requisite control. Because this state of affairs is not likely to inspire the confidence of the American population, the ideological institutions frame U.S. policy as invariably promoting the causes of justice, human rights, and democracy. The mainstream press, much of academic scholarship, and intellectual commentary generally constructs and conforms to a doctrinal system that serves established state and corporate power and fails to expose that power to the kind of sustained, critical scrutiny that it naturally expends on official enemies.[72] The recent past and current events regularly are shaped in a manner conducive to upholding the position that the United States pursues an essentially benevolent role in international affairs, although it may occasionally fail in this unique quest because of individual error or misjudgment.[73]

Chomsky and Herman contended that in the social-historical context of the United States in the Vietnam War era there were three kinds of atrocities, or bloodbaths, that occurred in the world: benign, constructive, and nefarious. "Benign" bloodbaths were those about which the U.S. government did not much care, because they did not affect primary U.S. elite interests of "maintaining the disparity." Accordingly, these violations of human rights did not arouse the U.S. government or political commentators. "Constructive" bloodbaths were committed by the United States or by its trusted allies (and so supported by the United States), because they served elite interests in preserving the kind of stability noted above. In the ideological system, these atrocities were ignored, downplayed, or even denied as atrocities because they revealed the values and interests operative in the real world of policymaking. "Nefarious" bloodbaths were those outrages committed by official enemies of the United States. These abuses were denounced loudly in the U.S. press and, perhaps, exaggerated if the truth alone was not enough to instill in U.S. citizens the proper fear and contempt for the perpetrators. The demonization of these enemies also served the domestic function of making the United States stand out even more favorably in comparison to such evil countries (as well as justifying ever-increasing "defensive" military budgets to contain these threats).

According to Chomsky and Herman, the war that the United States led against Vietnam, Laos, and Cambodia during the 1960s and 1970s constituted a "constructive" bloodbath: Elite media and scholarship faithfully supported the war effort in the struggle against Communism. Also, General Suharto's mass murder of up to a million Indonesians and his openness to U.S. investors was much admired in the West and also was considered "constructive."[74] Post-1975 Vietnam and Cambodia (under Pol Pot) were framed as "nefarious" bloodbaths, with the media effacing the role of the United States during its war in destroying much of pre-1975 Indochina. East Timor, under a brutal occupation by Indonesia, was an example of a "benign" bloodbath; many U.S. intellectuals who denounced the Khmer Rouge said nothing about the slaughters committed by a major Western ally. The authors point out that the extent of attention to one atrocity (say, Cambodia) over another (East Timor) is not accidental. The reason for the selective indignation is the simple criterion of utility to U.S. power. The ideological institutions focus on the crimes, real or alleged, of enemies and minimize those atrocities committed, supported, or tolerated by the United States.

In their 1988 study *Manufacturing Consent: The Political Economy of the Mass Media*, Herman and Chomsky elaborated on a "propaganda model" to explain how U.S. media coverage favors government-corporate interests.[75] This model proposed that the news that citizens receive must pass through several filters, two of which are the ownership by wealthy persons and companies and the profit orientation of the media corporations. In a subsequent essay on the model's cogency, Edward Herman emphasized that the propaganda model

> does suggest that the mainstream media, as elite institutions, commonly frame news and allow debate only within the parameters of elite interests; and that where the elite is really concerned and unified, and/or where ordinary citizens are not aware of their own stake in an issue or are immobilized by effective propaganda, the media will serve elite interests uncompromisingly.[76]

In a case study of how the media participate in propaganda campaigns, Herman and Chomsky used the paired expression "worthy and unworthy victims" to show how the government and mainstream media distinguished categories of people suffering from violence and repression.[77] Herman clarified this use of terms: "We used the concepts of 'worthy' and 'unworthy' victims to describe this dichotomization, with a trace of irony, as the differential treatment was clearly related to political and economic advantage, rather than anything like actual worth."[78] Thus, "worthy victims" are the victims of our official enemies and their nefarious bloodbaths; their plight merits substantial, outraged, and even distorted coverage. Comparably, one could identify "worthy refugees" as those who flee from Communist terror and are welcomed to the United States as further proof of Communist inhumanity. Similarly, "worthy dissidents" are those like Andrei Sakharov and Václav Havel whose heroism under Communism receives expressions of praise and solidarity from Western intellectuals.

But "unworthy victims" are those people who suffer from policies of the United States or its allies. That is, they are unworthy of our attention and concern, reflected in the media's minuscule, sporadic reporting in which U.S. responsibilities are minimized or denied. Correspondingly, refugees who flee from the terrors of U.S. allies are deemed not welcome, because they might tell the wrong story about why they fled their homelands. Also, dissidents from the U.S. sphere of influence do not merit impassioned editorials, television coverage, or congressional admiration. Herman and Chomsky maintained that

> the observable pattern of indignant campaigns and suppressions, of shading and emphasis, and of selection of context, premises, and general agenda, is highly functional for established power and responsive to the needs of the government and major power groups. A constant focus on victims of communism helps convince the public of enemy evil and sets the stage for intervention, subversion, support for terrorist states, an endless arms race, and military conflict—all in a noble cause. At the same time, the devotion of our leaders and media to this narrow set of victims raises public self-esteem and patriotism, as it demonstrates the essential humanity of country and people.[79]

One of the themes of this work is how Elie Wiesel and the Jewish victims of Nazism went from being "unworthy victims" in the 1940s to "worthy victims" in the United States in the late 1970s.[80] Indebted to Herman and Chomsky's radical interpretative framework and their extensive documentation, as well as that of other scholars and activists, I raise in this book different social, political, and cultural questions about Wiesel's work of remembrance and responsibility than have heretofore been addressed by his generally admiring Jewish and Christian interpreters.

In an interview with Harry James Cargas, Elie Wiesel expressed his concern that our response to today's victims not be selective: "Some people are sensitive only to one category of victims and not to the others. That is wrong. . . . If one is sensitive to one injustice, one must be sensitive to all injustice, which will never be at the expense of others."[81] Surely, this constitutes an immensely demanding job description. But one is confronted with the sobering reality of having only so much time and energy. How does one respond to so many cases of victimization that occur daily throughout the world? Noam Chomsky offered a helpful perspective on this issue of focus and responsibility:

> My own concern is primarily the terror and violence carried out by my own state, for two reasons. For one thing, because it happens to be the larger

component of international violence. But also for a much more important reason than that; namely that I can do something about it. So even if the U.S. was responsible for 2 percent of the violence in the world, it would be that 2 percent I would be primarily responsible for. And that is a simple ethical judgment. That is, the ethical value of one's actions depends on their anticipated and predictable consequences. It is very easy to denounce the atrocities of someone else. That has about as much ethical value as denouncing atrocities that took place in the 18th century. The point is that the useful and significant political actions are those that have consequences for human beings. And those are overwhelmingly the actions which you have some way of influencing and controlling, which means for me, American actions.[82]

Moral responsibility toward victims has been a chief theme in Elie Wiesel's public work of testifying, teaching, writing, and engaging. I now turn to an early stage of Wiesel's career, long before he received presidential accolades and expressions of Christian repentance, when he began to serve as the emissary of the unworthy Jewish victims and to criticize the bystanders who had done nothing to interfere with genocide.

The Impassioned Advocate

Jewish Solidarity

Of course, since I am a Jew profoundly rooted in my people's memory and tradition, my first response is to Jewish fears, Jewish needs, Jewish crises. For I belong to a traumatized generation, one that experienced the abandonment and solitude of our people.

—Elie Wiesel, *From the Kingdom of Memory: Reminiscences*

Below his breath, the Jew asks of his gentile neighbor: "If you had known, would you have cried in the face of God and man that this hideousness must stop? Would you have made some attempt to get my children out? Or planned a skiing party to Marmisch?" The Jew is a living reproach.

—George Steiner, *Language and Silence: Essays on Language, Literature, and the Inhuman*

In the decades after World War II, Elie Wiesel gradually made a fundamental commitment to express solidarity with Jews anywhere they were suffering. Recalling how so few Europeans came to assist his people and resist their murderers, Wiesel did not want to commit the same scandal of indifference to fellow Jews. Certainly since the 1960s Wiesel spoke out on behalf of Jewish causes with increasing fervor. However, after he received the 1986 Nobel Peace Prize, he occasionally was criticized by some people for his "Judeocentrism," the charge being that he apparently did not concern

himself with issues unrelated to Jewish needs. Wiesel defended his Jewish priorities in his memoirs, affirming that inasmuch as it was natural
for Nelson Mandela to struggle against apartheid, Martin Luther King
to fight against White racism, and Václav Havel to work on behalf of liberation for those in Czechoslovakia, so, too, it was natural for Wiesel to
dedicate his energies to his own people's welfare.[1] Of course, in different ways, each of the men Wiesel cites responded to issues beyond those
urgent ones involving his own people, for example, Martin Luther
King's concern for the Vietnamese suffering under American military
attacks in the 1960s. They and Wiesel would concur that it is not a matter of "either/or," but "both/and": both solidarity with one's own people and with others who are suffering from violence and injustice. In
Wiesel's energetic commitment to the Jewish people, he consciously
embraced a twofold role. Within the Jewish community, he tried to be
critical, even as he encouraged different divisions of Jewry to accept and
appreciate one another. Outside of the Jewish community, he defended
Jews before an insensitive or hostile gentile world. Wiesel acknowledged
that there was an ethical struggle in balancing these roles of "critic
within" and "defender outside": "What I try to do (it's very hard) is to
reconcile the two attitudes: not to be too strong, too sharp, too critical
when I am inside and not to be a liar on the outside."[2]

This tension between loyalty to one's people and commitment to the
truth is clarified by philosophers Agnes Heller and Ferenc Fehér in
their advocacy of citizen ethics and civic virtues. In an analysis of the
virtue of solidarity, the philosophers retrieved two understandings from
modern history.[3] First is the notion of an in-group solidarity in which
acts of concern are extended to the members of one's own ethnicity,
religion, class, or political group. One recent example of this is the U.S.
Christian churches coming to the aid of fellow Christians suffering
from hunger, torture, disappearance, and murder in Central America
throughout the 1980s. A second view is of a universal solidarity in which
concern is extended to all those in need of such assistance, regardless of
their particular identity. Here, a contemporary instance is the American Jewish mobilization in support of Kosovar refugees during the ethnic cleansing campaigns of Yugoslavian President Slobodan Milosevic
in the spring of 1999. And yet, Heller and Fehér note that there were
distinct problems with both forms of solidarity. In the first case, "[b]oth
Fascists and Stalinists held group solidarity in awe," one consequence
of which was that one would never criticize the leaders and functionar-

ies of the party.[4] In the second case, universal solidarity was often cheap, in that its adherents spoke on behalf of many oppressed people and yet did not take initiatives to help an individual in true need in their own immediate circles.[5]

Heller and Fehér thought that these limitations of solidarity needed to be overcome and that a new synthesis was necessary in which solidarity was linked to the modern values of life and freedom, along with other virtues such as tolerance and justice. In their view, solidarity then meant a willingness to offer aid to those groups and movements that were struggling to reduce violence and oppression in society and its institutions. In addition, solidarity "does not include unqualified support for the in-group (nor for that matter, any other group or movement); rather it excludes unqualified support."[6] Solidarity also required coming to the aid of those people threatened by violence and injustice, standing with the oppressed, and offering them protection against their persecutors. It is just this kind of demanding solidarity that so few Germans and other Europeans offered to Jews during the Third Reich.[7] In the next three chapters, I investigate how Wiesel has attempted to balance the strenuous imperatives of in-group Jewish solidarity with those of a more universal solidarity with non-Jews.[8] In this chapter, I take up Wiesel's practice of solidarity with his people on three fronts: his ongoing concern for the Jewish dead, the Jewish survivors, and Russian Jews. To probe more fully Wiesel's commitment to the Jewish people, in Chapter 4 I consider his relationship to the State of Israel. Throughout, I situate Wiesel's discourse and practice in the political context of "worthy and unworthy victims."

Respecting the Dead

By the time Wiesel published his Yiddish memoir on his death-camp experiences, he had supported himself already for a few years as a journalist for an Israeli newspaper in France. When he made the United States his home base in the late 1950s, he began writing for the *Jewish Daily Forward*. It was for the *Forward* that Wiesel faced one of his most challenging assignments: covering the trial of Nazi bureaucrat Adolph Eichmann in Jerusalem in 1961. Although Israelis had been wrestling with the impact of the Holocaust since the State's founding, Prime Minister David Ben-Gurion wanted to ensure that his nation and the world made a definitive confrontation with the recent past and so support the necessity of the Jewish State.[9] The trial was a galvanizing experience in Israel as it gave survivors permission to speak publicly about the catastrophe, with the understandable reticence and numbness of the survivors giving way to anguished expression. From that trial also came the controversial reporting and subsequent book by political philosopher Hannah Arendt entitled, *Eichmann in Jerusalem: A Report on the Banality of Evil.*[10] That last expression was given wide currency, as Arendt's major thesis was that Eichmann was no monster, but an uninspired bureaucrat carrying out his orders efficiently, like bureaucrats everywhere—it was just that his orders called for the total elimination of Jews.[11] In addition, Arendt raised critical questions about the collaborative role of the Jewish councils with the Nazis in facilitating the murder of the Jews. A public brouhaha ensued in which many Jews accused Arendt of showing terrible insensitivity toward the Jewish victims.[12] Both the Eichmann trial and the Arendt book precipitated an outpouring of commentary and polemics.[13] One question that was raised repeatedly was why the European Jews had not resisted their Nazi persecutors. In an Israel that prided itself on rejecting the weakness and passivity of the Diaspora, this question could function as ideological self-justification. But in the United States that question also was debated, and in 1964 Wiesel intervened with an essay properly entitled, "A Plea for the Dead."[14]

Wiesel began by recounting his arrival at the Auschwitz death camp and the ensuing conversation there among Jews on the relationship between dignity and death. He reported how the inmates greeted the new prisoners who did not know where they had arrived. The hardened survivors informed them: "Someone is waiting for you here. Who? Why, death, of course. Death is waiting for you."[15] The new Jewish inmates' eyes were directed to a fire, where, evidently, they, too, were to meet their fate. Fifteen-year-old Wiesel refused to believe that Jews could be burned alive; he expressed this incredulity to his father who did not answer him. Then several young people in the group of new arrivals issued a call for the Jews to resist. These youths urged rebellion as a way to die with honor, rather than with resigned acceptance. But the fathers of these youths discouraged them by recalling the Talmudic wisdom that, even in extremis, God had the power to intervene: "We must not rush things, we must not lose faith or hope."[16] This argument of the elders ultimately persuaded the youths not to pursue their resistance, which would be doomed before the overwhelming power of the Nazis. What was certain was that the Jews had come face-to-face with their destruction.

After beginning in this utterly grave and sober tone, Wiesel turned his attention to the controversial question: How could the Jews of Europe be like sheep to the slaughter? Wiesel clearly was agitated by the way in which supposedly conscientious people raised this issue without any modesty. He mimicked such facile questioners: " 'Tell us, speak up, we want to know, to suffer with you, we have a few tears in reserve, they pain us, we want to get rid of them.' "[17] For Wiesel, such an indecent attitude revealed that something had changed from wartime indifference to immediate postwar revulsion to a current chatty voyeurism. Wiesel worried that the Holocaust had become trendy. He recalled the time "when this subject, still in the domain of sacred memory, was considered taboo, reserved for the initiates, who spoke of it only with hesitation and fear, always lowering their eyes, and always trembling with humility, knowing themselves unworthy and recognizing the limits of their language, spoken and unspoken."[18]

In contrast, though not specifically citing Hannah Arendt, Wiesel referred to all the self-assured questioners who claimed that the Jewish victims "by participating in the executioner's game, in varying degrees shared responsibility" for their own deaths.[19] He linked this preoccupation with blaming the Jews for their own death to a long history of anti-Semitism in which Jews had been accused of committing numerous crimes and offenses, from the crucifixion of Jesus to recent social revolutions. He considered that the present garrulousness was just another manifestation of that historical enmity in that any outrageous opinion about the Jews was to be allowed free and easy circulation.

In this early intervention on the meaning of the Holocaust, Wiesel opposed those who spoke about the murdered Jews without demonstrating the proper sensitivity. With his survivor's mystical rhetoric in stark contrast to the alleged superficial banter of the commentators and spectators, Wiesel issued this request and warning:

> Let us leave them alone. We will not dig up those corpses without coffins. Leave them where they must forever be and such as they must be: wounds, immeasurable pain at the very depth of our being. Be content they do not wake up, that they do not come back to the earth to judge the living. The day that they would begin to tell what they have seen and heard, and what they have taken to heart, we will not know where to run, we will stop up our ears, so great will be our fear, so sharp our shame.[20]

However, in lieu of the dead coming back to afflict the living was Wiesel himself, a survivor who, unlike some intellectuals, was capable of testifying such that his listeners *ought* to feel such fear and shame. Grouping together unnamed "eminent scholars and professors" and "illustrious writers," Wiesel asserted his own modesty when it came to approaching the Auschwitz experience: In contrast to those purveyors of "formulas and phraseology," he could not fathom the mystery of evil that had engulfed so many Jewish parents and children.[21] Instead, he aligned himself with the biblical Job who had asked agonizing questions alternating with silence.[22] Moreover, whereas Job was to be silent for seven days, Wiesel believed that, given the magnitude of the Holocaust, humanity ought to maintain respectful, repentant silence for centuries. Against the impudence of the scholars, Wiesel inveighed: "We dare say: '*I know*'? This is how and why victims were victims and executioners executioners? We dare interpret the agony and anguish, the self-sacrifice before the faith and the faith itself of six million human beings, all named Job? Who are we to judge them?"[23] Wiesel also objected to the savants' assumption that their theories explained the event, as he countered that, in the death camps, no law could be extracted from those events. Such answers were an affront to the mystery of mass murder. Wiesel admitted he had wrestled with such questions for more than two decades and that definitive answers remained impossible before "a mystery which exceeds and overwhelms us."[24]

By invoking his Job-like status and connection to the murdered six million Jews, Wiesel reconstituted himself as their humble defender, as he reprimanded those he deemed to be the contemporary successors of Job's supposed friends who pontificated and proffered easy but insulting answers. Wiesel did not speak only in his own voice in this challenge to the impertinent. Rather, he invested his discourse with the awesome aura of the entire population of Holocaust victims. Sociologist Pierre Bourdieu offered a broader description of this kind of relationship between the spokesperson and the group:

> It is in what I would call the *oracle effect*, thanks to which the spokesperson gives voice to the group in whose name he speaks, thereby speaking with all the authority of that elusive, absent phenomenon, that the function of priestly humility can best be seen: it is in abolishing himself completely in favor of God or the People that the priest turns himself into God or the People. It is when I become Nothing—and because I am capable of becoming Nothing, of abolishing myself, of forgetting myself, of sacrificing myself, of dedicating myself—that I become Everything. I am nothing but the delegate of God or the People, but that in whose name I speak is everything, and on this account I am everything. . . . Paradoxically, those

who have made themselves nothing in order to become everything can invert the terms of the relation and reproach those who are merely themselves, *who speak only for themselves*, with being nothing either *de facto* or *de jure*.[25]

In this post-Eichmann trial context, Wiesel the survivor abolished himself in favor of "six million human beings, all named Job." Central, then, to this early symbolic conflict over the interpretation of the Holocaust was the struggle over who could be a legitimate interpreter, who had the right and the authority to speak. In his own self-presentation, Wiesel, who suffered under this vast evil, who survived to testify, who could not even begin to fathom it, was, in his trembling humility, more trustworthy than all the philosophers and social scientists who spoke "only for themselves," or who spoke from their academic and disciplinary specialties.[26]

Later in his essay, summoning his first memoir's motif that the world was silent while the Jews were slaughtered, Wiesel asserted that people now should observe a solemn silence. But if people still felt a need to ask questions so insistently, then they could at least spare the Jewish survivors such incivility. And because so few people took the trouble to pose such questions to the Nazi executioners, they could instead ask intrusive questions of the complicit bystanders. For example, the Allied governments knew what was happening:

> In London and in Washington, in Basel and in Stockholm, high officials had up-to-date information about every transport carrying its human cargo to the realm of ashes, to the kingdom of mist. In 1942–1943, they already possessed photographs documenting the reports; all were declared "confidential" and their publication prohibited.[27]

Then, tacitly agreeing with Arendt's conclusion that Eichmann was a "small man," Wiesel noted that Germany was replete with such men who simply did their work that facilitated the extermination of the Jews. He contended that "the fate of the Jews interested no one," that "[t]he Allies could not have cared less about what the SS did with its Jews," and that Himmler believed that his leading role in the genocide in no way disqualified him from negotiating a separate peace with the Allied powers.[28] Nazi policy had been attuned to public reactions: After each implementation of anti-Jewish measures, time was allowed for gauging the reactions of the international community. Although there had been occasional expressions of popular indignation, these had not been sustained with any efficacy over a long period. This being the case, the Nazis were convinced that that still another measure, even more severe, could be attempted. Wiesel conjectured that if only one unambiguous action had been taken by the civilized West, the Nazis might have been forced to recoil from their plans or at least modify them. From the Nazis' viewpoint, this lack of Western action indicated that the Jews were expendable to the Allied powers. Wiesel then made an acerbic comment on the press coverage of that time: "One need only glance through the newspapers of the period to become disgusted with the human adventure on this earth: the phenomenon of the concentration camps, despite its horror and its overwhelming ramifications, took up less space, on the whole, than did ordinary traffic accidents."[29] Perhaps reflecting his exposure to French existentialism over a decade earlier, Wiesel reframed the victims' alleged passivity by speculating that the Jews, knowing that the world had abandoned them, went to their death as an "act of lucidity, of protest, and not of acceptance and weakness."[30]

Wiesel continued his critique of the silence of the bystanders by noting that the Nazis had made some attempts at bargaining over Jewish lives, but that the Allied countries did not make room for the desperate Jews. He pressed the theme of unworthiness:

> [The Jew was] a kind of subhuman species, an unnecessary being, not like others; his disappearance did not count, did not weigh on the conscience. He was a being to whom the concept of human brotherhood did not apply, a being whose death did not diminish us, a being with whom one did not identify.[31]

He considered that this extreme degree of human indifference to the Jews indicated a "sickness," or "madness" as Franklin Delano Roosevelt, Winston Churchill, and Pope Pius XII failed to muster indignation and the Allies neglected to make any efforts to interfere with the functioning of the death camps.[32] Wiesel knew the justifications people used to defend themselves from such accusations as his: They did not know that such atrocities were occurring, or, if they had heard of them, they could not believe them. Ever on the offensive, Wiesel countenanced none of it: "I could answer that they did not want to know, that they refused to believe, that they could have forced their governments to break the conspiracy of silence."[33]

In light of what was known about the murderers' zeal and the bystanders' incapacity to be troubled, Wiesel wondered whether it could really be a serious topic for discussion that the Jews had not resisted their persecutors. Still, he noted that in some camps Jews had resisted. The intellectuals whom Wiesel had admonished had skipped over these facts of resistance to "illustrate a sociological theory, or to justify a morbid hatred which is always self-hatred."[34] When he chastised these thinkers, he proposed the only permissible posture: "We can only lower our heads and be silent. And end this sickening posthumous trial which intellectual acrobats everywhere are carrying on against those whose death numbs the mind."[35] And returning to the issue of judgment, Wiesel recalled a Talmudic teaching that proscribed judging others until one had been in their place. The world did not befriend the Jews at their hour of greatest need and "[b]ecause they had no friends they are dead." He implored: "So, learn to be silent."[36]

In this assertive cri de coeur, Wiesel reacted to both the civic silence that facilitated the Holocaust, as well as what he perceived was an indecent loquacity after the Eichmann trial. Against the intellectuals, Wiesel described the Holocaust as a sacred mystery, beyond mundane social analysis. He also challenged the intellectual confidence of those investigators who, evidently, had not been left shaken by the Holocaust. When he made these attacks, Wiesel declared his own greater authority to speak—based upon his experiences as witness and survivor—compared with those analysts who had not lived in the concentration-camp universe. In contesting the intellectuals, Wiesel presumed a monolithic community of Holocaust survivors, of which he himself was the humble representative, wounded spokesperson, and resolute defender. Such a move was somewhat risky, given the plurality of interpretations of the Holocaust and its lessons by different survivors.[37] One example is the famous Nazi hunter, Simon Wiesenthal, who opposed in crucial particulars Wiesel's own interpretations.[38] Wiesel avoided engaging by name the scholars, intellectuals, and thinkers who profaned the dead; by evading specifics and citations, Wiesel positioned himself, almost like the subject of the Holocaust itself, outside the normal bounds of discourse, in an untouchable realm.[39]

Wiesel had not entered this debate as a detached rationalist. He gave voice to outrage: He condemned the Allies for their indifference to Jewish suffering. Despite his later, frequent confession of political ineptitude, Wiesel exhibited an acute awareness of political action, both in Nazi Germany and in the Allied nations; there was nothing obscure about these public policies of Nazi dehumanization and Allied indifference. From the vantage point of the executioners and the bystanders, the Jews had been unworthy: unworthy of life from the point of view of the Nazis, and unworthy of Allied rescue, which might have exacted too strong a political cost at home. Wiesel was convinced: Instead of silent bystanders at that time and supercilious judges in the present, what the European Jews needed then were risky acts of solidarity, and what they deserved in the present was a demeanor of respect and silence.

In this "plea for the dead," then, Wiesel took on those with more recognized intellectual authority, those established, mainstream "professors," by countering their perspectives with his own explicit religious criteria of witness and interpretation.[40] But he also made a much broader and deeper critique of Western culture and its humane pretensions, as he spoke from the periphery as a representative of the West's perennial "Other," the Jews. In a few short years with even greater involvement of the United States in Vietnam, many Americans began to question, for the first time, a history they had long assumed was glorious and righteous. Wiesel's anguished, heterodox essay starkly called into question such national and cultural triumphalism.

Defending the Survivors

A decade after his distressed 1964 plea, Wiesel's own personal fortunes had changed considerably. Beyond his own individual circumstances, though, the issue of the Holocaust had increasingly become a topic of both serious and popular consideration, in no small part because of the 1967 Arab–Israeli War. Israel became a closer ally of the United States after the Jewish state demonstrated its military superiority against the Arab nations. However, the earlier springtime threats disseminated over Arab radio stations to drive the Israeli Jews into the sea galvanized the world Jewish community to rally to Israel's defense. After the Arab armies were defeated, the Jewish community in the United States and elsewhere began to mourn and investigate the momentous tragedy that their people had suffered only twenty-five years before. Israeli politicians also realized that Holocaust remembrance could help in justifying their policies of occupation in the name of "security" for a country of Holocaust survivors. After the 1967 war, both within and beyond the Jewish community, there was an increasing openness to Holocaust remembrance, both sincere and self-serving, by Jews and non-Jews. As a survivor who had made the United States his home, Wiesel was in a favorable position to respond to this developing interest.

In 1970 he published an article, "Holocaust: Twenty-Five Years Later," in the Jewish monthly *Hadassah Magazine*, which later became the title piece in his collection of short writings, *One Generation After*.[41]

Therein, Wiesel confessed that he was weary from the demanding effort of testifying to seemingly deaf ears. Also, he intimated that he soon would end his own preoccupation with the Holocaust: "one will speak differently about the holocaust. Or not at all. At least not for a long time."[42] But Wiesel did not go down that road. He could not ignore the greater interest in the European trauma as he frequently was invited to speak at synagogues, civic groups, and universities.[43] One manifestation of this growing public receptivity was a major symposium held in 1974 at New York's St. John the Divine Cathedral, where Wiesel gave an important address.[44] Certainly, neither Wiesel nor anyone else could control the direction of the growing examination of or even fascination with Nazism's crimes. And so he felt compelled to write "A Plea for the Survivors."[45] In this long essay, Wiesel pointedly addressed those who had not been a part of the Holocaust, perhaps those people who recently had become interested in the Holocaust and jumped on the bandwagon of its supposed "popularity."

Wiesel's opening was urgent, as he asserted that the Jewish survivors of the Holocaust were in need of defense. They were aging and often met one another only at funerals of fellow survivors. Years before the expression "political correctness" gained currency, Wiesel believed that compassion seemed de rigueur for everyone but the European Jews: "While it is fashionable these days to soothe the sensibilities of all minorities—ethnic, social, religious and others—few seem to worry about offending that particular minority [of Holocaust survivors]. Its suffering is exploited, distorted, monopolized, embellished or debased, according to the need of the moment."[46] Some survivors felt such despair that they committed suicide rather than continue to face their painful memories and insensitive inquirers.[47] Characteristically, Wiesel acknowledged that he felt sadness, not rancor or anger. The cause for this sadness was how the story Holocaust had been told and received. He presumed that the telling of the tale should have been the occasion for a powerful conversion in all those who heard it. And he confessed that the survivors still felt too traumatized to oppose with any vigor the trivialization of their experience. Consistent with his 1964 essay, Wiesel issued his own indictment of how people had responded to their suffering: "For you, it is one calamity among so many others, slightly more morbid than the others. You enter it, you leave it, and you return to your ordinary occupations."[48] For Wiesel, there was a basic choice: either one treated the Holocaust as a supremely awesome event or one viewed it as a topic à la mode, subject to all the vagaries and inanities of fashion. To Wiesel's dissatisfaction, the Holocaust was going through another vogue with incessant talk, opinions, commentary, and lack of respect, all of which wounded the Jewish survivors. Wiesel discerned that the days were gone in which the survivors were entitled to special privileges. Instead, he noticed that Jewish survivors were being harshly judged. Again, Wiesel challenged the presumption of such critics: "who gives you the right to judge them?"[49] In this atmosphere of judgment, of the desanctification of the Holocaust survivors, Wiesel rushed to their—and his own—defense.

Wiesel emphasized that, while in the camps, the prisoners survived only by contingency. He raised questions that marked the distance between ordinary people and himself: "How can one forget the passion, the violence a simple crust of moldy bread can inspire? Or the near-worship evoked by a slightly better dressed, better nourished, less beaten inmate?"[50] He wondered if those not so initiated could ever know what he and his comrades knew. He then suggested that the everyday life of the Holocaust survivors is framed within a ghetto not observable by others. According to Wiesel, one could not understand the survivor, for "[i]n spite of appearances, they are not of this world, not of this era."[51]

In the next section of this plea, Wiesel turned from the victims to the bystanders. The Jews in the concentration camps believed that the outside world did not know what was happening to them because there had been no interference with the Nazi mass murder. Their assumption was that if the Allies had known, something would have been done immediately. But the Jews had been wrong: "People knew—and kept silent. People knew—and did nothing."[52] Wiesel held that the current shameful treatment of Holocaust survivors was at least consistent with that meted out to the Jews during the war:

> At that time, as far as the Allies were concerned, the victims were already counted as dead. No effort was initiated, no political or military operation undertaken to save them. Among the thousands and tens of thousands of strategic and diplomatic plans elaborated in Allied headquarters, you will not find many designed to rescue the Jews from death: they were not considered worth the effort and surely not the risk. Not one commander shifted his troops in order to liberate this or that camp ahead of schedule. The living dead did not warrant such action.[53]

But it is not only the Allied governments that once again came in for Wiesel's censure. He disbelieved that Jewish leaders like Nahum Goldmann knew and remained silent: "how is one to understand, to rationalize their inaction, their passivity, their lack of vision and daring, of anger and compassion?"[54] Wiesel remembered other historical periods of terrible Jewish suffering; at those times, persecuted Jews found succor and respite with Jews in other locales, but, during the Holocaust, "secure Jewish communities took no interest in their distressed brothers' plight."[55]

Wiesel was searing in his criticism of how business as usual proceeded in American Jewish communities: "Jewish leaders met, threw up their arms in gestures of helplessness, shed a pious tear or two and went on with their lives: speeches, travels, quarrels, banquets, toasts, honors."[56] He critiqued American Jews for their shows of concern, their recourse to platitudes, and their lack of strategies concerning the life-and-death issues of rescue, public opinion, and U.S. government intervention. And although Wiesel was motivated by what he perceived to be simply a humanitarian set of concerns—at odds with anything suspiciously "political"—he next showed more than a little political imagination:

> How can one help but wonder what would have happened if . . . if our brothers had shown more compassion, more initiative, more daring . . . if a million Jews had demonstrated in front of the White House . . . if the officials of all Jewish institutions had called for a day of fasting—just one—to express their outrage . . . if Jewish notables had started a hunger strike, as the ghetto fighters had requested . . . if the heads of major schools, if bankers and rabbis, merchants and artists had decided to make a gesture of solidarity, just one. . . . Who knows, the enemy might have desisted.[57]

But demonstrations, public fasting, and gestures of solidarity were not forthcoming, and the Nazis proceeded methodically with their goal of exterminating the Jews. In this section of his essay, Wiesel stressed that the pillars of the so-called free world should have felt shame for writing off the European Jews as already dead and for not valuing their lives enough to intervene.

He then focused on the Jewish survivors who thought that the world would extend special kindness to them. But they received no preferential treatment, which surprised Wiesel, who assumed that their suffering in the Holocaust would have conferred privileges. But instead of special treatment, the survivors were ignored and marginalized. He recalled how Jews languished in displaced persons camps because no country would accept them and because their former homes and communities had been eradicated. He noted that the "United States, as in the thirties, distributed its visas parsimoniously, and with shockingly bad grace."[58] He continued to mock the West for its treatment of the refugees and survivors who were deemed too much of an embarrassment to bring into the full life of society.[59]

Wiesel recognized that some part of survivors' material needs had been met, though often with second-hand items and with little respect for the recipients' dignity. He was further angered that Diaspora Jewish doctors did not come to the aid of Jews still suffering in the liberated camps and rabbis did not spend the holy days with the survivors in Bergen-Belsen: "nobody felt the need or took the time to be with them and share their joys, as well as their mourning."[60] Further, Wiesel disapproved of how Holocaust survivors came to be used and exploited for political aims. Considered pariahs, they were treated without any love or affection, and Wiesel finally confessed to his reader: "How can we not be angry with you for that? How can we not remind you of it?"[61] He acknowledged the bystanders' rationales of fear and ignorance for not helping the Jews during the cataclysm, but he deemed it simply inexcusable how the survivors were treated after the war's end. He declared that all the survivors wanted was the attention of those who had not been in the concentration camps because these Jews had a unique message of utmost importance: "They merely hoped to justify their survival by accomplishing a mission that mattered more to them than their survival."[62] Here, Wiesel again spoke for all Holocaust survivors as an unanimous group, assuming that they all shared the same mission and motivation: to have an attentive audience who would heed their stern revelations about what humanity was capable of inflicting and enduring.

Wiesel anticipated his readers' response that people had shown an interest in the message of the Holocaust survivors, evidenced in the circulation of writings, dramas, and movies about the tragedy. But he ridiculed the claim that there could be any such genre as "Holocaust literature," because "Auschwitz negates all literature as it negates all theories and doctrines; to lock it into a philosophy means to restrict it."[63] Not stopping with the impossibility of Holocaust literature, he also denied any "theology of Auschwitz," which recently had been developing. Wiesel wrote in an apocalyptic rhetoric, so different than the rationalistic, categorizing tendency of "the scholars": "If you have not grasped it until now, it is time you did: Auschwitz signifies death—total, absolute death—of man and of mankind, of reason and of the heart, of language and of the senses. Auschwitz is the death of time, the end of creation; its mystery is doomed to stay whole, inviolate."[64] The survivor was torn between the realization that Auschwitz could not be communicated and the imperative, nevertheless, to "bear witness" as a way of resisting the oblivion that the Nazi killers had hoped would be the fate of the Jewish people. And still, survivors' testimonies and writings were riven by a sense of their own inability to transmit that experience to those who had not been there.

Alluding to the even more disputatious issue of legitimate interpreters, Wiesel remembered that talented writers once regarded the Holocaust with "sacred awe." They did not attempt to deal with it, he claimed, because even the most gifted imagination was dwarfed by the concentration-camp experience. The first testimonies and memoirs by the survivors themselves were accorded high regard. Since that time, the Holocaust had become "[a] desanctified theme, or if you prefer, a theme robbed of its passion, its mystery. Eventually people lost all shame. Today anybody can say anything on the subject and not be called to order, and not be treated as impostor."[65] Wiesel took it upon himself to call such shameless people to order. In addition to how the Holocaust was exploited by novelist and politician, Wiesel objected to the increasing frequency with which people assumed the identity of "survivor," even though they had never been in a death camp. He made plain that he did not object to attempts to confront the Holocaust and to investigate it from a variety of angles, in all of its expressions. But his concern was still for the appropriate emotional disposition: fear, trembling, and humility, instead of detachment, confidence, and arrogance. Some people earned Wiesel's respect, because they manifested this sensitivity and respect; others, however, "used" the Holocaust for base purposes. Although the Holocaust was featured in film and publishing, "[t]he days when people held their breath at the mention of the Holocaust are gone. As are the days when the dead elicited meditation rather than profanation."[66] Accenting this theme of profanation, Wiesel also singled out the outrage inflicted on survivors by those who denied that the Holocaust occurred or others who gave them cheap advice to get on with their lives and leave the past behind.

Wiesel was most opposed to those self-appointed spokespersons who talk in place of Holocaust survivors about their experience. In this part of his defense, Wiesel returned to the debates generated by the Eichmann trial. He saw the Holocaust more and more presented as a "spectacle" and claimed that the struggles of the survivors were never a serious concern to others. Wiesel adduced the evidence in the form of the invasive, even hostile, allegations directed toward the survivors:

> You argued that the boundaries were not clearly defined: that after all, all the victims were not innocent, just as all the killers were not guilty; that after all, under different circumstances, the victims might have turned into killers. I have heard this more than once, from more than one intellectual. I consider it an unfair, unworthy and despicable hypothesis, one that slanders the dead posthumously and attempts to dishonor the survivors.[67]

Wiesel expressed anger at hearing such obscenities. But as if to further instill shame in his reader, he stated that, in reality, the Holocaust survivors had felt gratitude for those who had lived outside of the Holocaust experience and, moreover, that "they loved you for having led a human existence during the catastrophe. Oh yes, they loved you for not having suffered."[68] Here, Wiesel's discourse displayed a structural ambivalence, as it juxtaposed rage and tenderness toward his readers: To perpetuate Holocaust memory, Wiesel obviously needed to appeal to a nonsurvivor audience. But, as his plea made clear, that audience often revealed itself to be untrustworthy.

Wiesel then closed with a scornful summary of how one should act toward the survivors: Leave them alone if one cannot communicate with them on their own terms, and accept that there is a gulf between their experience and one's own. He dramatically urged his reader not to speak until the last survivor has died and "joined the long procession of silent ghosts whose judgment one day will resound and shake the earth and its Creator."[69]

Whereas some survivors of trauma may have attempted to take refuge in forgetting, Wiesel chose an opposite course: Remembrance of the Holocaust became a sacred duty. Even though by 1975 Wiesel had achieved some modest fame and success as a writer and speaker, he still had a profound sense of victimhood, personally and collectively, which was passionately conveyed in this second plea. Alvin H. Rosenfeld offered an astute commentary on the nature of Wiesel's own vision:

> *Holocaust writers, in short, are one-eyed seers, men possessed of a double knowledge: cursed into knowing how perverse the human being can be to create such barbarism and blessed by knowing how strong he can be to survive it.*
>
> How, though, can we put our trust in one-eyed seers, men of impaired and only partial vision? How can we not trust them, for they are the prophets of our time—maimed into truth by the crack of the gun butt. To see with

them may indeed mean to risk seeing under the handicap of a shattered vision, but to foreswear what they have seen is to court blindness altogether.

If all Holocaust writers are in some sense one-eyed seers, what is the extent and what are the forms of impairment in the writings of Elie Wiesel? And how well does he cope with it?[70]

One of the forms of impairment may be Wiesel's own contradictory responses to the relationship between suffering and privilege. On the one hand, he asserted in a generalization that all the survivors wanted was to offer their moral message to humanity. In subsequent speeches and essays, Wiesel frequently affirmed, "Suffering confers no privileges; it's what one does with suffering that matters." In effect, this principle serves as an unsentimental rebuke to special pleading based on suffering. But, on the other hand, Wiesel expected that survivors would be accorded special privileges and recognition for all they endured; instead, they were ignored or treated shabbily by both fellow Jews and non-Jews.

Wiesel's essential positions did not change in the ten years between his two pleas. This time, he came to the defense to plead for the Jewish survivors whom he believed were still without honor in the United States. For Wiesel, the Jewish victims under Nazism were still being victimized, taken advantage of, denied respect, and it was because of this shameless treatment that he felt obliged to scold the public for its insensitivity. This intervention calls to mind Abraham Joshua Heschel's description of Wiesel's prophetic precursors of the Hebrew Bible:

> The prophet is intent on intensifying responsibility, is impatient of excuse, contemptuous of pretense and self-pity. His tone, rarely sweet or caressing, is frequently consoling and disburdening; his words are often slashing, even horrid—designed to shock rather than to edify. . . . Reading the words of the prophets is a strain on the emotions, wrenching one's conscience from the state of suspended animation.[71]

Truly, this essay still makes for uncomfortable reading as one confronts Wiesel's indictments against unfeeling fellow citizens as he attempted to intensify their sense of responsibility to the Jewish survivors. Wiesel used disparagement to silence and shame those who talked about the Holocaust without the necessary humility and so further harmed the survivors. He clearly believed that there is a hierarchy of permissible speakers on the Holocaust and, as with any hierarchy, deference is owed to those with authority, in this case, those who could bear witness to the event. Those self-interested usurpers of such authority had to be put in their place.

Complementing Heschel's biblical view of the prophet, Otto Maduro described the sociological role of a prophet in a religious community:

What does a prophet do? The prophet is the person (or group) capable of rendering explicit what is implicit, of uniting what is disunited, and of formulating, in words and deeds, a set of unsatisfied religious demands. The subjects, lay and clerical, of the unsatisfied demands find their demands expressed in this prophetic formulation. They can mobilize their energies around the prophet's words and deeds.[72]

Wiesel's plea was written in 1975, and it was at that time that he was helping to make explicit the implications of the Holocaust, for both the Jewish community and a broader audience in the United States. Among Jews, one major dimension of this formulation was a growing centrality of the Holocaust. The survivor became the prophet around whom the Jewish community could mobilize its energies as the Holocaust became more and more a central pillar in American Jewish identity.[73] In his study of survivors, Henry Greenspan observed a shift in the reaction to Holocaust survivors, from one of stigmatization after the war to romanticization increasingly after the late 1970s.[74] Alvin H. Rosenfeld also confirmed this change in status: "beginning in the late 1960s and continuing up to the present day, a radical change of attitude has take place, so much so that today the 'survivor' is a much-honored figure and, in some instances, enjoys something close to celebrity status."[75] This is certainly true in Wiesel's case, as a few years after his second plea, the secondary literature of exegesis, commentaries, and encomia about his work began to be published in the United States.

In the United States, the Holocaust was no longer taboo; it had entered the "profane" precincts of modern publicity and the culture industry. Whereas somber commentators such as Wiesel, with excruciating personal experiences, contributed to the growing market for Holocaust testimony, others, perhaps less demanding and circumspect, produced their own intellectual and cultural goods for public consumption. For example, a few years after this plea, Wiesel wrote an article in the *New York Times* critiquing the prime-time television docudrama, "Holocaust." Wiesel found much that was inaccurate and offensive about this representation, even though it introduced a large American audience to a crucial period of recent history.[76] What Wiesel faced in the mid-1970s (and what he continued to confront over the next two decades) was the disconcerting ambivalence of the "success" of Holocaust remembrance in American culture.[77] Once the Holocaust began to be remembered outside of groups of anonymous survivors and beyond the Jewish community, such memory inevitably became "used" in a variety of ways, from that of respectful warning to that of shameless sensation. Three years after his second plea, Wiesel faced a tremendous opportunity and challenge: President Jimmy Carter wanted to convene a group of survivors and other citizens to propose a way for the United States to remember the Holocaust. At that point, it was clear that there were strong possibilities both for further sanctification and profanation.

In the pluralistic and capitalistic marketplace of America, Wiesel found himself in battles on many fronts over the nature, lessons, and representations of sacred Holocaust remembrance.[78] But during this same period, Wiesel also involved himself in another battle that summoned his energies and solidarity: the ongoing subjugation of Jews in the Soviet Union.

Mobilizing for Russian Jewry

When people think of Jewish suffering in the twentieth century, they immediately think of the Holocaust in German-occupied Europe. However, Jews suffered terrible indignities and brutalities throughout the century in Russia and the Soviet Union: czarist repression, vicious pogroms, revolutionary violence, mass murder during the Holocaust, the banning of the Hebrew language in schools and publications, along with purges, scapegoating, and persecution under Stalin.[79] For a time after World War II, secular Jews had negotiated their passage into middle levels in the professions and government. But by the mid-1960s, Russian Jews had begun to face restrictions in employment and education; further, they experienced constraints in expressing their religious convictions and engaging in cultural activities without state interference. Although there was a broad restriction on emigration for all minority ethnic groups, Jews were viewed even more suspiciously because a majority of Jews resided outside the Soviet Union, in countries opposed to Communism, such as the United States and Israel.

In 1965 Wiesel made his first trip to the Soviet Union at the urging of two members of the Israeli Ministry of Foreign Affairs. He wrote of his impressions during this trip in a series of articles for the Israeli newspaper *Yediot Aharanot*, the collection of which was translated first into French and then English as *The Jews of Silence* in 1966.[80] Wiesel's choice of title showed a conscious thematic link to the "silence" that characterized his 1956 Yiddish memoir about Auschwitz. He informed his readers that this work was not political analysis but rather a witness's report. And although Wiesel's journalism dealt with some of the pivotal political events of the mid–twentieth century, his focus during this mission was on something altogether different: "Having never been involved in political action, I hope that what I have written here will neither exacerbate the cold war nor be used for political purposes. I have never engaged in propaganda, and have no intention of beginning now."[81] Wiesel had heard reports of the difficulties faced by the Soviet Jews; he decided to see for himself. He felt that it was not enough to proffer gestures of solidarity from the comfort and safety of New York, where a demonstration on behalf of Soviet Jews had been held in early 1965 at Madison Square Garden. He was not interested in meeting with Soviet officials or prominent Jews who might be put forward to repeat the party line. Instead, he went in search of those anonymous Jews who, he hoped, would indicate to him, and by symbolic extension, to the West, what they needed from world Jewry.[82]

What Wiesel found in Russia astonished him. Despite years of atheistic propaganda, Jews still wanted to remain Jewish, even if they had precious few resources to guide them on their spiritual and cultural quests. The dramatic highlight of Wiesel's trip was the feast of Simchat Torah, which celebrated the giving of the Torah to the Jews. At the Moscow synagogue, Wiesel was amazed to see thousands of young Jews come out to sing and dance in the streets: They threw caution to the wind and proudly affirmed that they, too, were part of the Jewish people. This overt demonstration of Jewish commitment deeply encouraged Wiesel: "Everyone has judged this [younger] generation guilty of denying its God and of being ashamed of its Jewishness. They are said to despise all mention of Israel. But it is a lie. Their love for Israel exceeds that of young Jews anywhere else in the world."[83] He also believed that Soviet officials were utterly inept if they thought that they could dissuade Russian Jews from caring about the State of Israel:

> The Russian authorities do not understand that the Jews and they are speaking two different languages, are talking about two different things. They fail to understand that it is possible to malign the earthly Jerusalem without injuring in the slightest the Jerusalem which Jews treasure in their dreams as a city innocent of any stain or flaw; their fidelity to that Jerusalem is in essence fidelity to themselves. It is for this reason that they value anything that comes from Israel and honor anyone who comes in its name.[84]

Throughout this journey, Wiesel interpreted the burdens and glories of Soviet Jewry in a language that went beyond mere political categories.

In an apt comment in the *New York Times Book Review*, historian Walter Laqueuer commented that *The Jews of Silence* "is a powerful and moving little book, very well translated from the Hebrew. It is based on mystic belief, and one hesitates to discuss it in rational terms."[85] Certainly, traveling to Russia as a journalist, survivor, and mystic, Wiesel became awestruck by the miracle of Jewish survival under oppression.

And yet, despite this display of Jewish fervor, Wiesel found fear among these Jews as well. Sensing an ally in their presence, they came to him and left terse messages about the struggles they were facing. Both inside and outside synagogues, Wiesel often was besieged with questions about Jewish life outside of Russia, particularly about the extent to which American Jews were working on their behalf. Wiesel expressed shame at the lackadaisical response back home:

> I could not bring myself to tell them that only a few thousand Jews went to Washington to take part in the protest march; that the Jews of New York were apparently too busy to fill Madison Square Garden for the demonstration held in early 1965 for the Jews of Russia. I lied to them, exaggerating the figures, telling them that a hundred thousand Jews had assembled on that evening. They looked at me in simple amazement. What? Only a hundred thousand? A hundred thousand out of three million? Is that all?[86]

When Wiesel went on to pose questions to them, often they were silent, cautious, and diffident. But he understood the dangers they faced—a well-known ring of informers and secret police.

Although Wiesel was sensitive to the echoes of Jewish history, he nonetheless felt that the suffering of the Russian Jews was of an entirely different order from what Jews had experienced under the Nazis. Stressing that "[a]n abyss of blood separates Moscow from Berlin," Wiesel contended that, although the Russian Jews face hardships and trials, it was nothing like what his generation knew in Europe.[87] Hence, he was hesitant to invoke analogies to the Holocaust:

> I do not like to draw extreme parallels between the condition of the Jews in Russia and that of the European Jews during the Holocaust. The analogy is illogical, unfair, and unreal. But from a subjective and emotional point of view it is impossible to escape the impression that the two communities have something in common—a sense of total isolation.[88]

The challenge Wiesel took upon himself was to break this sense of total isolation. But he contemplated whether Western Jewish protest might bring further harm to the Jews in Russia. Upon asking the Russian Jews themselves what they wanted from Jews abroad, "[t]heir answer was always the same: 'Cry out, cry out until you have no more strength to cry. You must enlist public opinion, you must turn to those with influence, you must involve your governments—the hour is late.' "[89] Wiesel took these appeals seriously and promised those Russian Jews who had confided in him that he would warn Jews at home and try to involve them in this struggle for human rights.

Upon his return to the United States, Wiesel threw himself into organizing. If he previously had been a Jewish witness to the Holocaust, he then became an activist on behalf of Jews suffering and forgotten in the present. Some grassroots groups already had begun to raise the issue of the Soviet Jews; soon after, some eager Jewish students joined the cause.[90] Along with the noted scholar Abraham Joshua Heschel, Wiesel spoke out on behalf of the Russian Jews' rights to their culture, religion, and emigration.[91] He described his own burst of activity in trying to galvanize American Jews to join in solidarity with their Russian brothers and sisters:

> I wrote article after article in the *Forverts*, *Yedioth*, and *Hadassah* magazine, circulated appeals and petitions, rushed from demonstration to demonstration and convention to convention: rabbinical associations in Toronto, Miami, and New Jersey, institutes and conferences of philanthropic groups. I accepted all radio, television, and press interviews on the subject.[92]

Among these audiences, Wiesel recounted his adventures among the courageous Jews, and he told of their underground writings, their fears, and their religious zeal. But he felt despondent, as his first forays into raising consciousness often were met with shrugs and indifference. On the ambiguous meaning of his book's title, Wiesel affirmed that "what torments me most is not the Jews of silence I met in Russia, but the silence of the Jews I live among today."[93]

In 1966 Wiesel took a second trip to Russia to see if there had been any improvement in the condition of the Russian Jews.[94] He had brought a copy of the recently published *The Jews of Silence* with him as evidence of keeping his commitment to the Russian Jews. However, the book was confiscated by the KGB and Wiesel himself was trailed by the secret police; for a time, he feared that he would not be able to leave the country. He also was discouraged to find that Jews still suffered discrimination, that they were not allowed to have their own publications or radio or television programs. In effect, they were forced to deny their Jewish heritage. But he was roused by the continuing defiance of the young Russian Jews: "Their salvation, then, will come from within themselves, not from us [in the West]. They may already have realized how futile it is to rely on us—either on our help or on our sympathy— and so have take destiny into their own hands."[95] Still Wiesel continued to work on their behalf, even as he disavowed any political dimension to what he was doing; he interpreted this work as purely ethical. In 1967 he advocated the following strategy: "We must give voice to our indignation and our despair, in order to arouse public opinion, including above all the sympathy of friends of the USSR and of enlightened Russians themselves, rather than play at some *Kriegspiel* with Brezhnev and Kosygin."[96] Wiesel combined a mystical sense of fraternity with the Soviet Jews as well as a political savvy—however much he chose to downplay it in other situations—about how to make a realistic difference.[97] Still, he assessed that work in the 1960s as a failure.[98]

The Soviet trials in Leningrad in 1970–1971 sparked greater interest in the movement, as several Russian Jews were charged with treason and received harsh sentences. With international outrage at this injustice, the increasing Russian phenomenon of dissent (by such figures as physicist Andrei Sakharov), and the emerging Soviet–U.S. détente, Soviet policy softened and larger numbers of Jews were permitted to leave the Soviet Union. Wiesel was exhilarated by how far the Soviet Jews had come in just a few years. At the time of his first visit, Jews had made a bold gesture on Simchat Torah and had demonstrated proudly on that one night, but then had retreated to being "Jews of silence" the rest of the year. By 1973, young Jewish refuseniks—men who were refused exit visas to Israel—were going on hunger strikes, staging demonstrations and protests, calling for international support, all of which inspired people in the West. Wiesel claimed that the young Soviet Jews had been the first "dissidents," long before Solzhenitsyn became a familiar name in the United States.[99]

In an open letter "To a Young Jew in Soviet Russia," Wiesel affirmed that, "[t]hanks to you I can dream again, and for that I am also grateful. You have allowed me to share your dreams, and on that level, every dream becomes adventure."[100] Given the official Soviet antipathy to religion, it had been thought that Judaism was becoming extinct in the land of Marxist-Leninist dogma. As a survivor who had beheld too many tragedies, Wiesel was gratified to witness the Jewish youth's enthusiasm for Judaism, its tradition, memory, and peoplehood. He admired their nonviolent resistance to an oppressive regime, even when there had been little international support. He had been cheered by their adamant support of Israel during and after the June 1967 war.[101] Gradually, the Soviet Jews became a rallying point for divided Jewish communities in the United States, bridging both religious and secular, old and New Left. It was the simplicity of their cause that generated such spirited support, because they only wished to live as Jews in Russia with other Jews, to be free from harassment or to be allowed to leave. Wiesel claimed in his letter that "we are witnessing a renewal of Jewish life, of Jewish culture in Western countries, and in large measure it is a renewal for which we are indebted to you."[102]

Wiesel himself had been making his own contribution to the renewal of Jewish culture with his own increasingly popular lectures on religious themes as well as his activism for Russian Jews. But he felt more was demanded of him as a writer, so, in addition to his journalism and public speaking, he tried an entirely new genre, drama, and wrote a play, *Zalmen, or the Madness of God*, a distorted version of which was staged in Israel with some success, much to Wiesel's dismay.[103] Later, he wrote a novel, *The Testament*, which dealt with the years of the Stalinist terror against the Jewish intelligentsia and the tension such Jews felt between nonbelief and fidelity to tradition.[104] The hero of Wiesel's novel was based in part on the famed Russian Jewish writer Peretz Markish who gradually distanced himself from Communist ideology to become more closely allied with the Jewish tradition. Considered a traitor by Stalin, Markish was executed. In a 1988 appeal, which showed his unwavering commitment to Jewish memory, Wiesel requested of Soviet President Mikhail Gorbachev that Markish and twenty-three other Jewish writers who had been maligned and executed by Stalin's orders be granted a posthumous rehabilitation. The Soviet president and promoter of glasnost granted Wiesel's request.[105]

In pursuing a policy of détente with the United States and Western Europe, Soviet leader Leonid Brezhnev had aimed to placate Western opinion and had allowed increasing numbers of Russian Jews to depart for the State of Israel. But if Brezhnev thought that this gesture would stem the growing movement for emigration, he was mistaken.[106] Soviet Jews persisted in agitating for even greater emigration, and, increasingly, over the course of the 1970s and 1980s, more and more people in the West took notice of the grievances of the Soviet Jews. In 1972 Senator Henry Jackson introduced an amendment linking the lifting of emigration restrictions on Soviet Jews to the granting of trade privileges to the Soviet Union.[107] A few years later, President Jimmy Carter's administration recognized the Soviet Jews' plight as a major human rights issue. The struggles of Soviet Jews and other Russian dissidents and victims were featured prominently in the mainstream press. For example, in their 1979 study, Chomsky and Herman reported:

> [T]he *trial* of a single Soviet dissident, Anatol Shcharansky, received more newspaper space in 1978 than the several thousand official *murders* in Latin America during the same year, not to speak of the vast number of lesser events such as tortures and massive disappearances. Information on Latin American horrors is readily available from church and other sources eager to tell the ghastly story, but—to put the matter baldly—the sponsors of class warfare under subfascism are hardly eager to focus attention on its victims.[108]

This concern for Soviet Jews continued under the Reagan administration, which adhered to a virulent anti-Soviet line in rhetoric and policy. In a letter to the Union of Councils for Soviet Jews, President Ronald Reagan reaffirmed his administration's own commitment: "We must maintain our witness and our efforts. Strenuous efforts to advance the human rights of Jews in the USSR, including the right of free emigration, will remain at the forefront of our human rights policy and an integral part of our whole policy toward the Soviet Union."[109] As had occurred with Holocaust remembrance, so, too, had Soviet Jewry: Issues of deep personal concern to Wiesel had at last received considerable publicity. He could remember, with some annoyance, when he testified and very few people even listened. Earlier, he had also been quite critical of major American Jewish organizations: "Until 1970, they refused even to establish an American Conference on Soviet Jewry."[110]

In a 1986 op-ed for *The New York Times*, Wiesel reflected this major shift in the reception of Soviet Jews, embodied most dramatically in the case of Anatoly Shcharansky.[111] Shcharansky was a Russian Jewish dissident who had been maligned, imprisoned, and sentenced to thirteen years of hard labor. In his article, Wiesel celebrated Shcharansky's release from prison and his arrival as a free Jew in the State of Israel. He emphasized the role of public pressure in helping to secure Shcharansky's freedom: "We knocked on every door, moved every stone, invoked every argument. Rallies were held, high officials approached, protests made, petitions signed, vigils encouraged."[112] He noted that a key in the final triumph of the dissident's release was President Reagan's own entreaty at the recently held Geneva Summit. But even though Wiesel applauded Shcharansky's arrival in Israel, he also was committed to remembering other Jewish refuseniks and dissidents who still were imprisoned, exiled to labor camps, or harassed on a daily basis. Wiesel added his now-familiar leitmotif: "Without our support, without our solidarity, they could not carry on."[113]

Wiesel singled out the case of Vladimir Slepak as deserving the consideration of his American audience. Slepak was an advocate of Jewish cultural freedom in the Soviet Union since the 1960s and he had watched many other Russian Jews leave for Israel, but he himself was never allowed to emigrate. Capitalizing on the publicity of the Shcharansky case, Wiesel issued an appeal for Slepak:

> Let us mobilize our energies, our contacts, our professional connections, our academic links, our economic resources. Let us mobilize our passion and our anger on his behalf. And on behalf of all the others who implore us to use our freedom for the sake of theirs. Let us be bold and imaginative. Why not organize a mass rally in Washington? Would it not be right to follow the civil rights march of the 1960's with a human rights march in the 1980's?[114]

As he had in the 1960s, Wiesel once again turned to the power of publicity to make a difference in the lives of troubled Jews. But both the fortunes of Wiesel and the Soviet Jews had risen in the United States—both were now seen as voices of conscientious heroism and both were able to warrant the attention of government officials as well as the mainstream media. If, in 1966, Wiesel had been writing on behalf of Soviet Jews for small Jewish magazines such as *Hadassah*, twenty years later he had access to the most influential newspaper in the United States to promote the human rights of Soviet Jews as an issue in which all Americans ought to have an interest.[115]

Wiesel also remained faithful to the Soviet Jews at the time of the Nobel Peace Prize ceremonies in December 1986. After receiving the prize, Wiesel and his wife returned to their hotel and telephoned their Soviet Jewish friends, refuseniks who still lived in isolation and fear. At the time of his own great personal triumph and prestige, Wiesel shared his honor with those who still were repressed in their country. In his lecture the following day, Wiesel stressed:

> We wanted them to know that, especially on this day, we were thinking not only of our joy but also of their plight. We went on calling them, one after the other. At one point they began calling back. The whole afternoon was a dialogue of human solidarity. If ever your prize had concrete, immediate meaning, distinguished members of the Committee, it was yesterday afternoon: to those Jews in Russia it meant that here in this place we care, we think of them, and we shall never forget.[116]

Throughout his public career over the last three decades, Wiesel has demonstrated a lasting solidarity with Soviet Jewry. Unlike so many people during the period of the Holocaust, Wiesel consciously refused to engage in "business as usual." He issued indictments of contemporary "Jews of silence" whose indifference was reminiscent of an earlier silence. And, as his influence and renown spread outward from Jewish circles, he made appeals to all citizens to support the aspirations of Russian Jewry to affirm their own culture or to join their friends and families in the West or Israel.

In his activism on behalf of Soviet Jews, Wiesel typically claimed to privilege moral considerations before political ones, the latter being viewed as somehow suspect or tainted. He had expressed concern that his 1965 testimony be used neither as propaganda nor be turned into a weapon in the cold war. But Wiesel combined both moralistic rhetoric and political skill in his solidarity with Russian Jews. If the injustices they faced were to be remedied, raising consciousness in synagogues, community federations and press clubs, and universities and newspapers was a crucial first step in the United States. In these early years, Wiesel worked tirelessly in the Jewish community, but, as his stature grew after the late 1970s, increasingly he found himself in a position to use his contacts with agents of state power, from Gorbachev to Reagan, to draw attention to these causes. Although Wiesel—and many others—had a driving moral motivation to work in this kind of solidarity movement, one also needed to consider the wider political context to account for the gradual U.S. embrace of the Russian Jews. In the post–Vietnam War era, such attention to and regard for the victims of our official enemies did serve propagandistic ends. In contrast to our oppressive enemy, the USSR, the U.S. government could present itself as humane and altruistic, because the Carter administration promoted human rights and the Reagan administration conducted a moral crusade against "the Evil Empire." In his study of the U.S. movement of solidarity with Soviet Jews, William Orbach observed,

> At first, the American government supported the movement, which counteracted Soviet propaganda claims of American oppression of blacks to prove its pro-Semitism and anticommunism. Such policies cost the United States nothing while the call for freedom and morality, always viable, proved particularly appealing after Vietnam and Watergate.[117]

In other words, Soviet Jews were politically safe and U.S. rhetoric could be expended on the nobility of their cause. Wittingly or not, Wiesel was drawn into political processes, ideological issues, and ethical choices as he worked for the "Jews of silence."

Consider, for example, the matter of immigration. Russian Jews typically immigrated to Israel and some settled on expropriated Palestinian land in the Israeli-occupied West Bank and Gaza Strip. Long before the current "peace process," Israel had seized Palestinian land, among other reasons, to provide space for absorbing new Jewish immigrants. With these illegal settlements establishing "facts on the ground," the Palestinians suffered the consequences of this Jewish "right of return," which enables a Jew anywhere in the world to immigrate to Israel. Although Wiesel pursued his solidarity work for moral, religious, and humanitarian reasons, the success of this work has had emphatically political effects, both for the Russian Jews who enjoy a new citizenship in Israel and for the indigenous Palestinians who, in both the Occupied Territories and in Israel proper, suffer from the increased numbers of Russian immigrants, as far as educational resources and occupational opportunities are concerned. Given the munificent amount of U.S. aid to Israel, some portion of which has been used for resettlement of the Russian Jews on Palestinian land, it has been the U.S. taxpayer who has helped pay for the humanitarian "return" of Russian Jews to Israel with the consequent dislocation and impoverishment of Palestinians.[118]

Since the 1970s the Russian Jews gradually were considered "worthy" victims in the United States; yet there were other people who suffered comparable or worse treatment than that meted out to the Russian Jews and who might have been deserving of American attention. Most pertinent in this regard are those people who have been persecuted frequently by governments that are allies of the United States: Iranian dissidents under the Shah of Iran, Nicaraguans under the Somoza dictatorship, or East Timorese Catholics under Indonesian occupation. The legitimate American Jewish concern for the Russian Jews came to coincide with and serve U.S. ideological interests. But Palestinian refugees had nothing to offer the U.S. government. Hence, there were no U.S. initiatives to back the emigration of Palestinians from other Arab countries to return to their homes and land in either Israel or Palestinian territory. Also, not only was there no U.S. interference with ongoing Israeli dispossession of Palestinians but also there was bounteous aid and ideological support from the U.S. government to the Jewish state throughout this period.[119]

Prophetic activity often has been described as "comforting the afflicted and afflicting the comfortable." In many of his interventions of Diaspora solidarity, Wiesel had engaged in such prophetic action. By his pleas and his defense of Jewish victims in the 1960s and 1970s, Wiesel had attempted to give comfort to the survivors whose ordeal had not ended in 1945 but continued, materially, psychologically, and socially. In addition to his affirmation of Holocaust survivors, Wiesel also "afflicted the comfortable," by reminding his audiences that the European Jews had been considered expendable by the world as well as Hitler, and that, after the war, the survivors had been met with shameful indifference.

Unlike the rabbis or leaders of Jewish institutions and organizations, Wiesel had no official position in the Jewish or broader American community in the 1960s. He could only speak out of his own personal experience as victim and survivor. But, drawing upon this personal authority, he called attention to an event that posed theological, cultural, political, and institutional challenges to American Jews, as well as the Christian Churches, and the United States more generally. Wiesel's early defense of the Jewish victims underscored a disruptive message: Life ought not go on as if the Holocaust had not happened. Further, his own excruciating experiences attuned him to those still considered outcasts in the world Jewish community. In addition to his solidarity with the Russian Jews, he also spoke out on behalf of Ethiopian Jews[120] and urged greater efforts at solidarity with Jews in Arab countries whose situation there Wiesel admitted in 1971 was an "echo of the Holocaust."[121] Furthermore, in these contemporary cases, Wiesel often evinced a strongly critical edge in his assessments of Diaspora Jewry for its impassive attitude toward other Jews. Defender of and advocate for Holocaust victims and Jewish survivors, Russian refuseniks, and Ethiopian and Arab Jews, Wiesel persisted in plaguing comfortable consciences by speaking out for those Jews he felt were abandoned or forgotten.[122]

Solidarity with his own people has been a major focus in Wiesel's public work. In the early years of his public career as writer and witness, Wiesel was speaking mostly to other Jews about the greatest catastrophe in Jewish history or attempting to mobilize his own community to ease the burdens of Soviet Jewry. And after the 1960s, Wiesel continued to be a spokesman for Holocaust survivors across a range of issues that extended beyond the Jewish community. Nevertheless, in a 1974 interview, he confided to his interlocutors: "I don't think [the Jew] should become obsessed with only Jewishness. I think he should be obsessed with everything else as well. I am. I was obsessed by Biafra; I think I was among the first to fight for Biafra. I saw the children's pictures in the newspapers and I couldn't sleep."[123] I next consider Wiesel's obsession and solidarity with those non-Jews who also suffer in the post-Holocaust world.

The Cosmopolitan Witness
Global Solidarity

We must always take sides. Neutrality helps the oppressor, never the victim. Silence encourages the tormentor, never the tormented. Sometimes we must interfere. When human lives are endangered, when human dignity is in jeopardy, national borders and sensitivities become irrelevant.

—Elie Wiesel, *From the Kingdom of Memory: Reminiscences*

We tell the story not only for the Jewish people; we tell it for the world. Only the tale of what the world has done to our people can save the world from a similar fate. It is very ambitious, I know. It is arrogant. We want to save the world from destruction. And perhaps only we can.

—Elie Wiesel, *Against Silence: The Voice and Vision of Elie Wiesel*

fter Elie Wiesel was named the winner of the 1986 Nobel Peace Prize, Robert McAfee Brown, an eminent Christian theologian and one of Wiesel's most sensitive interpreters, addressed the matter of "Wiesel's politics." Acknowledging that Wiesel did not consider his own work political, Brown agreed that Wiesel's self-perception was partially true, because the Jewish survivor did not "stump for candidates, engage in party politics, or slavishly follow an ideological line."[1] This kind of politics represented a distasteful partisanship that Wiesel eschewed, given the urgency and purity of his mission of

Holocaust remembrance. McAfee Brown offered another insight, though, into what did make Wiesel a political actor:

> He is one of the most intensely political people of our time; everything he does flows from an "ideological" bottom line that might be summarized this way: All persons are worthy of infinite respect. *All* persons, not just Jews, not just survivors of the death camps, but all persons, starting especially with victims.[2]

Whereas McAfee Brown honored such integrity and consistency, Alexander Cockburn, a columnist for the progressive weekly *The Nation*, offered a different appreciation of Wiesel. The muck-raking journalist claimed that, even though the Nobel Prize Committee celebrated Wiesel's work on behalf of humanity, "it is difficult to find examples of Wiesel sending any message on behalf of those victimized by the policies of the United States, and virtually impossible when it comes to victims of Israel."[3]

With this chapter, I engage this conflict of interpretations regarding Wiesel: universal conscience or selective moralist. I examine how Wiesel offered solidarity to other peoples: "One of the main tenets of my life has been: '*Lo ta'amod al dam reakha.* . . .' Do not be indifferent to the bloodshed inflicted on your fellow man (Numbers 19:16). Not to take a stand is in itself to take a stand, said Camus."[4] Because Wiesel has espoused many causes, I seek to be representative, not exhaustive, in this analysis: Paraguay in the early 1970s, Vietnam and Cambodia in the late 1970s and early 1980s; and Central America in the early and mid-1980s. In these cases, I consider Wiesel's distinctive narrative, rhetorical tropes, ethical stances of duty and responsibility, as well as his political appraisal of the conflict at hand. Also, I show how Wiesel has negotiated political pressures, capitalized upon opportunities, mobilized popular opinion, and responded to U.S. foreign policy.

A Final Solution in Paraguay

Wiesel, distressed by the suffering of the starving children in Biafra in 1970 whose photographs he had seen, spoke out on Biafra, making this one of his first forays into a non-Jewish issue of human rights.[5] A few years later, Wiesel became aware of an ongoing atrocity in Latin America. Paraguay had long been ruled by General Alfredo Stroessner, who had come to power in a 1954 military coup. His fiercely anti-Communist regime terrorized the population with torture, arbitrary arrests, and death squads. Under his rule, even former Nazi officials found safe haven from prosecution. During Stroessner's reign, the eradication of the Aché Indian tribe was part of his nation's "development" policy, as the indigenous people were considered an obstacle to the clearing of forests so necessary to the special interests of mining and cattle raising.

Wiesel contributed a short epilogue to a collection of testimonies by the International League of Human Rights about the suffering and disappearance of this tribe.[6] He admitted that his study of this documentation prompted strong feelings of repugnance. Perhaps remembering a refrain expressed by some Europeans a few decades earlier, he challenged his own profession for being ignorant that "a so-called free country," Paraguay, "was enforcing or tolerating measures of the same murderous racism, which my generation endured and fought."[7] Expressing his disbelief that such evil could exist three decades after Nazism, Wiesel felt forced to look back on his own experiences:

> Until now, I always forbade myself to compare the Holocaust of European Judaism to events foreign to it. Auschwitz was something else, and more, than the Vietnam War; the Warsaw Ghetto had no relation of substance with Harlem—deplorable and misplaced comparisons which often reveal the ignorance, the arrogance of those who formulate them. I found these offensive, revolting. The universe of the concentration camps, by its dimensions and its design, lies outside, if not beyond history. Its vocabulary belongs to it alone.[8]

In this reflection, Wiesel objected to Holocaust analogies invoked in recent years by Black Power activists and anti–Vietnam War protesters. But in this response to the abuse and murder of the Aché people, Wiesel readily made links with the European Holocaust, an analogical practice he subsequently would monitor in others with considerable passion.[9] Having read the accounts of what the indigenous people endured, Wiesel was startled by the similarities to his own experience: "Yes, the world impregnated with deliberate violence, raw brutality, seems to belong to my own memory. On one side the victims, on the other side the torturers."[10] The Aché victims had been subject to humiliation, starvation, cultural eradication, manhunts, slavery, and the abuse of women and children by their Paraguayan torturers.

Wiesel further connected his European experience to the Aché's by noting that Dr. Josef Mengele had been living an untroubled life in Paraguay. Wiesel even wondered if Mengele—who determined upon the victims' arrival at Auschwitz who would be sent immediately to the gas chambers—and other Nazi criminals contributed their experience and expertise to the bloodbath. Wiesel did not deny the facts: "it is indeed a matter of a Final Solution. This tribe is being exterminated so that nothing will remain, not even a cry or a tear. Efficient technique tested elsewhere is used here: the individual is dragged away from his tribe, from his family, from his past."[11] Wiesel also perceived another parallel to his generation's experience during the Holocaust. The media, national governments, the intellectuals, and the United Nations were all oblivious to this outrage; once again, the world remained silent. In his criticism of the contemporary nonresponse to the suffering of the Aché tribe, Wiesel recalled the customary apologia after the Holocaust era when people tried to exonerate themselves by asserting that they did not know. He countered that the excuse of ignorance no longer obtained with the knowledge afforded by the International League's documentation: "But now, after having read these testimonies, we know. Henceforth we shall be responsible—and accomplices."[12]

Wiesel humbly called attention to his own ignorance and lamented other people's indifference, including that of "politicized intellectuals." He could not understand how and why the democracies tolerated this assault on the indigenous people. Still, Wiesel did not venture to comment on or examine why some people were ignorant and others indifferent to the Aché. Indeed, Paraguay was not the only sanctuary for Nazis; other counties such as Chile and Argentina welcomed them after World War II, often with the aid of the Vatican and the U.S. government.[13] General Stroessner's Paraguay had been a long-time U.S. ally whose anti-Communism held him in good stead and whose openness to U.S. corporations was appreciated and rewarded, a familiar pattern throughout much of Latin America. In this intervention when he was not yet a widely known figure in the United States, Wiesel showed his alertness to unworthy victims, as the Aché had nothing to offer the powerful, either materially or ideologically, at home or abroad. They were the expendable victims for whom no intervention—by the U.S. government—and no outcry—by the U.S. media—were worth the trouble.

In this appalling case, Wiesel sounded themes that recur in his future human rights rhetoric. One major emphasis is that nothing had really changed, people had not learned from the Holocaust, and the world once again chose silence while the innocent were humiliated and slaughtered. Many Europeans and Americans had claimed that they did not know what was happening to the Jews under the Nazis. It is obvious, however, that the phenomena of ignorance, indifference, and bystanders did not originate in the Holocaust period. Historical precedents about silence other than during the Holocaust also could have been invoked. Traditionally both Europeans and Americans had exhibited complicity, ignorance, and indifference to the vast suffering and violence inflicted on numerous indigenous peoples in the Americas going back to Columbus's invasion. Wiesel owned his ignorance about the inhuman treatment of this one tribe, but, as Cherokee activist and author Ward Churchill pointed out, the Holocaust survivor did not make the broader connection between this recent murderous policy and "the entire genocidal sweep of history in Iberoamerica—a process of which the Aché slaughter is only the tiniest of recent parts."[14] Historian David Stannard also commented on Wiesel's epilogue and confession of ignorance and went on to make a more general point about this latest atrocity and its historical context:

> How many Americans today have heard of the Aché Indians? Or of the scores of other separate and independent indigenous peoples of Central and South America who have been totally exterminated, under equally ghastly conditions, during our lifetimes? Or of those who are being destroyed in the same way even in the far north to Tierra del Fuego in the far south, and on the 16 million square miles of land between—who were liquidated by outside invaders and settlers during past centuries? There is nothing left of them. Not a trace. Others cling on to existence, their numbers tiny fractions of what they were before the waves of violence swept over them.[15]

Such critical voices as Stannard and Churchill expanded Wiesel's Holocaust-based critique of the "civilized West" to include the colonial powers (and American successor) that pursued such conquests and the destruction of expendable peoples with patriotic fervor and self-righteousness.

Parallels in suffering and abandonment between past Holocaust and present Aché victims were all too clear to Wiesel. But there were two discontinuities he did not note. First, unlike World War II when the United States was at war with the Nazi regime committed to genocide, the U.S. government in the case of Paraguay was a strong backer of the dictator who presided over this reprehensible policy. Revealingly, the U.S. government that supported the civil rights of Soviet Jews did not respond to the misery of the Aché, for such a response, it maintained, would constitute an unwarranted intrusion into Paraguayan affairs. Second, whereas the U.S. press had at least reported the ongoing atrocities against the European Jews in the 1940s, the U.S. media, with rare exceptions, did not report what was happening to the indigenous people of Paraguay, except to repeat the optimistic reports of the State Department or to criticize the Paraguayan leaders for past errors.[16] In fact, if the Aché people's misery was too widely publicized, their fate could prove to be damning to both Stroessner and his U.S. supporters. But that was not too likely; the book for which Wiesel wrote his epilogue was not reviewed in the *New York Times* and had sold fewer than two thousand copies.[17]

Southeast Asian Refugees

Shortly after Wiesel wrote his epilogue on the Aché people, the official U.S. war against Vietnam ended in April 1975.[18] Although many U.S. citizens may have breathed a sigh of relief at the end of the long-standing national nightmare, the nation of Vietnam would continue to attract significant U.S. media coverage after the Communists came to power. Moreover, the U.S. government continued to pursue its regional goals relative to the new government, given the U.S. opposition to any rule by Communists or independent nationalists. The Communist government faced an immense task of social reconstruction, as Vietnam had been bombed relentlessly and destroyed during the U.S. war. Apart from the severe environmental devastation, the cities and countryside were teeming with refugees, orphans, drug addicts, and prostitutes. Hence, it would be gravely inaccurate to assume that suffering in Vietnam began after 1975, with no antecedent causes, certainly none to be laid to rest at official U.S. policy.[19]

While Elie Wiesel had been involved most heavily with the issue of Soviet Jewry, the U.S. government had been waging war in Indochina. During this period, American and European dissidents called for a war crimes tribunal against the U.S. government, thus evoking the Holocaust and subsequent Nuremberg trials. In accusing the United States of war crimes and crimes of aggression, these investigative critics identified, among other hideous practices, U.S. bombardment of civilians, torture of prisoners, systematic destruction of the institutions of civil society, forced labor, and the use of experimental weapons. In his remarks at the tribunal, philosopher Bertrand Russell explicitly made the connections between World War II and Vietnam:

> Moral purpose cannot be separated from the concern for truth. The burning children of Vietnam are martyred by the Western world. Their suffering,

like that of the gassed Jews of Auschwitz, is a basic feature of the civilization
that we have built. . . . It is our culture that is at stake. It is our barbarism that
menaces it. It is not possible to organize a society for plunder and mass
murder without terrifying consequences. Our scientists and engineers, our
chemists and researchers, our technology and economic system have been
mobilized for murder. In Vietnam we have done what Hitler did in Europe.
We shall suffer the degradation of Nazi Germany unless we act. *Untermensch*
is a word which lives again in the vocabulary of powerful men in Washington
who speak of "yellow dwarfs" and "coonskins." The pity is not in the
suffering of Vietnam. Her people resist and are heroic. The pity is in the
smug streets of Europe and the complacent cities of North America so
debased as to be indifferent even as our own fate is enacted in Vietnam.[20]

Some young people in the growing antiwar movement also made the
explicit connection between past and present. One was Mark Rudd,
whose family included Holocaust survivors. Rudd, a student leader at
Columbia University in 1968, had stated, "But we were not going to be
good Nazis. I was not going to stand by and watch American planes
drop napalm on innocent women and children. I was not going to let
my country burn innocents alive and do nothing."[21]

In addition to his work on behalf of Soviet Jewry and civil rights for
Blacks in the American South, Rabbi Abraham Joshua Heschel also
mobilized against this war in Vietnam. He challenged those in the religious community who supported U.S. policy when he affirmed: "To
speak about God and remain silent on Vietnam is blasphemous."[22] Heschel was influential in the group Clergy Concerned About Vietnam,
which included such other peace activists as Jesuit priest Daniel Berrigan. In his memoirs, Elie Wiesel recalled how Heschel struggled with
his own commitments, both to Israel and to the Vietnamese people:

> One Shabbat afternoon he confided to me that Israeli friends had asked
> him—possibly on the initiative of American officials—to keep a lower profile
> in his struggle against Lyndon Johnson's policy in Southeast Asia. "What can
> I do?" Heschel asked. "How can I keep silent when week after week
> thousands of Vietnamese civilians are being killed by our bombs? . . . How
> can I proclaim my Jewishness if I remain insensitive to the pain and
> mourning of men, women, and children who have been deprived of sleep by
> years of nighttime bombing?" He was genuinely distressed and since he was
> asking my opinion, I gave it to him. Press on, I told him, even at the cost of
> annoying the administration.[23]

In Wiesel's own published work, it is difficult to find any developed
position of his own annoying of the Johnson and Nixon administrations
about the agony of the Vietnamese, at least before 1970. Because of his

tireless activities on behalf of Russian and Israeli Jews, Wiesel may not have had the time and energy to join Heschel in the growing movement in opposition to Johnson's and Nixon's war. In a 1971 interview with Harry James Cargas, however, Wiesel claimed, "There is a political silence which is criminal: today to be silent when so many injustices are being performed and perpetuated: in Russia against the Jews; in Vietnam against the Vietnamese; in all kinds of countries against minorities. To be silent about it is criminal."[24] In later public talks and addresses, he made some passing references to the suffering of the Vietnamese people.[25]

Eventually, Wiesel did speak out more on Vietnam, but it was a few years after the U.S. government withdrew in 1975. At that time, U.S. media attention focused on the peril faced by Vietnamese refugees fleeing the allegedly atrocious Communist regime that reunited North and South Vietnam. In the summer of 1979 Wiesel involved himself in the issue of the Vietnamese boat people.[26] Invited to testify on the issue before the U.S. Senate, Wiesel began his remarks by identifying his "yardstick" of judgment: "We who live with the memory of the Holocaust, we who judge all things by its shadow and in its light are particularly distressed by the specter of silence and apathy which greets the fate of the 'boat people.' "[27] The Vietnamese boat people triggered Wiesel's own memories of abandonment and he criticized the fact that immigration quotas prevented these refugees from finding safe haven. He next invoked his recently conferred status as the chairman of President Jimmy Carter's Commission on the Holocaust to speak in that name of that commission to call for all nations of the world to offer asylum and refuge to the boat people "so that we may not once again be divided into a world of perpetrators, victims, and bystanders."[28] To Wiesel, it was clear that the boat people were the victims. The bystanders also were identified easily—the nations of the world that were not taking them in. Wiesel did not identify the perpetrators, but, because he was speaking before the U.S. Senate, one assumes he considered them to be the Vietnamese government. Wiesel then expressed his confidence that President Carter, whose administration had adopted the rhetoric of promoting human rights, would take leadership on this issue and work to "grasp this clear opportunity to learn from the history of the Holocaust not to err again."[29] Prudently, Wiesel did not mention that the U.S. leadership did not have to go all the way back to the Holocaust period, for only ten years before, the U.S. leadership had clear opportunities "not to err again," even as it carried out its murderous attack on Indochina. The current U.S. government and media concern with Vietnamese refugees did not begin before 1975, although there were millions who had lost their homes and had become refugees because of the savagery of U.S. attacks. In commenting on the conditions that led to the people leaving Vietnam, antiwar activist David Dellinger explained, "we can't overlook the greater role of the United States in first destroying much of the country and its economy and then imposing a murderous economic boycott."[30] But these history lessons were not admissible before the U.S. Senate. By the time of Wiesel's intervention, American political discourse characterized the Vietnamese boat people as "worthy victims" of the Communist enemy.

In the *Los Angeles Times* on 8 July 1979, Wiesel published an opinion column entitled, "The Victims of Injustice Must Be Cared For." Therein, he referred to the press and television coverage of the men, women, and children who lived behind barbed wire or who risked life and limb on the high seas trying to escape from Vietnam. He reported from eyewitness accounts that hundreds of people were dying daily. By the time that the United Nations had initiated a conference on this crisis later that month, thousands more already had died. Seemingly reminiscent of the international silence regarding the Aché, Wiesel could not fathom the tardiness of the international community: "Why so late? Why the delay? With so many innocent lives at stake, why wasn't this meeting organized earlier? What does it take to make the U.N. leadership realize that such an emergency warrants greater haste?"[31]

Wiesel then revealed his disappointment that President Carter and other statesmen, while at a meeting in Asia, failed to visit Vietnamese refugee camps in Malaysia and Thailand. He wished that some gesture would have been made, if only to offer consolation to the Vietnamese that their predicament was acknowledged and that other human beings were concerned about their suffering. This kind of visitation might have given the victims much needed moral reassurance. Wiesel assumed that appearances by Jimmy Carter and Pope John Paul II (who had recently visited Auschwitz) also would have had the positive effect of pressuring Vietnamese officials to act with greater consideration toward the refugees. As the gravity of this situation reactivated his own sense of heart-breaking loss, Wiesel articulated his responsibility:

> Of course, I will be the last to make analogies about what happened in the 1930s and now. We ought not to use the Holocaust terminology for other tragedies.

And yet, how can we witness the conditions of today's boat people without remembering those who, one generation ago, were not given shelter anywhere and whose misery and death were met with organized complacency?

How can we watch them, wounded and frightened children, without thinking at the same time about other children, of another generation, who were disowned by an allegedly civilized world?

Granted, the tragedies are different in essence and scope—but the universality of man's indifference remains the same.[32]

Wiesel guarded the uniqueness of the Jewish Holocaust even as he conceded that similar political dynamics were operative, a case in point being the UN conference on the issue in Geneva later that month. Wiesel cited the 1938 Evian Conference and expressed his hope that the approaching conference would not be a repetition of that earlier diplomatic disaster in which Western countries ultimately refused to offer aid and relief to Nazism's Jewish victims. Wiesel trusted that "[t]he Geneva conference will bring results because the Evian meeting brought none."[33] Wiesel's memorial and mystical logic was that, if the conference participants would only remember the failure of forty years earlier, when the Jews were cast aside, then they would necessarily be committed to finding a solution for these Vietnamese refugees.

In this article, Wiesel perceived the unfolding tragedy of the Vietnamese in the light of his own wretched experience in Nazi-dominated Europe: There was nowhere to run, no one to offer help or resistance. Convinced that Holocaust remembrance had the capacity to alter history, Wiesel speculated, "[i]f the fate of the boat people does inspire a vast movement of solidarity and compassion throughout the Western world, it is because the life and death of another people, only some forty years ago, was met by society's indifference."[34] Wiesel then claimed that the link between the ignominy of the past and the possibility of the present is the Jewish survivor, the witness who bore an epistemological advantage: "More than others we know, yes, we know, that we must save these new victims from death or rejection and despair: not to do so would mean to betray them—and those who were betrayed before them."[35] If Wiesel betrayed the Vietnamese by his silence and indifference, he would also betray history's previous victims, his own Jewish people. For Wiesel, fidelity consists of fusing the memory of past atrocity to present responsibility. Explicit in his avowal is the claim of a rare authority that compels him to wake up and mobilize his readers to influence governments to offer aid to the Vietnamese boat people.

At an address in Warsaw in late July 1979, Wiesel shared further reflections on his time in Geneva where he had served as a member to the American delegation to the Conference on the Boat People. Noting that Vice President Walter Mondale had been the chairman of the U.S. delegation, Wiesel applauded Mondale's persuasive and eloquent speech. The reason for Mondale's exemplary discourse? Wiesel attributed it to the vice president's appropriation of the Holocaust "as the basis and texture of his speech."[36] Mondale used the Holocaust as the framework for stressing the urgency of the Vietnamese predicament and he, too, invoked the Evian Conference as an obvious precedent not to be repeated. Wiesel then restated his Holocaust hermeneutic: "[Mondale] spoke of the tragedy today in the light of the greatest of all tragedies of the past, the Holocaust."[37] Whereas in the case of the Soviet Jews Wiesel's work was motivated by assertive in-group solidarity, here, his own particular interest—remembering the Holocaust—was put to the service of a more universal solidarity with the Vietnamese, albeit at a time when their suffering had become ideologically useful to the U.S. government. But another side of the equation must also be recognized, one important for understanding Wiesel's strategies and stakes in the U.S. public sphere: Solidarity with the Vietnamese was then put back in the service of remembrance of the world's greatest tragedy, the Holocaust.

During this same period in which U.S. media attention focused on Vietnamese fleeing the new Communist regime, Pol Pot's Khmer Rouge came to power in Cambodia in April 1975. Soon thereafter, there were allegations of genocide being perpetrated by the Communists in the course of the revolutionary transformation of their society.[38] Once again, Wiesel gravitated to this widely publicized ordeal of a people facing reeducation camps and mass murder. In a December 1978 interview, he exclaimed incredulously, "That the United States government has not done anything to stop the massacre in Cambodia is something I cannot understand. And the UN of course has other things to do than think of Cambodia."[39] Although Wiesel had made a specific—although highly unrealistic—proposal of action regarding the Vietnamese refugees (universal asylum), he did not specify what exactly the U.S. government, the United Nations, or anyone else should have been doing to stop the killing. Once displeased by President Carter's failure to visit Vietnamese refugee camps in Thailand and Malaysia, he decided to witness in January 1980 against what he again perceived to be worldwide indifference to the Cambodians. He became a part of an international delegation to march for the "survival of Cambodia," organized by Doctors Without Borders and the

International Rescue Committee. Composed of intellectuals, journalists, and doctors, the delegation went to offer food and other supplies to those in the refugee camps at the Thai–Cambodian border. Upon his return to the United States, Wiesel wrote an extensive account of what he found there, once again published in the *Los Angeles Times*.

Wiesel started by posing the apocalyptic question—"Can a people die?" He remarked that the causes of Cambodian suffering had been one after another: American bombing, Vietnamese arms, and, most significantly, Pol Pot's killers.[40] He sounded his perennial theme: "If the world does not shake off its indifference, this people will die."[41] At the time of this visit in early 1980, Wiesel understood that the situation had somewhat stabilized—the Khmer Rouge gangs were on the run after Vietnam invaded Cambodia in 1979, famine was decreasing, and the capital city of Phnom Penh was recovering slowly. Yet the desperation Wiesel saw in the faces of the refugees was poignant enough to motivate his own work of witness:

> So it was because I believed and at the same time could not believe [this mass suffering] that I went to Thailand. To see, to listen, to bear witness.
> And to keep *you* from saying later on that you didn't know.
> As always, that is what people say: "We didn't know, how could we know?" Well, now you will have to find another excuse. For now you know.[42]

Even though the Western press had recently focused on the misery of the Cambodians (as it had of the Vietnamese refugees) in the form of murder, torture, hunger, and disease, Wiesel refused to let his readers' consciences off the hook: "Don't say, don't say again that you didn't know. When a people dies, today, in the middle of the 20th century, *it is known*."[43] Writing a few years after his epilogue on the Aché, Wiesel took a more rigorous and forceful stand against bystander rationalization.

Wiesel visited three camps, one for Cambodians fortunate enough to immigrate soon to a Western nation, another for Khmer Rouge refugees, and a third with more than a hundred thousand people. At each stop, Wiesel made a special effort to reach out and communicate to the children in the educational classes and hospital. He wondered about some of the young Khmer Rouge boys that he met: "is it possible, then, that these children could have committed the atrocities about which we all know?"[44] Although some refugees were reticent, others told Wiesel of their own witnessing or surviving of atrocities. Wiesel expressed his admiration for the international brigades and volunteers who had come to care for the refugees and assist them in relocation. Nevertheless, despite these occasional, individual successes, Wiesel still was concerned about how to prevent such massive death of the Cambodian people. He admitted a commonality between the misery and abandonment experienced by the Cambodians and by his own people in Europe. But he was careful to restrict the use of the terms "Auschwitz" and "Holocaust" to the events that took place in Europe, not those taking place in Southeast Asia, even though, he proclaimed, Auschwitz's "bearing is universal."[45] In another article published in *The Jewish Chronicle* in 1980, Wiesel maintained that "there is no comparison. The event which left its mark on my generation defies analogy. Those who talk about 'Auschwitz in Asia' and the 'Cambodian Holocaust' do not know what they are talking about. Auschwitz can and should serve as a frame of reference, but that is all."[46] Earlier in the decade, Wiesel had objected to people who had made offensive analogies between the Holocaust and the domestic American scene, from Harlem to anti–Vietnam War protesters. But as Pol Pot's infamy was exposed, it was not surprising that he would be demonized like Hitler and that Holocaust analogies would proliferate and become au courant—to Wiesel's evident dismay.[47]

Still, because of his experiences and his testimony about Auschwitz, Wiesel felt that "it was impossible for me not to try to confront this mass of suffering which defies us, and which sometimes accuses us." His memories prodded him to go to the border and serve "by my presence, by my own person" as a "link."[48] Namely, it was his duty to join the warning that was Auschwitz to the agony of Cambodia. Wiesel was convinced of the necessity of his presence, but he had no illusions about the power of the delegation to change the situation. He suspected that in a few weeks the media would turn to some other issue as people grew tired of hearing about Cambodia. But he did not regret having made the trip, even though he believed that there might be few fruitful consequences from this initiative of solidarity. In response to fellow activists, Wiesel explained his recurrent rationale, which is comparable to his untiring speaking out on the Holocaust: "I realize I can't make my society change, but I can't let that society change me."[49] Wiesel exuded resignation about the difficulty in doing anything beyond offering a symbolic march to save a people from massive suffering even as he mustered moral resistance to remaining indifferent and at a safe distance from their agony.

This linkage between Auschwitz in 1945 and Cambodia in 1980 was strengthened by the coincidence that Wiesel's visit to the border occurred on the anniversary of his father's death in January 1945. Although he offered his own personal prayers, Wiesel wanted to offer the solemn Kaddish for the dead. To do so, he needed to find nine other Jews to form a minyan. This was not an easy task among the delegation, but Wiesel finally was able to find the number required by Jewish law. Wiesel asked the tenth man who had joined them for whom he was saying the Kaddish, a mother or father, perhaps. The young man replied, looking toward the refugees at the border, "It is for them."[50] Although Wiesel had his own doubts about the effectiveness of his visit to the refugee camps, his prayer and presence reconstituted the memorial bond of solidarity, to family and foreigners, to the past and present alike.

Wiesel's interventions on behalf of suffering refugees in Southeast Asia reflected both his long-standing commitment to remember the Holocaust and to use that experience as a frame of reference for contemporary affairs. In both cases, Wiesel safeguarded the Holocaust experience from profane analogies increasingly invoked in the public domain, even as he connected that incomparable catastrophe to these current instances of suffering with his denunciation of public indifference and silence. By this time, Wiesel was able to promote both memory and solidarity in a more public way than even in the early 1970s (when he spoke out on Biafra and Paraguayan human rights violations), because he himself gained increased visibility and honorary status in the United States as a respected Holocaust survivor. So he could write for major national newspapers, testify before the Senate, and serve the United States government both as a delegate in international conferences as well as chairman of the President's Commission on the Holocaust.

Regardless of how much Wiesel personally felt moved by the experiences of these victims, these interventions of witness and solidarity did not occur in a political vacuum. Wiesel may have seen his efforts here as exclusively humanitarian, comparable to his work with Soviet Jews, far from having any suspect "political" dimensions. But the travail of Vietnamese boat people and Khmer Rouge victims were already ideologically framed issues of human rights in the United States. Because these refugees were victims of official Communist enemies, their plight warranted much coverage and aroused extensive indignation. Wiesel's anguished, moralizing discourse—and his avoidance of any penetrating political questioning of U.S. policy (as opposed to U.S. inaction) past and present—was welcomed on the available market for commentary on the misery of these victims of Communism. And yet, there were many other examples during the same time period of refugees who warranted little or no attention in the U.S. media and to the U.S. government, such as the 250,000 refugees created by Israel's bombing of Lebanon in 1978, the 15,000 Haitian "boat people," or the 140,000 refugees from the Philippines.[51] Because these people were not fleeing from Communist terror, but from governments friendly to the United States, they did not readily warrant testimony at international conferences, detailed media coverage, or senatorial expressions of solidarity.

At the same time that U.S. attention was riveted on the worthy victims of Communism, another atrocity was taking place in the same region. The Indonesian government invaded and annexed East Timor, the former Portuguese colony, in 1975–1976 and engaged in full-scale aggression to "pacify" the indigenous population.[52] Church and human rights groups estimated that 200,000 out of a pre-invasion population of 615,000 died from the mass killings and famine. Similar to Paraguay, Indonesia was a trusted ally of the United States and so received significant military and ideological aid, at the time of near-genocidal attacks by the Indonesians in 1978. About Cambodia, Wiesel had claimed, "Don't say, don't say again that you didn't know. When a people dies, today, in the middle of the 20th century, *it is known.*" Yet, contrary to Wiesel's assertion of widespread silence, the genocide committed by the Khmer Rouge was well known and volubly discussed. However, the tragedy of the people of East Timor was downplayed and ignored by the U.S. media. Unlike the situation in Cambodia, where there were no serious proposals on how best to stop the Khmer Rouge, a remedy in East Timor was comparatively simple: If enough citizens spoke out to pressure the U.S. government (and those of Canada, France, and so on) not to send arms to the Indonesians, and to enforce—rather than water down—the UN resolutions condemning Indonesia, more Timorese lives could have been saved. Evidently, the "civilized West," to use Wiesel's sardonic expression, had more important concerns than the East Timorese.

Central America in the 1980s

If it took the war in Southeast Asia during the 1960s to make many Americans aware of the existence of that region, the same might be said for Central America in the 1980s.[53] In both decades, the U.S. government made each area its prime testing ground in foreign policy. The official rationale for the policy of war in Southeast Asia as well as U.S. intervention in Central America was the battle against Communism. The antiwar movement of the 1960s challenged the accuracy and legitimacy of this government doctrine, leading to government officials referring to the need to combat the "Vietnam Syndrome," simply put, the U.S. public's opposition to military violence abroad.[54] Both the Carter administration's touting of human rights and Ronald Reagan's crusading against the "Evil Empire" could be seen as efforts to recover from this popular suspicion and direct attention to regimes that were truly abominable. Nowhere was this focus more clearly demonstrated than the Reagan administration's support for anti-Communist governments and insurgents in Central America.[55] Throughout the decade, there were significant debates and controversies involving U.S. economic and military aid, negotiated settlements, death squads, freedom fighters, and international law. The U.S. media focused attention extensively on the conflicts in El Salvador and Nicaragua, less so on Honduras and Guatemala. Intellectuals, journalists, and academics debated the merits of Reagan policy, while ordinary U.S. citizens traveled to the countries, organized caravans of material aid, and engaged themselves in the various congressional debates over U.S. funding. The U.S. Catholic and Protestant churches took a major lead in offering solidarity to fellow Christians in Central America, because those Christians in base communities had played a vital role in empowering people to defend their rights—which provoked violent repression by the U.S.-backed government and military forces.[56] Thus, a region that few U.S. citizens cared about before 1980 became a subject of intense and spirited conflict between civil society and the U.S. government.

After decades of supporting the brutal Somoza family dictatorship, the U.S. government grew concerned with the advances of the revolutionary Sandinista movement. As late as 1979, the Carter administration hoped to work out an arrangement whereby there could be "Somocismo without Somoza."[57] The United States wished to preserve the preferred form of stability, in other words, the status quo without the depredations of the corrupt Somoza regime in which radical social change—the kind advocated by the Sandinista Front—could be avoided at all costs. This U.S. goal was frustrated, however, with the Sandinista victory in July 1979. By the time the Reagan administration had come to office in 1981, former Somozan National Guardsmen had gathered in Honduras and begun attacks against the Nicaraguan government. Nicaragua became a litmus test of U.S. resolve to oppose and repel Communism, now portrayed as a grave danger to American security. In the relentless U.S. propaganda campaign, not only were the counterrevolutionaries ("contras") consecrated by President Reagan as "freedom fighters" on the moral level of the American Founding Fathers, but the Sandinistas were correspondingly demonized as running a totalitarian government bent on domination of the entire Central American region.[58] U.S. military aid to the government of El Salvador was justified officially by the charge that Nicaragua was sending destabilizing aid to the Salvadoran revolutionaries. The contra armies were the chief instrument of U.S. policy against Nicaragua in that they terrorized the civilian population and diverted vital national resources away from social reconstruction to military defense.[59] Contras regularly engaged in rape, torture, and kidnapping of civilians, as well as destruction of farms, health centers, and cooperatives. They never posed a serious challenge to overthrowing the Sandinistas, but with U.S. intelligence, military aid, and ideological support, they amply interfered with the plans the Sandinistas had for transforming their overwhelmingly poor country, left in ruins by the Somoza dictatorship.

In this politically charged atmosphere, Elie Wiesel made a trip with Joachim Maître to the Honduran jungles to meet with leaders of the Miskito Indians who had lived primarily on Nicaragua's Atlantic coast.[60] Wiesel reported his reflections on his encounters with the Miskitos in the *Los Angeles Times* in February 1984.[61] There he noted that the people had become exiles living in Honduras where they were attempting to "rebuild [their] homes and [their] dreams, which a regime marked by violence on the other side of the Nicaraguan border tried to change and even to destroy."[62] Wiesel stated that the Miskitos had come to Honduras when they were forced from their homes by Sandinista military rationales; he also pointed out that they had been persecuted for ethnic and cultural reasons. At the refugee camp, Wiesel had encounters that were similar to his visit at the Thai–Cambodian border. Men, women, and especially children suffered the pangs of deracination; they wanted only to continue their traditional way of life removed from the political conflicts and pressures of modern, revolutionary society.

Wiesel described how some Miskitos initially had identified with the Sandinista revolution, because the Somozan regime had victimized them as well. The Sandinistas even offered some government positions to the Miskitos, but conflicts ensued when the Sandinistas relocated the Miskitos to increase protection at their borders, given the frequency and ferocity of contra attacks. Wiesel next offered a litany of Miskito suffering after they had resisted the Sandinista orders: Their homes were burned, people were arrested, and individuals suffered various humiliations and executions. As a result, some Miskitos organized themselves into secret guerrilla actions against the new government. Wiesel asserted that in December 1983 the Sandinistas forced the Miskitos to march toward Honduras during the three days of which they were attacked by the Nicaraguan army. Sympathetic to their suffering and endurance, Wiesel mused: "How did they manage not to give in to defeat, the fear? How did the children manage not to panic? They smile: When one is Miskito, one can do anything."[63]

He then shared some of the testimony he heard from those Miskitos who were then battling the Sandinistas because their Indian identity was being violated. Wiesel considered the possibility that the Miskitos were exaggerating but then dismissed it because would not be consistent with their character. He seemed grateful that they were not prone to using the inflated rhetoric of genocide, which could only diminish the unique and transcendent stature of the Holocaust. He candidly ranked the Miskito tragedy far behind that of Cambodia, which may account, he reasoned, for the world's indifference. Although Wiesel often expressed his bewilderment at politics, he managed to grasp the predicament of the Miskitos: "An armed movement cannot remain neutral. By fighting the Sandinistas, the Miskito are defending U.S. interests. Just as the former are manipulated by the communist world, the latter probably are by the Western powers."[64] Wiesel assumed that the Sandinistas were manipulated, but suggested that the Miskitos only "probably" were so manipulated by Western powers. But he quickly moved from political analysis to what really concerned him, the civilians, especially the children, who suffered in this conflict. Wiesel quoted an Indian who told him that the surroundings in Honduras reminded him of his childhood home and that although the Miskitos might be able to re-create much of their previous life there, they could not bring everything with them, for example, their cemetery.[65]

By coming to the Honduran jungle, Wiesel hoped to extend solidarity to another people that suffered, to assure them that others cared about their dislocation. Wiesel's intervention lacked any specific Holocaust discourse that he had deployed in past interventions, if only to debunk pundits who claimed that Vietnam or Cambodia was somehow comparable to Auschwitz. But in his scant reference to the geopolitical context of the Miskito–Sandinista conflict, Wiesel avoided tackling the serious issue of how U.S. power and propaganda were then mobilized against Nicaragua because it was attempting to chart an independent course in Central America after decades of subservience to the United States. Although he noted with approval the modesty of the Miskitos in not claiming extermination or genocide, others were not so cautious and reserved. For example, shortly after Wiesel wrote his article, President Reagan claimed: "There has been an attempt to wipe out an entire culture, the Miskito Indians, thousands of whom have been slaughtered or herded into detention camps where they have been starved and abused. Their villages, churches and crops have been burned."[66] It was no accident that the Miskitos received the solicitude of the U.S. government, because their torment could be attributed to the Communist Sandinistas. In June 1985, the president upped the rhetorical ante by charging that the Sandinistas were waging "a campaign of virtual genocide against the Miskito Indians."[67] The human rights monitoring group Americas Watch refuted Reagan's charge and mentioned that even the Country Reports of the State Department did not make such audacious claims. Further, a human rights report released by the Organization of American States found one incident of noncombatant killing, while Americas Watch found one other. These reports indicated that the incidents were serious and worthy of condemnation, but were far from Reagan's insistence that thousands were being killed by ruthless, cold-blooded Sandinistas. Earlier, Jeane Kirkpatrick claimed on the MacNeil-Lehrer television program that "some 250,000 Mestizo Indians [sic]—are being so badly repressed that concentration camps have been built on the coast of Nicaragua in the effort to try to imprison them, to eliminate their opposition."[68] Although it is true that the Sandinistas did precipitate a conflict with their relocation of Miskito civilians during wartime, by December 1983, the government admitted its mistakes and attempted to rectify relations by declaring an amnesty for insurgent and imprisoned Miskitos.

In his solidarity and human rights work, Wiesel tried to present himself as a political innocent, positioning himself above mere "politics" so as to assert his moral connection to the victims, especially refugees, and to denounce civic indifference. As with his concern for victims in Southeast Asia, Wiesel's Honduran trip and reportage were shaped by the political context of the day. In 1965 Wiesel had hoped his report on Soviet Jewry would not be used for propaganda purposes. However, it would take some naiveté not to realize that a report on Miskito suffering, in the context of the Reagan administration's attacks on Nicaragua, would be further "proof" of the treachery of this alleged Soviet satellite. Once again, there was an available market for testimonies to purported Sandinista terror even though there were other issues involving innocent victims and moral responsibility. While it made unfounded charges of mass killings by the Sandinistas, the Reagan administration had been funding a terrorist proxy army to murder and torture civilians and disrupt the Sandinista social experiment. In the U.S. political economy of human rights, the non-Miskito, Nicaraguan civilian victims of the U.S.-backed contras did not merit concern; in fact, their executioners were trained and funded by the U.S. government.[69] Wiesel did not draw attention to the suffering of these victims, perhaps because he had cordial relations with President Reagan (whose administration favored the State of Israel and supported Holocaust remembrance)[70] and because Reagan had nursed a virtual obsession with the Sandinistas.[71] Although usually so careful to object to excessive rhetoric around the use of the word "genocide," Wiesel did not protest the preposterousness of Reagan's characterization of the Sandinistas of being perpetrators of this evil crime. Also, Wiesel did not comment upon this U.S. war *against* Nicaragua; instead, he focused on the beauty and burdens of the Miskito children and the refugees' need for cultural autonomy.

Subsequent years witnessed the continuing terrorism of the contras (funded by the U.S. Congress), the Reagan administration's refusal to heed a World Court condemnation for its illegal bombing of Nicaraguan harbors, and the chicanery of the Iran–contra deals.[72] I have been unable to find any reference in Wiesel's work to the U.S. government's support of terrorism and its own refusal to abide by the World Court decision. Wiesel's long-standing dictum—silence and neutrality only benefit the oppressors, never their victims—certainly had pertinence to the U.S. government's hostility toward Nicaragua. In some previous cases, Wiesel lectured the U.S. government for its lack of responses to human suffering; in the case of non-Miskito Nicaraguan civilians, Wiesel had nothing to say about the U.S. government's *agency* in causing such suffering. In his 1999 memoir, Wiesel recalled the Miskitos as being "expelled from their homes by Daniel Ortega's repressive regime, the latest 'forgotten' in our society, which often practices apathy and selective solidarity," which prompted him to ask, "why do so many civil rights activists look the other way? Because Daniel Ortega is of the left and violently anti-American, anti-imperialist, and therefore untouchable?"[73] This charge, though, could equally apply to Wiesel, as he offered solidarity to the one group of Nicaraguans that the Reagan administration found most worthy of temporary and expedient compassion. At this time, there were far more extensive atrocities being carried out in the region at the time Wiesel visited the Miskitos in Honduras, by the governments of El Salvador and Guatemala, which were engaged in vicious battle not only with revolutionary movements but with their own civil societies.

In addition to its attacks on the Sandinista government in Nicaragua, the Reagan administration maintained amiable relations with the governments of Guatemala and El Salvador. In these two countries, the United States offered military and economic aid for regimes that were engaged in serious human rights abuses even as they resisted grassroots demands for social change, particularly in the area of land reform.[74] For example, President Reagan defended the born-again General and Guatemalan President Efraín Ríos Montt in the early 1980s even as he was laying waste to the Indian highlands in a campaign often described as genocide—the U.S. concern for indigenous Miskitos in Nicaragua was not mustered in the case of indigenous Mayan Guatemalans who were destroyed by the U.S.- and Israeli-backed military regime.[75] Revolutionary movements calling for radical social change in these extremely poor countries battled the governments; U.S. aid poured in to protect these regimes from the dreaded revolutionary fate of Nicaragua. As a result of the ravages of war, systematic repression, and brutal destruction of entire villages, up to two million people suffered uprooting from their homes, and many of these refugees sought haven in the United States.[76]

The increasing numbers and desperation of refugees in the U.S. southwest provoked the conscience of U.S. Christians and others working close to these border areas. A religious movement arose to offer these refugees "sanctuary," with obvious political implications, for the church-based movement offered hospitality to people the Immigration and Naturalization Service (INS) declared "economic refugees" and "illegal aliens," who had no right to be in this country, unlike legitimate "political refugees" fleeing from Communist countries such as Cuba or the Soviet Union. For harboring the refugees, churches and synagogues in coalition with other organizations risked FBI harassment and legal charges. The allies of the refugees pointed out that such civil disobedience was justified, given the policies of the U.S. government that contributed to the flight of refugees in the first place and that sought to return them to likely persecution in their countries.

In January 1985 a conference was held in Tucson, Arizona, the early center of succor to the refugees and resistance to U.S. policy.[77] The conference was to give direction to what was becoming a national movement, with even mainstream congregations in the U.S. heartland becoming willing to defy the law of the land. Harry James Cargas, one of the Catholics involved in the incipient solidarity movement and a long-time friend and ally of Elie Wiesel, had alerted the Holocaust survivor to the suffering of the refugees and urged his participation at the conference. Wiesel attended the opening of the conference and gave an address to the audience composed of hundreds of ministers and activists, as well as sixty refugees who wore bandannas to protected their identity from the media. In his speech on the refugee, an apt symbol, he believed, of the calamitous twentieth century, Wiesel offered a series of reflections that once again revealed how thoroughly the Holocaust experience permeated his sensibility and solidarity.[78]

Wiesel commenced by stating his abiding identification with the refugees, for he, too, once had been a refugee. He described his own fear over the years at customs proceedings and encounters with police, because of his own frightful, stateless past during the 1940s and 1950s. He stressed the incongruous sense of space and time in the context of Switzerland and France during World War II. The French on one side of the border in their occupied country could look across to Switzerland and know that their people lived in freedom. He also pondered how the Swiss "could remain free and eat in the morning and at lunch and at dinner while looking at the other side, at occupied France. After all, they lived in the same time, and yet, time itself had its own divisions."[79] Wiesel also criticized the indifference of the privileged to those who were oppressed. But in his battle with indifference in the present, Wiesel shrugged off politics:

> Those who know me will confirm that I am not a political person. I have never been involved in anything political. I don't understand politics; to me, it is something extremely obscure. I come from a tradition that aims at conferring an ethical meaning on anything a person does or does not do.[80]

Wiesel instead considered that from an ethical point of view, he, as a Jew who once witnessed absolute evil, must be involved. He identified the authentic community as including those who suffer as well as their allies who try to lessen their suffering. When he turned to the Jewish religious tradition to discover meanings of "sanctuary," Wiesel retrieved one definition applicable to the case of refugees fleeing Central America: "Any human being is a sanctuary. . . . Any person, by virtue of being a son or daughter of humanity, is a living sanctuary whom nobody has the right to invade."[81]

Wiesel next reminisced about his family's own danger in 1944 in Sighet. He had believed readily that because he and his family had gone to great lengths to get properly documented citizenship papers, they would be safe. The Nazi official, however, simply tore up the papers and threw them away. Wiesel then recalled being stateless in France and he expressed his gratitude to the United States for accepting him as a U.S. citizen. He stated his wishes that someday soon the Salvadoran and Guatemalan refugees would feel the same appreciation that he felt for the United States. He articulated the visionary goal that, by the end of the twentieth century, refugees will no longer exist, for "[w]herever people come, they should be accepted in every society with friendship."[82] To achieve this goal, Wiesel believed that the American public had a vital role to play. If only U.S. citizens could be made aware of the situation and the agony of the refugees, they could pressure Congress to act. Specifically, Wiesel remarked:

> After all, Congress is our best ally. I am pleased to hear that Senator
> DeConcini has introduced a bill. I think we should work with all our friends
> in Congress so that the bill passes in the House and the Senate. I think that is
> the way we must follow. I think it can be done. It can be done because
> humanity is contagious. We have seen it.[83]

The contagious example Wiesel cited was his work earlier that year on behalf of raising awareness about the famine in Ethiopia: The American people had responded "beautifully" as they were unable to tolerate the suffering of the dying in Africa.

Wiesel next asserted that tragedies should never be compared, for each was sui generis. Moreover, it was up to the victims of each tragedy to give a name to their own suffering. Wiesel held that "[t]he least I can do is to accept your testimony, the testimony of the victims, and give it full credence, because you are both victim of and witness to your own cause."[84] Although not directly confrontational, he then effectively dissented from the Reagan administration's distinction between economic and political refugees. For Wiesel, if someone's hunger compels them to flee their homeland, that person deserves American support and respect just as much as those fleeing for political reasons. He then adverted to a conference that had been held recently in Washington on the "righteous Gentiles" of the Holocaust, those who had the courage to shelter Jews. Wiesel admitted his surprise that the righteous were not people of stature: "Most of them were simple people who didn't even know that what they were doing was courageous; they didn't even known that their acts were heroic."[85] In Wiesel's eyes, it does not augur well if simply acting in a human way was identified as heroic.

In previous cases of massive suffering like Biafra and Cambodia, Wiesel had been moved to engagement by the distressing pictures he had observed on television or in the press. On the issue of Sanctuary, he went to the conference, he said, because of the phone calls and letters that implored him to intervene and speak out. He shared this modest self-appraisal with his audience: "I am not sure that I can help you very much. I have no political power. All I have is a way of putting some words together, that's all."[86] He concluded his talk with biblical and Hasidic references to make the ethical point that his place was measured by his distance from those who suffer. When he sees someone who suffers, he has to work to reduce the distance between them and offer modest gestures at mitigating that person's pain and preventing that person's humiliation.

This address at the Sanctuary conference represents another instance of Wiesel's solidarity with unworthy victims of the United States who deserved, according to INS policy, to be repatriated to their homelands, a grave danger, refugees and Sanctuary advocates claimed, because of the likelihood of reprisal by the government or security forces. In attending this conference, Wiesel kindly offered sympathy to the victims and related his own European experiences to the grassroots Sanctuary movement. Throughout, he highlighted his ethical, emotional, and existential links to the refugees; but his insistence on not being "a political person" invites closer scrutiny. Although in the beginning of the speech Wiesel claimed that he had never been involved in anything political, he later recommended popular pressures to help pass the DeConcini bill, which aimed to end the deportations of the refugees back to El Salvador and Guatemala. To mitigate the suffering, political channels obviously were critical. Congressional opponents of the DeConcini bill would have, in all likelihood, seen Wiesel's advocacy as partisan, even if he himself viewed it as unproblematically moral. Even as he initially maintained to be uncomprehending before politics (as "something extremely obscure"), he nevertheless indicated that he knew how to play the political game and turn the refugees' grievances into a public issue by drawing on social connections with Congress so as to promote ameliorative legislation. In fact, at a press conference before his lecture, Wiesel called for the formation of a congressional committee to investigate the status and safety of refugees who were sent back to their countries: "If there is a danger to these people upon their return, we should know about it. Congress should know."[87] Sanctuary advocates had already maintained that refugees were in such danger, though it was doubtful, because these refugees were fleeing from trusted U.S. allies, that Congress would follow Wiesel's own course and "accept your testimony, the testimony of the victims, and give it full credence, because you are both victim of and witness to your own cause."[88] Clearly, Wiesel involved himself in political struggles as he lent his growing moral authority as a Holocaust survivor to an embattled, fledgling movement and urged citizens to influence Congress on a particular bill. His presence at the Sanctuary symposium also had this positive symbolic effect: He could not be accused of being a "Communist," a derisive label often attached to the Sanctuary movement by the government and other opponents.

There is yet another political dimension to Wiesel's talk in Tucson. Whereas Sanctuary itself was an explicit confrontation with U.S. domestic and foreign policy, Wiesel did not comment upon, much less endorse, the movement's civil disobedience. Instead, he urged working with Congress—"our best ally"—to change the law. Wiesel also avoided any explicit criticism of the Reagan administration for its policies that backed the Salvadoran and Guatemalan governments and that contributed to the massive exodus of a large agrarian population in both countries. Although Wiesel empathized with the dangerous plight of the refugees, he did not take a controversial stand by directly opposing U.S. government policy. He compassionately attended to the effects of those policies—the torment of dislocation—but he did not address the causes of the refugees' suffering. Wiesel's Sanctuary speech revealed how his own position on this issue was shaped not only by his instinctive gravitation toward refugees but also his respectable status as a U.S. government advisor on Holocaust remembrance.

One consequence of Elie Wiesel's growing celebrity has been an increased number of urgent requests to attend to one or another issue of human misery. So in between his enduring projects and initiatives of solidarity with other Jews, Wiesel has managed to circle the globe and respond to many cases of suffering, including in Latin America, Africa, and Asia, as well as in Bosnia and Kosovo, to which I turn in Chapter 5. Throughout such interventions, Wiesel has minimized politics and instead emphasized his moral role of witness. His time-honored strategy has been to listen to the cries of those refugees whose upheaval evokes his own. As he has moved from one crisis to the next, he has shared his time, energy, and skills with the victims and their allies. He often has been willing to lend his increasingly authoritative voice and prestige to bring attention to these suffering peoples. Not only has Wiesel used his memory of the Holocaust as the driving motive to come to the aid of Jews and others who were victims of violence, but he also has used these occasions to protect and promote the memory of the Holocaust. Even as Wiesel has impressed upon his various and growing audiences in the United States his conviction of the significance and singularity of the Holocaust, he has also monitored that very same audience who might engage in sacrilegious comparisons between contemporary atrocity and the Nazi extermination. A refrain in many of Wiesel's interventions has been precisely that the uniqueness of the Holocaust must be respected as a kind of sacred province; no irreverent analogies are permissible. As he said in 1999, "Now we are witnessing a nightmare in Kosovo; it demands action, not comparison."[89] Explicit in Wiesel's worldview and public formulations has been that the Holocaust is *the* measuring stick or framework for appraising contemporary civic responsibility; to challenge or to decenter its preeminence is deemed an insensitive if not an offensive act.

In regard to the question posed in the opening of this chapter: Has Wiesel limited his interventions of solidarity only to "worthy victims" of past and present official enemies of the United States? I do not think so. In addition to the Aché people in the 1970s, Wiesel also came to the aid of Jacobo Timerman, an Argentinean Jewish newspaper man in the 1970s and spoke out against the mass disappearances there; again, Argentina was supported by the United States during the years of its fierce repression against its own citizens.[90] In the 1970s and 1980s, Wiesel visited South Africa and wrote about the apartheid regime, a long-standing U.S. ally that was the beneficiary of the Reagan administration's "constructive engagement" in the 1980s.[91] I examined earlier Wiesel's appearance at the Sanctuary conference in 1985. In addition to such victims of "constructive terror," as Chomsky and Herman describe the violence of U.S. allies as filtered by U.S. propaganda, Wiesel wrote or spoke out on behalf of other victims of "benign terror." For example, he concerned himself with the people of Tibet suffering under a brutal occupation by the Chinese and he spoke out on Biafra in which U.S. interests were neither at stake nor likely to be advanced even by a show of indignation.[92] In the post–Vietnam War context in the United States, Wiesel's work on behalf of Jewish causes had gradually become work for worthy victims, principally Holocaust survivors, Soviet Jews, and the State of Israel. Also, his sympathy for the Vietnamese boat people, Cambodian refugees, and Miskito Indians are examples of his solidarity with worthier victims. I wish to repeat that the political-ideological designations "worthy" and "unworthy" reflect the concerns and priorities of dominant U.S. institutions.

Wiesel consistently has insisted that he only was concerned morally in these interventions, and so he was able to stand above disreputable politics. Unwittingly or not, however, Wiesel has been engaged in politics by virtue of one of his own moral apothegms, to wit: neutrality—not taking the explicit side of the victims against the oppressor—always benefits the privileged of the status quo. Neutrality can manifest itself in different ways. A characteristic feature of Wiesel's witness has been that while he pointed to the horrifying effects of suffering—and, in some cases, was critical of the United States for failing to intervene on the victims' behalf—he has not attempted any formulation about or assessment of the U.S. government's ongoing agency and complicity in the human rights violations concerning America's "unworthy victims." Instead of making an attempt at identifying what might motivate U.S. policy to be so unconcerned about Salvadorans, Vietnamese, East Timorese, and Aché Indians, as it once had been unconcerned about European Jews, Wiesel has reiterated anguished, emotion-laden questions of why no one does anything for the victims, why, in effect, the world continues to remain silent as it had during the Holocaust. In this way, his efforts at a more universal solidarity have mirrored his earlier pleas regarding the unworthy Jewish victims inasmuch as Wiesel's rhetoric was one of a plea to do something, *anything*, for the current victims.

Nevertheless, the civic responsibility Wiesel has wished to see develop requires an awareness of the causes that lead to such suffering, especially those causes for which U.S. citizens bear responsibility vis-à-vis our government's policies. To call attention to the "sins of omission" in U.S. policy is necessary but not sufficient for a more humane world. For we must also respond to the U.S. government as an *actor* in international affairs, not simply an occasionally confused, timid, or ineffectual bystander, and so grapple with the systematic features of U.S. policy that account for our government's "sins of commission." In such wise, we need to understand so as to change the U.S. government's transcendent goal of maintaining "stability," which resulted in the savage attacks throughout Indochina in the 1960s and 1970s and its decades-long support of corrupt and brutal dictators such as Somoza and Marcos.

Wiesel's enthusiasm for the United States grew more fervid in recent decades, not surprisingly as his stature in his adopted country increased considerably. But his spirited sense of patriotism toward the United States has been rivaled by his long-standing ardor for the State of Israel. It is to the political conflicts of the Middle East that I now turn to explore Wiesel's solidarity with Israeli Jews and his relations to the Palestinian people.

4

The Diaspora Apologist
Israel and the Fate of Palestine

Do not ask me, a traumatized Jew, to be pro-Palestinian. I totally identify with Israel and cannot go along with leftist intellectuals who reject it. Perhaps another generation will be free enough to criticize Israel; I cannot.

—Elie Wiesel, *Against Silence: The Voice and Vision of Elie Wiesel*

How is it possible that a man so intelligent, knowledgeable, and informed could not have been aware of the anti-Jewish laws of Vichy? The plundering, the persecutions, the arrests, the roundups—how could he have failed to know about them?

—Elie Wiesel, on French president François Mitterand's World War II experience, *And the Sea Is Never Full: Memoirs, 1969–*

With the founding of the State of Israel in 1948, Elie Wiesel faced a major personal decision: whether to remain in France, or to make *aliyah,* or "ascent," and move to the new Jewish state. Since Wiesel's earliest years, Jerusalem had assumed a prominent place in his religious imagination: "Jerusalem had always figured in my most ardent and luminous dreams—Jerusalem my lullaby, my prayer. The mere evocation of its song made me feel elevated, transformed."[1] Even before the establishment of the state, Wiesel offered his services as a translator in Paris for the Irgun, a right-wing Zionist group skilled in terrorism.[2] Later, as a journalist, Wiesel would make many trips to Israel and often be enraptured at what was taking place there. But there were times, too, when he was chagrined, for example, at the second-class status meted out to Holocaust survivors or at the decision of David Ben-Gurion's government to accept reparations from the West German government in the early 1950s.[3] Despite his love for Israel, Wiesel could not bring himself to move there; he finally became an American citizen in 1963. Nevertheless, he maintained many connections with Israelis from all walks of life, including prominent government officials, like Golda Meir, with whom he had lively conversations. Wiesel had long nurtured a keen and passionate interest in the affairs of the Israeli people; this commitment redoubled because of transformative events in the spring and summer of 1967.

The Mystical Triumph of 1967

The third Arab–Israeli War was the pivotal event of recent Middle East history, so much so that the current peace negotiations and resistance to those negotiations cannot be understood apart from the quick succession of events that occurred in June 1967 and its aftermath.[4] Israel had been threatening Syria for months, alleging that it was a haven for terrorists and that it was violating the 1949 armistice agreement.[5] To stand up to Israel's threatening stance to its Arab ally Syria, Egypt's General Gamal Abdel Nasser requested the removal of the UN emergency forces from the Sinai and began to concentrate his troops there in late May. Nasser also blocked Israeli access to the Straits of Tiran so that Israeli shipping vessels could not send strategic materials that could be used against Syria. Three weeks before the war broke out, Arab pronouncements had grown increasingly alarming: Israel would be destroyed. From the perspective of world Jewry, this Arab threat to eliminate Israel was terrifying.[6] From the perspective of U.S. intelligence, however, the threat was mere posturing, as the United States assumed as a matter of course that Israel was quite powerful enough to thrash Arab opponents in any war.[7]

On June 5 Israel's surprise attack rapidly destroyed much of Egypt's air force and the Jewish state was well on the way to redrawing the boundaries of the Middle East conflict. Only the day before, Wiesel had been giving the commencement address at the Jewish Theological Seminary in New York and exhorted the students that if there should be a war, they should immediately set to work for Israel. The next day as the war began, Jews throughout the Diaspora mobilized on behalf of Israel. Even though Wiesel discovered that the Israelis had routed the Egyptians very early on, he decided that he still had to go to Israel. He was not optimistic but filled with a dread that was impervious to the Israeli Army's lightning victory:

> As I listened to Arab speeches and observed the passivity of Western governments, I told myself it was happening all over again. Clearly the Jews would fight courageously, as they had in the Warsaw ghetto, but they would be outnumbered, as before. The well-equipped Arab armies would crush Israel in the end. Then the so-called civilized world would shed crocodile tears and deliver grandiloquent funeral orations on our death. I say "our" death because, like so many of my contemporaries, I associated mine with Israel's. For me it was inconceivable to wish to live in a world that had no place for a sovereign Jewish state.[8]

As he would do consistently in the future, Wiesel interpreted the contemporary scene in the Middle East in light of his own experience during the Holocaust. "It was happening all over again" meant that the Jews were threatened with extermination and that they were outnumbered and outarmed by preponderant military forces. The Warsaw ghetto was not only bitter past but also imminent future. Initially, as he journeyed to Israel, Wiesel could not admit a dramatic difference since the 1940s: Jews now lived in a state and so had armed forces, superior to those of the allegedly "well-equipped Arab armies." Because of this anticipated replay of fearful history, Wiesel thought that he had to go to Israel and share his people's fate, whatever might be in store. Similar to his earlier missions to the Soviet Union, Wiesel realized that it was "incumbent upon the Jewish writer to be witness to all that has haunted the people of Israel from its beginnings. That is his role—not to judge but to testify."[9]

What Wiesel found when he arrived in Israel overwhelmed him. Contrary to his most despondent imaginings, the Israeli Jews had indeed emerged utterly victorious over their Arab enemies. He was further astounded that the Jews had captured the Old City of Jerusalem, formerly under Jordanian control. For Wiesel, Jerusalem had a mystical resonance that linked past and future in the Jewish imagination: "The Jew in me loves Jerusalem with a different, unique love."[10] To see Jews of all ages and kinds gathering at the Wailing Wall, the remnant of the Second Temple, was tantamount to a miracle.[11] He gave animated testimony:

> I saw Israel at war; I can therefore testify in its behalf. In the Old City of Jerusalem, barely reconquered, I saw hardened paratroopers pray and weep for the first time in their lives; I saw them, in the thick of battle, gripped by

an ancient collective fervor, kiss the stones of the Wall and commune in a silence as elusive as it was pure; I saw them, as in a dream, jump two thousand years into the past, renewing their bond with legend, memory and the mysterious tradition of Israel. Do not tell me they were moved by a will for power or material superiority. Their will sprang from spirituality and the harrowing immediacy of their past. Their experience was of a mystical nature. Even the non-believers felt transcended by their own acts and by the tales they told about them afterwards. The words on their lips sounded strangely fiery and distant. . . . Humanity has never known victors less arrogant, heroes more sober and eager for peace and purity.[12]

In immediate response to this rendezvous with legend, memory, and the mysterious tradition, Wiesel began writing a novel, *A Beggar in Jerusalem*.[13] Wiesel disputed simplistic equations between the Holocaust and the State of Israel, denying that the latter was somehow recompense for the former. Nevertheless, he interpreted Israel's impressive victory in the same religious terms as he comprehended the Holocaust. If the Holocaust was a mystery of absolute evil, the Israeli victory was a mystery of absolute good. Wiesel believed that Jewish history and memory, including that of the Holocaust victims, had been mobilized in the service of Israeli military power.[14]

Wiesel clearly chose to concentrate on the mystical resonances rather than the political implications of the conflict. As for the latter, Israel became an occupying power, seizing the Sinai from Egypt, the Gaza Strip and West Bank from Jordanian control, and the Golan Heights from Syria. In conquering Jerusalem, the Israelis laid the groundwork for its annexation and increased Jewish settlement around it. By interpreting the events through his Holocaust lens, Wiesel perceived Israel as the innocent David threatened by the Arab Goliath and ignored by the rest of the world. He defended the Israeli soldiers' spirituality, denying that the Israelis were interested in material profit or power. Others, however, had a different assessment. Yeshayahu Leibowitz, an influential Israeli philosopher and social critic, took exception to the rhapsody so characteristic of witnesses like Wiesel:

Within a short period of time there will be no Jewish workers in Israel. The Arabs shall be the workers; the Jews shall be the managers, inspectors, officials, and policemen and mainly secret service men. A State governing a hostile population of 1.5 to 2 million foreigners is bound to become a Shin Bet [secret police] state, with all that this would imply to the spirit of education, freedom of speech and thought and democracy. This corruption, characteristic of any colonial regime, would be true for Israel. The administration will be forced to deal with the suppression of an Arab protest movement and the acquisition of Arab quislings. We must fear that even the army and its officers, a people's army, will deteriorate by becoming an occupation army, and its officers, turned into military governors, will not differ from military governors elsewhere in the world.[15]

Such sober political analysis—which appraised Israel as a state power in quite this-worldly terms—was not Wiesel's penchant. Some Israeli officials later conceded that the 1967 war was all about expansionist politics and propaganda, not mysticism and rapture. For instance, in 1972 General Mattityahu Peled stated, "To claim that the Egyptian forces concentrated on our borders were capable of threatening Israel's existence not only insults the intelligence of anyone capable of analyzing this situation, but is an insult to Zahal [the Israeli army]."[16] In addition, Ezer Weizman, one of the chief planners for the 1967 war, acknowledged that "there was no threat of destruction against" Israel.[17] Mordecai Bentov, a member of the Israeli Cabinet, admitted that the threat of extermination was "invented of whole cloth and exaggerated after the fact to justify the annexation of new Arab territories."[18] In 1982 Menachem Begin stated that "[i]n June 1967 we . . . had a choice. The Egyptian Army concentrations in the Sinai approaches do not prove that Nasser was really about to attack us. We must be honest with ourselves. We decided to attack him."[19] Both in 1967 and after, Wiesel's interpretation of the war, so attuned to innocence, peace, and purity, could not assimilate momentous political facts such as the Israeli violations of international law or its dispossession of Palestinians from their land in the Occupied Territories.[20]

After the war, Wiesel noticed that some people did not share his conviction that Israel's victory was one of righteousness. In addressing these critics, Wiesel emphasized his complete loyalty to Israel. In a postscript to the 1967 war, he accused the world of being disappointed that the Arabs were not able to make good on their desire to rid the world of Israel; the Gentiles preferred the Jew as victim, "they love the Jew only on the cross."[21] Wiesel was distrustful that anyone could consider Israel an "aggressor," for he could not dismiss the Arabs' stated goal of extermination:

Their leaders have said it and written it, and you will never convince me they did not mean it. You see, I belong to a generation sensitized to the extreme, trained to attach more significance to threats than to promises. It is a fact that in times of danger, our friends and protectors, when in power, suddenly discover in themselves a hypocritical tendency to be cautious and wise.[22]

Wiesel believed that Christians and leftists all too easily dismissed or downplayed the seriousness of the Arabs' threat to Israel. He equated French president Charles de Gaulle's criticism of Israel in 1967 to that of Roosevelt's policies in 1942; in both cases, Wiesel felt hurt that "Jewish destiny was not a decisive factor for either leader."[23] In this instance, Wiesel confirmed his self-professed political naiveté in thinking that powerful political leaders, when formulating policy, gave priority to the wounded sensibilities of those who had suffered.

In the essay "To a Concerned Friend," Wiesel tried to reassure a non-Jewish friend (French writer François Mauriac) that he need not worry about Israel acquiring a conqueror's mentality. Wiesel stressed that the meaning of victory in the Jewish tradition is primarily victory over oneself. He stated that victory does not depend upon crushing one's opponent, "[f]or this reason too the Jew has never been an executioner; he is almost always the victim."[24] As far as Wiesel was concerned, this victory would not transform Israel into an oppressor. He encouraged his friend to inspect what was taking place in the West Bank; the flattering portrait Wiesel painted of the first days of occupation disqualifies any comparison with "conditions that prevailed in German-occupied Europe" (Wiesel evidently felt a need to nip in the bud any imminent analogies to the Nazi period).[25] He claimed to deplore all rulers of occupation but considered that this Israeli one was warranted by necessity. He also declared it to be "the most humane and least oppressive possible."[26] Wiesel viewed Israel as the victor that did not want a conflict; it was the Arab states that had been hostile to Israel. Moreover, after such provocation, Israel did not engage, Wiesel professed, in the kind of retributive barbarism one comes to expect in such conquests. In what would serve as his refrain on Israel in the troubled decades to come, Wiesel later stated that "the Jewish fighters did not become cruel. They became sad."[27] Implicit in Wiesel's letter is the assuredness that one need not worry about such sad, that is, humane, soldiers.

According to Wiesel, what Israel's critics found so hard to forgive was that Israel had not sacrificed its honor or its purity. He contended that "it is because Israelis commit no sacrilege and profane no mosques, that they are resented."[28] Once again, the Jew upset the conceptual categories of the West. He reacted to what he considered to be the condemnation of the Jew as a sort of "unworthy victor," unworthy of respect because, as victor, Israel had somehow held on to its humanity. In addition to being militarily triumphant, Wiesel maintained that

Israel is morally unimpeachable, unlike so many other states in the international arena. He accused Israel's judges of hypocrisy, such as the Soviet Union (the invader of Prague), the United States ("whose troops razed Vietnamese villages 'in order to save them,' as one officer put it"), and others.[29] Further, he recited a litany of political horrors around the globe about which "the world remained silent" even though people somehow found the time and energy to criticize Israel. Wiesel frowned at the seeming eagerness with which others uttered animadversions of Israel "[w]hose way of conducting wars and winning them is a reproof to those whose own battles brought no glory to the human spirit."[30] He characterized Israel's conquest to be a moral victory above all, for Israel's "national independence has not been achieved at the price of human dignity," an assertion, however, that seven hundred thousand Palestinian refugees displaced in 1948 might quickly have questioned.[31]

Wiesel averred that the Israeli occupation would be far more humane in comparison to the political conditions characterizing Arab regimes. And he enunciated the following principle, which linked the Holocaust and Israel: "The nations that kept silent during the Holocaust ought to keep silent now as well. The world that then condemned itself by its silence has lost all right to judge Israel now."[32] In Wiesel's formulation, the European Jewish experience dominates the Middle East: Because "the world" did not respond to European Jewish suffering during the Holocaust, that world has no right to find fault with Israel as occupier of Arab lands in 1967.

Wiesel then expressed hope in future reconciliation between the Jews and Arabs, "without the aspirations of the one limiting the other's."[33] He conceived that this was the true vision of Israel, but, regrettably, Arab leaders were influenced by extremists. Such leaders did "not take the hand extended them, and therein lies the tragedy."[34] Finally, Wiesel hoped to assuage his friend's unease with what may yet happen to the "Jewish soul":

> The mentality, the instincts of a conqueror are not acquired in months, or even years; it takes generations, and implies a tradition the Jews do not claim. The Jew who has resisted change throughout his millennial history, do you really suppose he would repudiate his heritage because of a few victories on the battlefield?[35]

In trying to reassure his friend, Wiesel overlooked that the Zionist enterprise had been a self-conscious repudiation of the allegedly passive Judaic heritage to which Wiesel referred here with pride. Moreover, the

Zionists and Israelis had achieved far more victories than the recent few on the battlefield that Wiesel celebrated here. For example, at the time of the Balfour Declaration in 1917, the Zionists received the blessing of the British Empire to facilitate its mission of acquiring a Jewish homeland.[36] Also, as a result of the 1948–1949 war, Israel had been able to take half of the land intended for a Palestinian state. Further, the Zionists in the prestate period and the Israelis thereafter used terrorism in pursuit of their political aims, a subject to which I return.

In his accounting of the road to war, Wiesel did not mention any part Israel played in inciting Arab fears. He did not ponder the illegality of an Israeli "preemptive" act of aggression. Rather, swept up in the euphoria, Wiesel contributed to the rhetoric that depicted the Israelis as not wanting the war, as being reluctant, morally superior warriors.[37] Although Wiesel deplored the hypocrisy of nations who castigated Israel as if their records were clean, criticism of Israel's war was not ipso facto anti-Semitism. In November 1967 the United Nations finally hammered out Security Resolution 242, which would become the basis for a peaceful settlement of the Arab–Israeli conflict and which underscored the inadmissibility of holding on to conquered territory. Wiesel did not remark to his "concerned friend" that shortly after Israel began its occupation, plans went through for Jewish settlements on occupied Palestinian lands; Palestinians were also the victims of Israeli collective punishment and deportation, all of which violated international law.[38] In retrospect, Wiesel's friend could be seen to have had some justified concerns about the Israeli conqueror's mentality and, more to the point, Israel's practical strategies to seize the choice parts of the Occupied Territories and to leave the rest to "autonomous" Arabs.[39] In 1967, then, Wiesel assumed the role of a mystic pacifist lauding the military triumph of an occupying power.[40]

Confrontations and Disputations

After the 1967 war, Israel normalized its occupation of the territories, which meant increasing Jewish settlement, continuing to expropriate Palestinian land, and monopolizing vital resources, such as water. Also, the occupation gave Israel both a source of cheap labor and a market for its goods. The resounding defeat of the Arab armies convinced the Palestinians in resistance that they had only themselves to depend upon for their struggle against Israel. By the mid-1970s, the Palestine Liberation Organization (PLO) began to propose an independent, secular, and democratic state in part of the former Palestine (that is, the West Bank and Gaza Strip); those proposals were rejected by Israel. In addition to this move toward diplomacy, Palestinian militants also pursued terrorist strikes against Israelis. One of the more notorious of these was the kidnapping and murder of Israeli athletes at the 1972 Summer Olympics in Munich. This tragedy was foremost in Wiesel's mind when he gave an address for the United Jewish Appeal (UJA) in December 1972. At the beginning of his speech, Wiesel explicitly stated his fundamental stance vis-à-vis Israel:

> My loyalty to my people, to our people, and to Israel comes first and prevents me from saying anything critical of Israel outside Israel. That is the price I pay for living in the Diaspora. As a Jew I see my role as a *melitz yosher*, a defender of Israel: I defend even her mistakes. Yes, I feel that as a Jew who resides outside Israel I must identify with whatever Israel does—even with her errors. That is the least Jews in the Diaspora can do for Israel: either speak up in praise, or keep silent. Therefore I believe if I have something to say about certain things I do not like about Israel—and there are some—I must first go there.[41]

Wiesel believed that his UJA audience was tantamount to Israeli territory, so he invoked his status as a Jewish witness and teller of tales to raise some difficult questions about Israel. What weighed most heavily on him was that Israel had sent athletes to Germany for the Olympic sports competition. Again, eschewing anger but expressing sadness, Wiesel objected that the members of the Israeli delegation marched in ceremonies on the Sabbath. Out of respect for traditional Jews—whom they also represented as Israelis—the athletes should have stayed home. He was also grieved that, on an Olympic delegation to visit Dachau, only four of the fifty Israelis went.

After the terrorist attack, Wiesel reasoned, such criticisms of the Israeli delegation were laid to rest. But before his Jewish audience, he felt compelled to make the connections between the Holocaust and the terror and bloodshed in Munich. He insisted that, after these murders, Jews should understand that they made a mistake:

> We were wrong to forget that Munich is a symbol. We were wrong to forget that Munich occupies a certain place in Jewish history, a history that refuses to be forgotten. Whenever we ignore it, it reminds us of its existence by giving us a slap in the face. We forgot Munich? History knew how to remind us. If we Jews in Israel and everywhere had remembered Munich and its terrible implications, the tragedy would have been averted.[42]

Here again, Wiesel resorted to a mystical reading of Jewish history, which used dispossessed Palestinian militants to remind Jews of how a prematurely normal relationship with Germany was itself a violation of Jewish memory. What is crucial is not so much the battle and grievance between Palestinians and Israelis, but the emotionally damning symbolism of Jews carrying on in Munich as if nothing had ever happened between *Germans* and Jews.

In the rest of the speech, he underscored the importance of Jewish unity and how a false messiah is always one that divides Jews from each other. He concluded by reminding his audience of the failure of Christianity as symbolized by Munich, not in 1972, but during the Third Reich. He told his audience that Auschwitz would not have been possible without centuries of Christian hatred for the Jews. Then, in terms reminiscent of his description of Israel's victory in 1967, Wiesel said:

> Call it masochism, if you wish, but I still prefer to belong to the victims rather than the executioners. I prefer to see a human being in every person and not an object.
> Call it masochism, but we are proud of having belonged to those who died and not to those who killed. We did not betray man or diminish him. Therefore, even Munich should be taught and given as an offering to our generation because then the young will understand that we must choose it retroactively as an act of conscience and freedom.[43]

In this speech, Wiesel elided the realities of the Middle East and instead magnified a central place for the Holocaust. By speaking of the Holocaust, he was able to continue to belong to the victims in the present. At a gathering of the UJA, it may have served a more unifying end to stress the Holocaust (and Christian anti-Semitism) than to attend to the conflictual particularities of the Middle East. Israeli critic Benjamin Beit-Hallahmi has commented on this use of the Holocaust in Middle East discussions:

> The Holocaust is thus an original sin against the Jews which justifies Zionism and Israel totally and completely. The unlimited credit of the Holocaust can always be drawn on. It is useful for Diaspora Jews, giving them greater immunity from anti-Semitism or criticism, and for Zionism, giving it an ultimate justification. There are no two sides to the Holocaust story. There is only one. But there are two sides to the Israeli-Palestinian conflict. So apologists of Zionism prefer to bring up the Holocaust, whether it is called for or not.[44]

In Wiesel's interpretation of Munich, he did not focus upon the political act of terrorism that grew out of the concrete consequences of the

Israeli occupation of the West Bank and Gaza Strip since 1967. Munich remained more a symbol of German brutality than of Palestinian defiance and terror.

One of the provisions of UN Resolution 242 was the insistence that Israel withdraw from occupied Arab territory. In February 1971 Egyptian President Anwar el-Sadat made a peace offering to Israel.[45] Although Israel considered it a serious offer, it nonetheless rejected Sadat's land for the peace initiative (which, not incidentally, made no mention of the Palestinian cause). Frustrated at being unable to gain back the Sinai through diplomatic channels, Sadat decided to use the "language of force."[46] In the October 1973 war, Egypt and Syria surprised Israel with their fighting capability. Although the Arab forces were eventually beaten back out of the Sinai and Golan Heights, they gave the Israelis a scare they had not encountered previously, except the rhetorical one that had been so alarming in 1967.

In the midst of the 1973 war, Wiesel made another fund-raising speech for Israel. In his remarks, he avowed that Israel was in great danger and that many enemies were preparing to enter the conflict. He admitted to a kind of impotence in the United States, where all he could do was write, make speeches, and sign checks. In this war, as in 1967, Wiesel was attuned to other than purely political and military considerations. As a guardian of Jewish memory, he found it telling that the Arab armies attacked Israeli-occupied Arab territory on Yom Kippur. As a witness to Jewish history, he said that the Arab surprise attack "was an assault on our past, on our state, on our national identity. I hate to draw parallels between one generation ago and now. I do not say that the Arabs are Germans and Nazis. I do not say that we now live another chapter of the Holocaust."[47] Nevertheless, Wiesel noted that the Nazis had learned how to strike at Jewish memory by scheduling deportations and operations on Yom Kippur and other sacred days of the Judaic calendar. He continued, "And now once again the enemy struck on Yom Kippur. Is it a coincidence?"[48] He then expressed his trepidation that, once again, the Israelis were left alone to face their enemies. Wiesel did not mention that since the 1967 war the U.S. government had counted Israel more fully as a strategic ally in the Middle East, granting it extraordinary economic and military support.[49]

In December 1973, Wiesel gave another speech for the UJA, and, in part of his address, he referred to the recent war: "Yes, sadness is the key word. That is what we have all felt since the Yom Kippur aggression against our people."[50] Wiesel was saddened by Arab aggression against Israel but not, evidently, by Israel's illegal occupation of the Arab territory it conquered and had refused diplomatically to cede to legitimate Arab demands. In his remarks after the 1967 war, Wiesel maintained that Israel had been ready to extend its hand; however, Israel had not been interested in Sadat's peace overture. Moreover, the overly confident Israeli military believed that, once again, the Arab armies did not constitute a serious threat, hence their unpreparedness in October 1973. Wiesel still avowed that all the Israeli Jews wanted was peace and that Jewish fighters were "sad warriors." He also recognized a major change since the 1967 rendezvous with destiny. Wiesel supposed that the splendor that came out of the 1967 war could not last long because of the world's envy and corruption. But he also felt that the 1973 war generated an even greater sadness because of "the most important event in our history: the Holocaust":

> If we won in '67, it was because the terms of reference were those of the Holocaust. In 1973 the terms of reference were those of '67. In other words, the Holocaust, which had been a most powerful motivation, had in the meantime lost its impact. We had allowed it to be distorted, used and misused. Our entire community had grown dangerously insensitive to an event that some survivors had naïvely thought would continue to haunt all Jews forever, if only to save them from indifference and complacency.[51]

Wiesel thus criticized the misuse of Holocaust memory and the violation of its transcendent stature. Although he did not go into specific detail as to how the Jewish community inappropriately used Holocaust memory, he nevertheless saw the diminishment of the memory's awesomeness as somehow responsible for the trauma Israel faced in this latest, costly war.

Alongside of these Arab states' conflict with Israel, the Palestinian movement was making its own progress in achieving publicity and legitimacy. In 1974 the PLO was recognized by many third world nations as the sole legitimate representative of the Palestinian people. As the United Nations had expanded to include many postcolonial nations, more of these countries viewed the suffering of the Palestinians with some sympathy. Increasingly, Israel was on the ideological defensive in international gatherings. The most controversial example of the gains made by the Palestinians and the losses suffered by Israel was the UN Declaration of 10 November 1975 in which the General Assembly referred to Israel as "the racist regime in occupied Palestine."[52] Zionism was characterized as a form of racism and a threat to world peace and so, all the signatory countries were urged to oppose Zionist racism and imperialism. The adoption of this statement had some symbolic power, but little practical effect, except for outraging Israeli Jews and their Zionist supporters. Wiesel joined the counteroffensive with a brief article, "Zionism and Racism."

Therein, he suggested that an international "plot" resulted in this condemnation and isolation of the Jewish state. He linked this resolution to the beginnings of the Nazi era, which distinguished Aryan and Jew and began to deny Jews full participation in German society. Wiesel's response to the UN resolution was to invoke the whole of Jewish history and anti-Semitism in which, according to the Jews' detractors, "the Jews are never entirely innocent, nor are the others ever entirely guilty."[53] For Wiesel, this contemporary act of defamation against Jews "must be viewed in a context of chilling horror," the context, that is, of the long experience of Jewish oppression.[54] His rhetorical strategy was to downplay and diminish the political context and implications of the present by joining this UN outrage to the accumulated infamy of past centuries of anti-Semitism. He recalled various instances of how the Jews were blamed for committing the crimes of their persecutors. He then addressed the disclaimer that the UN resolution was not about Jews per se but about Zionists. Wiesel dismissed this approach as a long-standing ruse of anti-Semites, to divide and conquer the Jewish community as he remembered how, during the Nazi era, Jews of one country were told that it was only Jews from another nation that constituted a "Jewish problem." He held that wherever a Jewish community was threatened, all Jewish communities were endangered. Hence, the attack on Zionism was an attack on all Jews. Wiesel's conviction of the mystical unity of all Jews corresponded to the Israeli/Zionist political claim that Israel was the state of all Jews around the world, though not the state of all its citizens.[55]

Deeply offended by the resolution, Wiesel could not believe that the Jews, of all people, could be considered racists. He concluded his article by describing Judaism as a messianic movement, one "of spiritual, national and political rebirth" and so could not countenance the charge of the UN resolution:

But racist, no—Judaism excludes racism. All men and all women of all colors and origins are accepted as equals. If there is a tradition that is generous and hospitable toward the stranger, it is the Jewish tradition.

I have never been a Zionist, not in the formal sense of the word. I have never belonged to a political organization. But faced with the anti-Zionist attacks by those who corrupt language and poison memory, I have no choice but to consider myself a Zionist. To do otherwise would mean accepting the terms of reference used by Israel's enemies. I wish our non-Jewish friends would do the same, and claim Zionism as a badge of honor.[56]

However, what was under criticism by the UN resolution was not Judaism, but the practices and ideology of Israel that officially distinguished between Jewish and non-Jewish citizens. Wiesel did not address the specific charges of Israeli practice; in all likelihood, he saw such a response as beneath him, given what he considered to be the scurrilous nature of the resolution. But in ignoring the political criticism and attacking the United Nations, Wiesel disregarded a long tradition in Zionist theory and practice that has been described as settler-colonial, which was influenced fully by the thought and practice of the European powers. The presence of the Palestinian Arabs as a majority of the population in the area was the problem the Zionists faced as they strove to create a Jewish state that benefited Jews and that correlatively saw the Arabs as non-Jews, hence, unnecessary to the state-building project.[57]

Wiesel denied being a Zionist and alleged never to have belonged to a political organization, evidently not considering his patriotic participation as an underground translator for the Irgun in the late 1940s. His own public mission included the combat against the poisoning of memory and the corruption of language, which he attributed in this case to the United Nations. Yet, Wiesel's loyalty to the State of Israel was so overriding that he had nothing to say about the Zionist poisoning of memory and corruption of language. To give one infamous example, a few years earlier, Wiesel's friend and Israeli Prime Minister Golda Meir remarked: "It was not as though there was a Palestinian people in Palestine considering itself as a Palestinian people and we came and threw them out and took their country away from them. They did not exist."[58] Because Wiesel did not or could not assess Zionism from the standpoint of its Palestinian victims, it may have been possible to wear Zionism as a badge of honor, as Wiesel counseled his non-Jewish friends to do.[59] But if one considered the effects of Zionism and Israel on the Palestinian population—ongoing dispossession, terrorism, military bombardments, humiliation, cultural denigration, torture, and, within Israel proper, second-class citizenship solely because they have been politically designated as non-Jews—then one could regard Zionism and an expansionist Israel in critical terms, as indeed many UN members did.

Again, Wiesel was justified in denouncing the hypocrisy of some of the UN supporters of this resolution, who used indignant rhetoric about Israeli racism as a cover for their own comparable or worse treatment of racial or ethnic minorities. In Wiesel's perspective, dominated by the Holocaust and fearful for Israel, this resolution assumed its place in an opprobrious history of vicious anti-Semitism. Even so, the UN resolution did signal a victory for the Palestinian movement in that it was recognized that Israel discriminated against its non-Jewish citizens in ways that some compared with South Africa's system of apartheid.[60] As a third world initiative, the UN resolution may be viewed in another context other than that of "chilling horror," namely that of solidarity with the suffering and oppressed Palestinians.

Wiesel attempted to address the Palestinian movement for liberation in his letter "To a Young Palestinian Arab" published in *A Jew Today*.[61] There, he expressed a desire to make human contact with the Palestinians and sought to further the goal of mutual understanding. He also had hopes that a real exchange might embody an inspiring example to others. He wished to confront the "pain" of the Palestinian, because that was what separated Jew from Arab, and, in so doing, to judge himself because another's suffering was a call to his own responsibility. With his habitual suspicion of political matters, Wiesel emphasized that his engagement came out of a moral commitment: "I draw this to your attention from the start, because I do not understand and am wary of politics."[62] Wiesel insisted that both sides had valid arguments. But for each Palestinian complaint, Wiesel countered with a corresponding Jewish trump that served to fault the Arabs: "if only they had taken into account Jewish suffering *also*, the Jewish right to also claim its sovereignty on its ancestral land."[63] Wiesel envisioned Israel solely as the party of peace and reconciliation. He also implied that the Palestinians have immense power because of their "weighty assets: money, oil, allies from the Third World," framing the conflict as one between the powerful Palestinians and blameless, moral Israelis, since all Israel had to offer was "a sense of history, a yearning for justice and, also, a sense of honor."[64] Wiesel preferred not to linger too long on such issues; rather, he wanted to deal with the conflict from "an exclusively human point of view."[65] He urged reciprocity; he would endeavor to consider the Arab cause as the Arab should attempt to reckon with the Jewish cause. Wiesel then made an overture of sympathy: What touched him deeply was the human, ethical dimension of Palestinian suffering. He admitted that as a member of a generation that had seen too much suffering and death, he could not but respond to another's misery. As a Jew, he was especially sensitive to the varieties of suffering, and not just within his own Jewish circle. He next described how the experience of the Holocaust informed his perspective:

> The Jewish soul is wounded, our memory badly scarred. We have lost too many children and too many illusions. That is a truth that must be said and repeated: I would be betraying myself if my loyalty toward my people were not flawless and limitless, if I did not devote myself without reservation to the cause of Jewish survival, that is to say, the cause of Jews living everywhere.[66]

Wiesel felt obliged to encounter the Palestinian and he claimed to understand the torments of homelessness and humiliation that have been the Palestinians' experience. He affirmed that Palestinians undoubtedly are influenced by their suffering, as Wiesel has been by his suffering as a Jew. He wondered why their common experience of suffering did not unite them, and he then suggested that they may have had different notions of suffering.

Wiesel portrayed how the surviving Jews of Hitler's death camps entered into the phase of their liberation. They had, he believed, a kind of invincible power. After what they had suffered, they were capable of condemning the entire world and no one could have stopped them. Yet rather than inflict a justified vengeance on an unfeeling world, the Jewish survivor chose to take a stand on behalf of humanity. Some of the survivors came to Palestine "not to displace you" but to "relive an ancient dream."[67] Other Jews chose different options than Zionism, but what consistently characterized these Jewish survivors was that rather than becoming inured to the suffering of others by staying immersed in their own misery, they instead became compassionate. Following this confident and sweeping generalization, Wiesel next identified the characteristic that distinguishes the Jewish position on suffering: "For you, it seems to justify everything; not for me. Suffering confers neither privileges nor rights; it all depends on how one uses it. If you use it to increase the anguish of others, you are degrading, even betraying it."[68]

Wiesel reminded his Palestinian audience that the Jews of postwar

Europe did not resort to retribution, except rarely. Keep in mind that Wiesel was referring to Jews in postwar Europe, in the immediate aftermath of liberation: Jews did not take vengeance on Germans, Poles, Ukrainians, on executioners, collaborators, bystanders in Europe. Wiesel then spelled out how the Palestinians had dealt with their suffering:

> I will not attempt to measure your distress, nor will I tell you ours is greater. This kind of scorekeeping is out of place and odious. But I will tell you this: I do feel responsible for what happened to you, but not for what you chose to do as a result of what happened to you. I feel responsible for your sorrow, but not for the way you use it, for in its name you have massacred innocent people, slaughtered children.[69]

Wiesel framed the Palestinians' response to their suffering as terrorism: They killed innocent Jews who already had known enough suffering and death. He thought that his Palestinian interlocutor would surely describe these violent acts as the work of extremists; however, he asserted that "they acted on your behalf, with your approval, since you did not raise your voice to reason with them. You will tell me that it is your tragedy which incited them to murder. By murdering, they debased that tragedy, they betrayed it."[70]

Although Wiesel started this letter hoping to connect at an ethical level with the Palestinians, gradually he moved into blaming the Palestinians and averted his eyes from the political causes of their grievances. In his hoped-for, human, moral encounter with the Palestinian, Wiesel instinctively adverted to the incomparable suffering of the Holocaust and the way Jews supposedly transcended that brutality in an amazingly humanistic way. He compared Palestinian responses to suffering under Israel with Holocaust survivors' responses to suffering in Europe. What he did not do was to raise the pertinent issue of what Zionist Jews in Palestine did with their European-based suffering before and after the Holocaust in their quest for a Jewish state outside of Europe and, after 1948, what Israeli Jews had done with their historical inheritance of affliction in relation to the indigenous Palestinians. Had Wiesel pursued this line of investigation, he would have had to surrender the moral high ground he assumed so unproblematically. He admitted that he felt responsible for Palestinian "sorrow," which, in historical terms, was caused by the mass dispossession since 1948 and military occupation since 1967. But he did not specify what he felt compelled to do as a result of feeling responsible for this sorrow and he did not acknowledge any wrongdoing by Israel as a direct agent in causing Palestinian suffering.

Political critic Edward S. Herman maintained that "[i]f 'terrorism' means 'intimidation by violence or the threat of violence,' and if we allow the definition to include violence by states and agents of states, then it is these, not isolated individuals or small groups, that are the important terrorists of the world."[71] In the U.S. ideological system, Herman noted that there are two kinds of terrorism: retail terrorism, that done by official enemies, small agents, and condemned by the U.S. government and media; and wholesale terrorism, that done by our own government, our allies, and thus not considered terrorism (but rather self-defense). In his rebuke of the Palestinian embrace of violence, Wiesel chose not to condemn how Jewish terrorists, such as Menachem Begin in the Irgun, used Jewish suffering under anti-Semitism and the Holocaust to engage in murderous activities against the British and the indigenous Arab population in Palestine. Indeed, there is a long-standing historical record of Israeli terrorism in which the bombardment and killing of civilians had been practiced under both Labor and Likud governments, from attacks in the 1950s on the villages of Kafr Kassem and Qibya to the bombings of Lebanese civilians in the 1970s up to the present time.[72] In his letter to the Palestinian, Wiesel did not comment upon various Israeli policies in the Occupied Territories during the 1970s, which were, apparently, enacted on his behalf as a Jew by the Jewish state, according to his own logic in criticizing the Palestinian. And this was evidently with his approval, because he had not raised his voice (outside of Israel, anyway) to reason with the Golda Meirs and Yitzhak Rabins, who promoted illegal Jewish settlement in the Occupied Territories, negated the existence of Palestinians, denied their right to return to their homes, and opposed their political right to exercise national self-determination. Although Wiesel was willing to criticize the violence of the weaker Palestinian "retail" terrorists, he said nothing about the violence of the far stronger Israeli "wholesale" terrorists, backed by the United States.[73]

Wiesel shared with the Israeli Jews a sense of foreboding after the 1973 war. Although much more powerful than its Arab neighbors, the Israeli military was not invincible, and the Arabs were not going to go away. Egypt had made overtures that it wanted to become a U.S. ally and exchange land for peace; only after the 1973 war did Egypt and Sadat finally become a force with which to be reckoned. After much diplomatic maneuvering, Sadat went to Jerusalem in 1977 to declare his resolve for peace with the Israelis. His symbolic meeting there with Prime Minister Menachem Begin was a steppingstone to U.S. President Jimmy Carter's convening of the Camp David process in 1978. The essence of that agreement was a separate peace between Egypt and Israel with the latter agreeing to return the Sinai, a main result of which was the isolation of Egypt in the Arab world for making peace with Israel.

Wiesel was in New York when Sadat traveled to Jerusalem to meet with Begin. Making an exception on this momentous occasion, Wiesel violated Sabbath laws and watched the television reports:

> I had to see it. And I had tears in my eyes. I do not cry. I do not like sentimentality. I had tears in my eyes not because of Sadat only. Of course not. I was moved because of the way he was received in Jerusalem. Four years earlier this man had given the signal for a bloody war—3,000 young Jews were killed, 6,000 were wounded, 10,000 families are mutilated because of him. And he came to Jerusalem, and he was received as a brother by that very people who should have hated him—with what affection, with what admiration, with what passion, with what love. Of this human miracle I was proud.[74]

Accordingly, the political dimensions of the visit were secondary to Wiesel compared with the humanity of the Israeli Jews who welcomed Sadat with such generosity. He even thought that it made sense to give a Nobel Prize to Jerusalem, because the city of peace "became a protagonist, a character in a drama."[75] Yet the Jerusalem Wiesel had in mind here was not a political entity, but a mystical one. Arab East Jerusalem already had been forcibly occupied since 1967 and the entire city was declared the eternal capital of the Jewish state, with Jewish settlements ever extending the boundaries of the city. The Jerusalem Wiesel applauded was a symbolic one, because the real Jerusalem was the site of a contentious political struggle between Israeli Jew and Palestinian, apart from the supposedly miraculous Sadat–Begin rapprochement. This struggle continues today.[76]

In the decade after the June 1967 war, Wiesel mobilized his energies on behalf of Israel as he had previously for the Soviet Jews. He acclaimed the 1967 victory even as he denounced the world for its vindictive envy of the rapidity and humanity of the Israeli victory. He acted as a staunch defender of Israel, willing to identify even with its errors. He steadily invoked the Holocaust in his defensive interventions on Israel's behalf, the effect of which was to minimize the political conflicts between Israel and the Palestinians and other Arab nations. Wiesel made some attempts to engage in what he considered humane encounters with the Palestinians, but, because of his total allegiance to Israel, he chose not to make any public criticism of the concrete effects of Israeli policy on the Palestinians. He typically interpreted charges against and resistance to Israel as the latest manifestations of an eternal anti-Semitism, rather than as rooted in an asymmetrical political status quo in which Israel stood as the dominant military power in the Middle East. Wiesel tended to evaluate Israel as a righteous victim, in visionary and romantic terms. His rare criticism of Israel, as in the case of Munich, was that Holocaust memory had not been accorded a central place in dictating policy vis-à-vis Germany. In the face of Israel's power and ongoing dispossession of the Palestinians, he legitimated Israel as a uniquely moral nation-state in the world. But the political realities to which Wiesel was inattentive would not go away in the 1980s, a decade as full of personal triumph for Wiesel as it was full of further tumult and tragedy for Israeli Jews and Palestinians.

From the 1982 Lebanon Invasion to the "Peace Process"

Wiesel's previous characterization of Israel as exemplary received its greatest test in 1982. Until then, U.S. foreign policy with Israel had been made a domestic issue to the degree that an Israeli lobby—made up of a variety of Jewish and non-Jewish groups and alliances—focused on the need for Israel's security before U.S. presidents, Congress, and the public.[77] Since the 1967 war, Israel had come to be more highly regarded by the American foreign policy establishment (as it served American power as a strategic asset in the Middle East), liberal intelligentsia (as it was touted as "the only democracy in the Middle East," as well as a uniquely benign occupier), and the general population (as it was seen as the legitimate response to the Holocaust, reflecting to some degree a repudiation of anti-Semitism).[78] But in the summer of 1982, Israel's heretofore grand reputation in the United States and elsewhere in the West would come under more critical scrutiny because of its invasion of Lebanon, siege of Beirut, and complicity in the Sabra-Shatila massacres.

General Ariel Sharon's 1982 "Peace for Galilee" operation was designed to deliver a crippling blow to the Palestinian guerrillas and civil society located in Lebanon.[79] The PLO also had made progress in being increasingly recognized as a moderate political actor. Diplomacy with

Palestinians leading to peace was greatly feared by Likud leaders who wanted to fill the Occupied Territories with Jewish settlements and maintain control of the area's resources. Likud, like Labor, was adamant in refusing to recognize Palestinian national rights in the West Bank and Gaza Strip.[80] Sharon's plan was designed to finish off Palestinian resistance and resolve for an independent homeland, eliminate Syria's presence in Lebanon, and establish an alliance with Christian Maronite elites. Overwhelming Israeli military superiority would quickly deal the Palestinians in Lebanon a deathblow and thus grant Israel a free hand to pursue its policy of Judaization of the territories. The Camp David Accords also had a significant effect, as they removed Egypt as a deterrent to such Israeli expansionism. Although Sharon characterized "Peace for Galilee" as "defensive," the Israelis' invasion resulted in two hundred thousand refugees and twenty thousand people suffering death or injuries.[81] Prime Minister Menachem Begin did not respond to international calls for peace and authorized the attack on West Beirut, which included the use of napalm and phosphorous cluster bombs.

Because the invasion constituted an undeniable and unprovoked aggression, international criticism was directed at Israel. During this time, some Israelis engaged in the kind of dehumanizing rhetoric that Arab leaders had directed at Israeli Jews in 1967. For example, General Rafael Eitan stated, "When we have settled the land, all the Arabs will be able to do about it will be to scurry around like drugged roaches in a bottle."[82] The Palestinians received some international sympathy because the Israeli invasion was so blatant and ferocious. Wiesel made a number of responses through interviews and articles in which he reiterated his own unwavering commitments to Israel. More than at any time in the recent past when he sought to justify Israeli actions, Wiesel was then on the defensive. In an interview in early September 1982, he depicted Israel as being "forced to take cruel and distressing measures," though he did not indicate why or how Israel, long lauded for its "purity of arms," was so forced to destroy a city full of innocent civilians.[83] But what Wiesel found most distressing over the course of the summer was the widespread expression of hate toward Jews and the State of Israel. He believed that the press was engaging in distortions and did not show Israel's perspective. He also indicted unnamed intellectuals strongly critical of Israel for not siding with the Jewish state when, according to Wiesel, it had been "in her death throes" during the 1973 war. He applauded Israel for remaining remarkable, as its democratic character had been preserved even during the 1982 war. Wiesel still avowed that no country is in a position to give moral lessons to Israel. Rather, it was this state that could rightly confront all others with its humane record.[84] Without apology, the noted Diaspora Jew rose to the occasion to come to the ideological aid of Israel at a time when it was engaged in massive state terrorism against Palestinian and Lebanese civilians.

The growing debate around Israel and the Lebanon war touched on a range of political, military, and ethical issues. Wiesel declared that he was not an expert in political or military affairs; he also conveyed that he was a pacifist and did not "like weapons" (incidentally, as such, Wiesel was precisely the kind of Diaspora Jew that Zionism had sought to overcome with the mercilessly tough Israeli Sabra). Still, Wiesel did not feel that he was in a position to judge the Israeli military: "I can pass judgment only from a historical point of view, and from that perspective I believe one cannot judge an ancient people on the basis of episodes. We are a 4,000-year-old people, and what we do today reflects a history of 4,000 years. Episodes are episodes."[85] As in previously controversial situations regarding Israel, he adopted a long-range historical perspective, which distracted attention from the fact that thousands of Palestinian and Lebanese civilians were killed in the Israeli attack. A major atrocity was reduced to an evidently inconsequential "episode" from the vantage point of millennia of Jewish history.

In the September interview, Wiesel's interlocutor pointed out that, "[a]s a survivor of the Nazi terror, you have taught that silence is the greatest sin, that it should always be avoided." He asked Wiesel if it was not those Jews, critical of Israel's cruel invasion, who were upholding Wiesel's own teaching. Wiesel responded by asserting that Jews should observe, "but not pass judgment. Our role is to witness."[86] He admitted to feeling hurt and grief over what he had witnessed, but criticism was out of the question. He was convinced that the world's criticism of Israel was an eager attempt to "demystify" the Jewish state. After the Holocaust, the roles were clearly established: Jews were victims, whereas others were victimizers, which gave Jews "a moral protection." Then Wiesel held that the world was enthused to see Israel behave like other nations, capable of the same foibles. The "moral protection" once granted the Jews was then null and void, Wiesel feared, as he imagined the world gladly asserting, " 'You see, the Jews are not better than us.' "[87] Wiesel's position amounted to the Holocaust providing Israel with a cover of collective exculpation: Because of what the

Jews suffered under Nazism, Israeli policies ought to have been protected from criticism.

Although Wiesel granted that there was a novelty in some Jews critically responding to the Israeli invasion, he decided to hold to his long-
standing duty:

> But I have a principle. I am not Israeli, I am a Diaspora Jew, and the price I
> pay, the price I chose to pay for not living in Israel, especially in times of
> danger, is not to criticize Israel from outside its borders. When I have
> something to say, I go there and say it. Sometimes I am received with anger,
> but I do it nevertheless. That is my taboo, and I stop on that line.[88]

And yet, with the most powerful military force in the Middle East, Israel
was not in a time of "danger," but that distinction surely belonged to
the Arab victims in Lebanon. Wiesel allowed that Israeli military
prowess did not readily impress him, for he "would prefer Israel to be a
nation of poets and writers, where everyone dreams mystical dreams,
but that is not possible."[89] In response to the question as to whether he
had ever had real contacts with Palestinians, Wiesel recounted a story
in which a Palestinian poet visited him and told him of the terrible treatment of Palestinians in Israel. Wiesel could not believe these detractions, and so he called Israeli friends to verify if the charges were true.
His Israeli contacts confirmed the allegations. The Palestinian youth
next asked Wiesel to sign a statement of intellectuals, evidently opposing the status quo in Israel. Wiesel asked him if his interest was in assist-
ing his friends or in getting involved in politics, it being clear that the
act of helping individual people had much greater weight in Wiesel's
eyes than a public statement that challenged Israeli policy. As Wiesel
was soon to visit Israel, he promised the Palestinian that he would intervene on behalf of the Palestinian's friends who were suffering. There he
spoke to Golda Meir and the Israeli chief-of-staff. He announced to
them that the situation had to change, but "[t]he majority of them
advised me to return to my poetry. But I did arrange the release of the
Palestinian's friends."[90] Wiesel's compassionate response was an individual intervention to a presumed anomaly. Initially, he could not
believe the allegations of the young Palestinian; he did not see that the
issue was not so much an individual one as a structural one stemming
from the nature of the Israeli state policy that had its own long-standing "Palestinian problem."

Two days later, Wiesel addressed the Israeli invasion in another newspaper article.[91] Wiesel once again stressed the fundamental sadness that

he felt.[92] At the root of Wiesel's sadness was his observation that too many people were forcing connections between the Israeli invasion of Lebanon and the Nazi period. What alarmed Wiesel was not the suffering of the Palestinians and Lebanese, but the rhetoric that subverted the purity and sanctity of Holocaust memory, as intellectuals and politicians made offensive comparisons between the Israeli invasion and the Warsaw Ghetto. Thus, Wiesel took his pressing task to have been not that of criticizing Israeli power, but of criticizing the rhetoric of those who had criticized Israeli power. Through this period, he clearly considered Israel to be the main victim, as it was not the Israeli invasion that he deemed excessive, but the analogical discourse of Israel's critics, some of whom were Israeli and, like Wiesel, Holocaust survivors.[93] For example, Wiesel did not denounce the Israeli rhetoric of hate and dehumanization of the Palestinians mentioned earlier, but he did rail against the animosity expressed by those opposed to the invasion. He interpreted the media depiction of Israelis as victimizers and Palestinians as Israel's victims as an incitement to hate all Jews. As far as the Holocaust survivor was concerned, Israeli and Diaspora Jews still remained the world's "unworthy victims."

Wiesel believed that the root of this irrational hatred was that people wanted to denigrate the Jews for their "righteous dignity during the Nazi era," hence, the critics' frequent use of the Nazi analogy. In this line of thought, because the Jews were no longer the victims, the Jewish community lost a certain moral privilege of not being able to judge the indifferent world; Jews were now being harshly judged and criticized. The Jewish monopoly on Holocaust rhetoric and the claim of Israeli righteousness were being contested, a fact Wiesel found both odious and ominous. Further, he recognized a changed landscape in that some Jews in Israel and the United States did not abide by Wiesel's principle; they issued their dissent and held demonstrations against the Israeli government. Wiesel wondered if it was imperative to make these public criticisms and went so far as to add that unconditional support and love of the Israeli state would have been better *regardless* of the suffering of the Lebanese and Palestinians.[94] While he emphasized that Jewish love for Israel ought to increase at this time of international disapprobation, he had no doubt that Jews had a responsibility for caring for Lebanese civilians. He affirmed that if international Jewry could find a way to initiate a kind of Marshall Plan, he would wholly support it. Here, as in his sanctuary talk in 1985, Wiesel revealed his proclivity for responding to effects while remaining aloof from analyzing systemic causes by advocating that Jewish doctors, teachers, and philanthropists offer their skills and service to the victims. As for the Jewish intervention of charity that he envisioned, his priority remained solidarity with Israel. What was becoming increasingly clear to the international community, however, was that the Israeli–Palestinian conflict required not simply gracious charity but also the political recognition of the Palestinian people's rights both to return to their homeland and to exercise self-determination on that land.

Soon thereafter, Lebanese Christian militias ruthlessly murdered hundreds of Palestinian civilians in the Beirut refugee camps of Sabra and Shatila. Although Israeli military forces did not take part in the actual atrocities, they trained, armed, and, in effect, allowed the Phalange killers to proceed with this mass murder. The butchery at Sabra and Shatila precipitated even more revulsion than that already expressed by world opinion against the Israeli invasion.[95] Once again, Wiesel was pressed for a response. He granted that, since 1945, he had not known a Rosh Hashanah as dark as the one of 1982. But even in the face of this massacre at the time of the Jewish New Year, Wiesel's devotion to Israel remained undiminished: "It is not that I accuse or indict anyone, and surely not the people of Israel, but I felt sadness, incommensurate sadness, almost disarmed."[96]

Such remarks indicate Wiesel's inability and unwillingness to speak critically in the face of the wanton destruction of Palestinian civilians, although he had demonstrated such trenchant criticism of Poles and Germans, popes and presidents, for not speaking out during the Nazi years. When confronted with the horror of a cold-blooded massacre of Palestinians in Beirut, Wiesel could not bring himself to address this atrocity; instead, he recalled the Holocaust: "Perhaps if we had told the story [of the Holocaust] more convincingly, if we had prevented the trivialization and cheapening of what was and remains a unique catastrophe, things would not have happened this way."[97] At a time when American Jews and non-Jews finally had to confront the violated humanity of the Palestinians, Wiesel adhered to his traditional modus operandi: Protect the state of Israel and protect the uniqueness of the Holocaust, no matter what, with protection of the Palestinians not being a manifest concern. He did not criticize Israeli politicians such as Menachem Begin for trivializing and cheapening the Holocaust by their repeated references to the Palestinians as Nazis and PLO Chairman Yasir Arafat as Hitler.

Perhaps had Wiesel and others resisted this trivialization, "things might not have happened in this way," namely, that Israeli soldiers would have stood by while the Palestinians were properly taken care of by a trusted and vicious ally. A year before, Zionist leader Nahum Goldmann articulated a quite different point of view: "To use the Holocaust as an excuse for the bombing of Lebanon, as Menachem Begin does, is a kind of 'Hillul Hashem' [sacrilege], a banalization of the sacred tragedy of the Shoah [Holocaust], which must not be misused to justify politically doubtful and morally indefensible policies."[98]

The Israeli invasion of Lebanon and the Sabra and Shatila massacres marked a turning point in the international community's perception of Israel. Although Wiesel interpreted this turning throughout the summer of 1982 as being grounded in irrational animosity for the Jewish people, the savagery of the invasion was undeniable, and the cost to the Palestinians and Lebanese was extreme. Nevertheless, U.S. policy during the Reagan administration continued to support the Israeli government with lavish funding, even as it denied the legitimacy of Palestinians' claims. In exchange for this U.S. support, Israel played an important service role for the United States, in providing arms to U.S. allies who had come under some congressional censure for human rights abuses. One of these countries was Guatemala. In the early 1980s under General Efraín Ríos Montt, the Guatemalan government was intent on eliminating "subversives" (that is, anyone involved in movements for land reform and social change) by a strategy of scorched earth tactics that razed an estimated 440 Indian villages to the ground.[99] It was this kind of state-sponsored terrorism that produced a mass exodus of refugees, leading to the sanctuary movement in the United States. At the time, Wiesel had been contacted by a Nobel laureate who provided him with information about Israel's role in arming the Guatemalan military during its decimation of Indians. The laureate urged Wiesel to intervene with Israel, because Wiesel was known to have close associations with high Israeli officials. Questioned about this request in an Israeli press interview, Wiesel responded, "I usually answer at once, but what can I answer to him?"[100] In her study of Israeli relations with Guatemala, Jane Hunter noted,

Throughout the years of untrammeled slaughter that left at least 45,000 dead, and, by early 1983, one million in internal exile—mostly indigenous Mayan Indians, who comprise a majority of Guatemala's eight million people—and thousands more in exile abroad, Israel stood by the Guatemalan

military. Three successive military governments and three brutal and
sweeping campaigns against the Mayan population, described by a U.S.
diplomat as Guatemala's "genocide against the Indians," had the benefit of
Israeli techniques and experience, as well as hardware.[101]

Wiesel's allegiance to Israel superseded solidarity with Guatemalan victims under siege, even though he would later consent to speak at the
Sanctuary conference in support of Guatemalan (and El Salvadoran)
refugees. There, Wiesel made no criticism of U.S. or Israel's policies in
creating the conditions that led to their exodus or in arming their people's murderers.[102]

Throughout the 1980s, Palestinians in the Israeli-occupied territories
continued to face harassment, expulsions, arbitrary arrest, restrictions on
movement, land confiscation, demolition of homes, and political repression. In December 1987, a spontaneous uprising of Palestinians began in
the Gaza Strip, which soon spread to the West Bank, taking the form of
a massive and, for the most part, nonviolent, civil insurrection against the
Israeli occupation.[103] The media showed vivid scenes of Palestinian
youths throwing stones and using crafty defiance against the powerful
Israeli army. Soon these demonstrations of Palestinian courage and desire
for independence led to greater sympathy for their struggle and in forthright criticism of Israel's harsh measures, such as Defense Minister
Yitzhak Rabin's insistence on ending the revolt with force, beatings, and
might. The stakes of the Israel–Palestine conflict were featured more
prominently in the U.S. media, and some American Jews became even
more vocal in their criticism of the Israeli occupation, with proposals of
a two-state solution being taken more seriously.

   In January 1988 Wiesel convened a group of Nobel laureates in Paris
to address the challenges of the next century. But there were some who
were not interested so much in these problems in the abstract, but were
more interested in the concrete circumstances of that moment. Wiesel
observed that interviewers and journalists kept pressing him about the
intifada and he pondered: "How can one tolerate armed soldiers hunt-
ing down youngsters, even if they are not only capable but determined
to wound and kill? On the other hand, how can one defend the provocative acts of the Intifada fighters determined to shed Jewish blood on the
West Bank?"[104] Later that spring when he was in Israel, Wiesel also visited the Gaza Strip and subsequently gave an eyewitness report in an
op-ed in the *New York Times*.[105] He began his testimony by reflecting

on the relative normalcy of Gaza, in contrast to its recently acquired reputation as a cauldron of Palestinian resistance. He noted that the Israeli military forces were "more felt than seen" as were "the implacable plight of tens of thousands of refugees who dwell in inhuman conditions in two camps nearby." Before traveling to Gaza, Wiesel made it a point to raise questions to Israeli political and military leaders about the intifada: "How long could this situation go on? . . . What is the meaning of all these clashes between Jews and Arabs, these security considerations, these moral principles?" He interviewed a Palestinian lawyer who expressed his desire for a demilitarized Palestinian state. Wiesel asked him if he realized the Israeli fears regarding its security and he reported the Palestinian's response: "Israel's military might ought to assuage all her fears." Wiesel also conversed with young Israeli soldiers and they covered many urgent subjects: "How should one deal with the sufferings of the Palestinians? Is insensitivity the answer? Isn't a Jew called upon to be sensitive to his fellow human beings? How then is one to reconcile the needs of security with Judaism's concept of humanism?" Wiesel was privy to a wide-ranging debate with the soldiers and he posed the "question of questions," reminiscent of the question that so antagonized Wiesel during the Lebanon invasion: How did the Israeli soldiers deal with the international criticism of Israel's response to the intifada?

The soldiers invoked the need for self-defense and pattern of reciprocal hatred, but as to how to move beyond the current impasse, they did not know. According to Wiesel, "their eyes reflected determination and sadness." But these soldiers felt their backs up against the wall inasmuch as the world media had publicized Israeli house demolitions, physical attacks, and the breaking of bones of Palestinians. Wiesel asked: "Who was not outraged by the reports about Arabs being buried alive by soldiers?" Even though Wiesel characterized these as "regrettable exceptions—immediately corrected by Israeli authorities," Israel was still being condemned. Whereas the United States was once condemned for its war in Vietnam and France for its policies in Algeria, Israel was now the latest object of criticism. And Wiesel was rankled by writers closer to home: "Some Jewish intellectuals who had never done anything for Israel but now shamelessly used their Jewishness to justify their attacks against Israel."

Wiesel then raised the obvious question—"Should Israel be above criticism?" He responded: "No one says that." Wiesel admitted Israel's

"short-comings" but he objected to how the Israelis were being presented as "blood-thirsty," or, in circles favorable to Arab causes, "Israel
is being compared to Hitler's Germany, its policy to Nazism and the
Palestinians of today to the Jews of yesterday. How are we to convince
Israel's political adversaries that the Holocaust is beyond politics and
beyond analogies?" Consistent with his outrage during the Lebanon
invasion, Wiesel tried to protect the Holocaust from these irreverent
comparisons. Perhaps Wiesel's discomfort at the proliferation of these
analogies led him to take a different stance from the one he adopted
during the 1967 war, when he himself used the Holocaust to gloss the
events of that war.

Wiesel then stated his sympathy for the Palestinians who had been
isolated and "betrayed by the whole world," including other Arab
nations. When they had been condemned to be nonpersons, he said,
"[w]hy shouldn't they have chosen violence as a means of attracting
attention to their existence and their dreams of obtaining national identity?" Wiesel's wording here is interesting—some Palestinians chose
violence because some Israelis denied their very existence (Golda Meir)
and both political blocs, Labor and Likud, attempted to crush the Palestinian dream of obtaining, not so much "national identity," but national
freedom. Wiesel went on to acknowledge that in modern civilization,
self-determination is "a sacred principle." He believed that it applied
also to the Palestinians, but he questioned exactly what this Palestinian
self-determination was, as he attested that the Palestinians had been
dangerously expanding their goals.[106] He referred to Mahmoud Dar-
wish, the Palestinian poet who created a controversy in Israel with his
poem urging Israelis to leave. On the basis of this poem, Wiesel
assumed that "Nablus and Gaza would no longer satisfy the Palestinians—now they are after Haifa and Tel-Aviv." Wiesel then reviewed the
formative history of the conflict—he claimed that Israel recognized a
Palestinian state when it accepted the UN partition plan in 1947.[107]
After the 1967 war, Wiesel alleged that, if the Israelis had not taken over
the territory, it would have been unlikely that King Hussein of Jordan
would have facilitated the emergence of a Palestinian state. Then, contrary to the overt Israeli strategy of taking the best parts of the Occupied Territories for settlements and monopolizing the vital resources,
Wiesel assured his reader, "Israel did not want those territories; they
were imposed on Israel in war." Such imputed passivity is at odds with
the explicit Israeli determination to create "facts on the ground" with

Jewish settlements. Even in 1948 David Ben-Gurion voiced greater territorial aspirations, as he resisted specific frontiers of the new Jewish state.[108] Moreover, as Israeli officials have since conceded, the territories were not "imposed," they were desired for political and economic ends and then taken.

Wiesel next disputed that Israel had "lost its soul," that Israeli soldiers had become sadists: "They do not enjoy fighting stone-throwing adolescents. But confronted by them, what should a soldier do? Retreat? How far? Run away? Where?"[109] He conceded that he did not accept all that Israel had done in response to the intifada, but he felt obliged nevertheless to come to the aid of the Jewish state.[110] He opposed "those who offer simplistic solutions; they are misleading and unworkable. If there is a realistic solution to the problem, I do not know it." Wiesel warily cited examples of those on the Israeli right who advocated the "transferring" all the Palestinians to Jordan and the liberals "who are ready to give up all the territories immediately." Consistent with his views during the 1982 Lebanon invasion, Wiesel also noted, apparently without irony, that "Israel is the only country that feels its existence threatened." Yet, apart from these subjective impressions, it was the Palestinians whose existence on their land was objectively threatened, as Israel continued to seize Palestinian territory and turn it over to Jewish settlers. Then Wiesel ignored PLO moderation by continuing to define it as a "terrorist" organization, as if to say that Israel did not need to negotiate with it. Internationally, the PLO had long been recognized as the legitimate voice of Palestinian nationalism, with Israel and the United States being the exceptions. Wiesel asked that if the PLO were not capable of entering negotiations with the Israelis, who could? He understood that there were some moderate Palestinians, but evidently outside the PLO. Here he did not voice doubt whether the recent Labor and Likud governments embodied such moderation, even though both ignored many UN resolutions censuring the Israeli occupation and harsh treatment of the Palestinians.[111] Still, Wiesel ended his article with a hope that a way could be found that would satisfy both sides: "More than ever, I would like to believe in miracles." Whatever the grounds for Wiesel's "hope," it remained true that there had been a record of Palestinian peace proposals going back to 1976. Moreover, a well-known international consensus had emerged in support of a two-state solution based on UN Resolution 242.

Over a year and a half later, as the intifada had changed the political contours and debate of the Israel–Palestine conflict, Wiesel introduced a symposium for the U.S. Zionist monthly *Midstream* on the current crisis.[112] He stated that Jews are entitled to discuss Israeli policy, because whatever happened to Israel would affect Jewish life everywhere. In the context of what he called the "recent Palestinian riots," Wiesel maintained that discussion by Jews about Israeli policy "must be anchored in a deep attachment to and love of the Jewish State." He then set the proper boundaries for those who may have participated in these discussions and how they should have done so. Only those who had expressed solidarity with Israel in the past were entitled to speak then, and their privilege was only to "voice their sadness when faced with certain events taking place in Israel." He denied a platform to Jews who to that point had not demonstrated their support of Israel, because they might have been employing their Jewish identity only to justify making a special criticism of Israel at that time of "danger." He reiterated his long-standing principle, "*In personal terms: I refuse to see myself in the role of judge over Israel. The role of the Jew is to bear witness; not to pass judgment.*"[113] Perhaps in response to those critics who had accused him of silence, Wiesel interpreted this principle as not constituting a "vow of silence." He seemed to validate his own principle that silence is abhorrent and he acknowledged that because so many people were suffering in the region, Jews had to respond publicly. What legitimately may have been expressed, however, was "our sadness, our pain, our frustration." Any expression of outrage toward Israeli policies was proscribed. He opposed the application of any Diaspora pressure against Israel, and he refused to get involved in supporting one political group over another: "Why should I, a Jew in the diaspora, go farther than Labor ministers who, for all practical purposes, submit to government solidarity?" Wiesel then asked whether debate be forbidden on Israel. He claimed that, to the contrary, he supported debate but objected to decisions being made in the Diaspora: "We may ask all the questions; but the answers belong to the Israeli people." He finished his brief remarks by repeating: "whatever happens in Israel and to Israel, I love Israel. There were times when I loved Israel with pride; there were times when I loved Israel with joy. Today I love Israel with anguish." Wiesel's stance prompts a basic question: Who benefited from this anguished call for silence? It was not the Palestinians who were held in administrative detention, whose land was expropriated, and whose homes were demolished.[114]

Certainly since the intifada, events moved at a dizzying pace in the Middle East: the August 1990 Iraqi invasion of Kuwait and the U.S.-led war on Iraq in 1991; the U.S.-brokered Madrid Conference; the Oslo Accords between Israel and the PLO; the reciprocal, reactionary violence of Jewish and Islamic fundamentalists; the assassination of Yitzhak Rabin; Israeli redeployments, and the battle over continued Israeli settlements and Jerusalem, even as the Palestinian Authority attempted to exercise control in territories partially ceded by Israel.[115] Wiesel's position on the Israeli–Palestinian conflict remained consistent with his long-standing defense of Israel, although there emerged some interesting shifts, admissions, and nuances not present in his public work before.

Wiesel's position on Israel had long been shared by many American Jews and liberals: do not speak critically about Israel and do not acknowledge fundamental Palestinian rights. As Wiesel grew in public stature with increased connections to American power, he became a part of the prevailing consensus on the assumed U.S. role in promoting a "peace process" between Israel and the Palestinians. He came to adopt the terms of the dominant U.S. discourse: to overcome the fanaticism of the extremists and terrorists, even as he continued to hope for miracles and exalt Israel's commitment to peace.[116] This discourse obscured how the "peace process" further marginalized the Palestinian people, with the dismissal of their fundamental rights.[117] Present on the White House lawn in September 1993 when Yasir Arafat shook the hand of Yitzhak Rabin, Wiesel placed his hope in these negotiations that might end the bloodshed between Jew and Palestinian. At that point, he became willing to reconsider his own long-standing views of PLO chairman Yasir Arafat. Wiesel's shift here was not surprising, because Arafat had been granted some legitimacy by the U.S. government and Israel, inasmuch as basically he acceded to the aims of the Israeli negotiators. Some Palestinians, such as Edward Said, critiqued Arafat's participation in the Oslo Accords as capitulation to the Israelis.[118] It is because of Arafat's willingness to play the diplomatic game by U.S. and Israeli rules that he was only then considered a "moderate." Reconsidering his critique of Arafat's terrorism in the 1970s, Wiesel offered another possible view of the Palestinian leader:

> I wonder whether I was right to be so wary of Arafat. Yes, he was responsible for deadly terrorist activities, which it was my duty to denounce. But at the same time, he was a freedom fighter in the eyes of his people. I was asked to meet Arafat many times. Was I wrong to refuse? Are those who claim to have chosen peace over terror not to be believed? Is Arafat, therefore, to be

looked upon as a moderate, a peacemaker, the head of a nascent state rather than of a clandestine military organization?[119]

It might be noted that much of the world looked upon Arafat as a moderate many years before, when the PLO was advancing toward a negotiated settlement with Israel, consistently rebuffed by Labor and Likud governments, as well as the United States.

Nevertheless, Wiesel had evinced greater discomfort about the evolution of Israeli society in recent years. In the second volume of his memoirs, he wrote freely about the many currents in Israeli society that disturbed him. He realized that by speaking plainly he was likely to antagonize some Israelis who had stated that unless he lived in Israel, he had no right to criticize what they do. Wiesel justified his speaking out this way:

> Oh yes, I know the formula, having used it myself at times. A person who does not live Israel's ordeals and challenges has no right to criticize its decisions. Never mind. I shall speak out, because the situation is too serious and the stakes too high for me to remain silent. An ancient philosopher said: When truth is in danger, silence equals guilt.[120]

Previously, Wiesel had not found the stakes too high when it was a matter of the humiliation and dispossession of the Palestinians. But he became so disturbed by what Israelis were saying about other Jews that he had to leave behind his long-standing formula and address these concerns in a forthright way.

One of the issues that bothered Wiesel was the hostility toward his own person, which he noticed after he won the Nobel Prize in 1986:

> And so I learn that Israel is the only non-Arab country where, along with the praise, there were negative articles on the Nobel committee's decision—not many, but enough to make me sad. A journalist from the extreme right scolds me for not living in Israel; one from the extreme left is angry because I have not sufficiently espoused the Palestinian cause. Once again I am told that by choosing to live in the Diaspora, I have sinned against Israel.[121]

Wiesel went on to lament the fanatic divisions between secular and religious, the frequent tone of rancor that does not allow for dignified discussion of serious matters, and Israelis' supercilious tone toward Diaspora Jews as second-class Jews.[122] Surveying these characteristics of Israeli society, Wiesel recoiled from these expressions, some excessive to be sure, of a lively and raucous political culture. But he was unnerved also by the fact that Israelis had perpetrated such horrendous murders: Physician Baruch Goldstein murdered Palestinians at prayer in Hebron in

1994 and Yigal Amir murdered Yitzhak Rabin in 1996. Both murderers were committed to a racist and extremist religious ideology that dehumanized the Palestinians and threatened other Israelis who had a different view on peace negotiations.[123] About Goldstein, Wiesel exclaimed, "There can be no justification for the murderous act of a religious man, a physician whose calling it was to save lives. What was it in Israel's political climate that made this criminal act possible?"[124]

Still, rather than remain focused on these troubling realities, he turned to "Israel's young people, who will soon be summoned by the army. I think of the dreamers in front of the Wall. I think of all those mothers and fathers who lost their sons in combat. In times of doubt it is their faces that represent the eternal image of Israel."[125] Such eternal images were more consoling than the then-reigning vituperation in Israel.

In the second volume of his memoirs, Wiesel wrestled more with his position on the Palestinians. Evidently feeling that he had to address this issue more directly than he had previously, he contended,

> Indeed, I can say in good faith that I have not remained indifferent to any cause involving the defense of human rights. But, you may ask, what have I done to alleviate the plight of the Palestinians? And here I must confess: I have not done enough.
>
> Is an explanation in order? In spite of considerable pressure, I have refused to take a public stand in the Israeli-Arab conflict. I have said it before: since I do not live in Israel, it would be irresponsible for me to do so. But I have never concealed how much the human dimension of the Palestinian tragedy affects me.[126]

But, as Wiesel mentioned previously, citing Albert Camus, "not to take a stand is a stand." Over the decades, Wiesel's loyalty to Israel dominated other considerations, such as the protection of the human rights of the Palestinians and their right to national self-determination in their own land. He refused to criticize Israel outside of Israel, for fear of giving aid and ammunition to anti-Semites who, he was convinced, gladly would have used his criticism for their own spiteful ends. Although Wiesel accepted that Jews had a duty to argue, and not always politely, with God, he did not advocate such public argument with the Israeli state.[127] He commonly blurred distinctions among Judaism, the Jewish people, the Israeli people, and the current Israeli government. Reflecting his deeply ingrained love of the Jewish people, Wiesel counseled that trust was to be placed in the Israeli people and, from his position in the United States, Wiesel acted as a champion of Israel's rectitude, no matter what Israel's policies.

Wiesel occasionally did express his existential empathy with Palestinian suffering but, as with the cases of solidarity I analyzed in Chapter 3, he did not concern himself with the historical and political causes of their suffering, except to blame the Arab nations or the Palestinians themselves. By bearing witness, he expressed paeans to Israel (as after the 1967 war), or, when things got out of hand, confessed anguish and sadness (as after the Lebanon invasion and the intifada). As he desired that Israel be a land of poets and dreamers, he did not really reckon with Israel as a powerful state, enthusiastically backed by the United States, with the same capacity for realpolitik characteristic of other governments in the international state system, that is, with its own political and economic interests. In his various defenses of Israel, Wiesel alleged that any assertion that the victim had now become the victimizer was tantamount to anti-Semitism, a useful rhetorical strategy for neutralizing criticism.[128] The historical record and ample documentation of Israel's policies of exclusion, dispossession, and violence—from the United Nations, international human rights groups, and Israeli human rights groups—could then quickly be dismissed as another expression of the world's contempt for the Jews.[129]

In articulating his position on the Middle East conflict, Wiesel positioned himself as a traumatized Jew, which served to explain why he could not be expected to be pro-Palestinian. Wiesel may have been incapable or unwilling to penetrate the systematic distortions in the Israeli narratives and to criticize the practices toward the Palestinians. But he opened himself to the criticism from others that his moral maxims—for which he has been respected both by powerful and powerless alike—were suspended when it came to his own favorite state of Israel. Wiesel's public career had been marked by his insistence that one must intervene on behalf of the victims, against the persecutors, so that one does not fall into the morally contemptible category of the "bystander." He himself would surely agree in principle that we ought to live according to a single standard of human rights intervention, not just when it is convenient, easy, or self-serving. But such a principle dictates that one's own in-group solidarities should not blind one to the responsibility to care for others outside that group, particularly when one's own group is oppressing those very others. Wiesel himself considered this universal principle—always side with the victims—as a necessity in one intervention after another. Yet he embraced this principle selectively in service to an Israel he perceived as perennially endangered. In his writing on the Holocaust and Israel, frequently he invoked the adage that suffering conferred no privileges, that what mattered was what one did with that suffering. Whereas Wiesel accused the Palestinians of putting their suffering to ignoble ends, that is, terrorism against Israeli Jews, Wiesel deployed his Holocaust suffering in the service of a state whose record of human rights violations and diplomatic recalcitrance was well documented, although very largely ignored in the mainstream American media. On the matter of Holocaust remembrance in the United States, Wiesel came to play a central role of guarding the sacred boundaries of the event. He especially opposed any sacrilegious encroachment by others, whether by inappropriate analogy or failure to respect the event's uniqueness. And yet, Wiesel's Middle East commentary was marked regularly by the invocation of the Holocaust, which eclipsed the contemporary geopolitical context of the Arab–Israeli or Israel–Palestine conflicts. Even as the Holocaust was unique in all of history, so too the Jewish state was morally exceptional, if not unique, which accounted for Wiesel's willingness to grant it a singular immunity from criticism. Wiesel considered Israel not just as a morally superior country, but one that still was viewed in a hostile manner by the international community, and so all the more deserving of his—and other Jews'—total solidarity. By seeing Israel as the enduringly unworthy victim in international affairs, Wiesel ignored that Israel was the dominant power in the Middle East, with innocent victims of its own, principally the Palestinians.

5

The Worthy Victim
Moral Authority and State Power

Rabban Gamliel, son of Rabbi Yehuda the Prince, said: "Be careful in your relations with those in power; they draw you close or allow you to approach them only when they need you. They are your friends when your friendship is useful to them and affords them pleasure, but they forget you when you are in trouble." I have thought of this often. Is it wise for a writer to come too close to power? Is it prudent to be a friend to princes?

—Elie Wiesel, *All Rivers Run to the Sea: Memoirs*

I too think the intellectual should constantly disturb, should bear witness to the misery of the world, should be provocative by being independent, should rebel against all hidden and open pressure and manipulations, should be the chief doubter of systems, of power and its incantations, should be a witness to their mendacity. For this very reason, an intellectual cannot fit into any role that might be assigned to him, nor can he ever be made to fit into any of the histories written by the victors. An intellectual essentially doesn't belong anywhere; he stands out as an irritant wherever he is; he does not fit into any pigeonhole completely.

—Václav Havel, *Disturbing the Peace: A Conversation with Karel Hvízdala*

115

Since the June 1967 war, the Holocaust has been discussed increasingly in the United States.[1] One could point to the existence of a Holocaust culture industry reflected in the publication of innumerable books, histories, and testimonies on the tragedy; symposia and university courses; interfaith conferences; museums and memorials; and popular and documentary films.[2] Some commentators point to the "Americanization of the Holocaust," in that the European tragedy has been made to appeal to American aspirations, self-perceptions, and comfort levels.[3] Without question, Elie Wiesel has played a significant role in this cultural transformation of the Holocaust from being a taboo to its secure place in American public life as tragedy, warning, and symbol of humanity's ultimate debasement. The sociopolitical conditions have changed so dramatically since the early 1960s that Wiesel and the movement for remembrance have achieved a important rank in the "political economy of memory" in the United States.[4] In pursuit of his mission, Wiesel has made thousands of interventions: in religious audiences among Jews and Christians; in the media through op-eds and articles; in universities through lectures; and, increasingly in the last twenty years, in the political field, in international forums for human rights, and through speeches before and meetings with U.S. presidents and Congress. He has legitimated writers with his own imprimatur, inspired networks of allies across civil society, and helped to lead the movement to institutionalize the remembrance of the Holocaust.[5] For these many efforts, Wiesel has received extensive honors and acclaim as a moral paragon.

In light of this widespread approbation, some of Wiesel's earliest statements and pleas on the Holocaust and its victims are worth recalling: His indictments were severe, his rhetoric was outraged, and his work was an affront to the comfortable pieties of Western civic pride. How did someone with such a disturbing message become so lauded? How did this alternatingly diffident mystic and defiant advocate come to be so accepted by American leaders and taken into their confidence? How did Wiesel's strictures against criminal silence fare as he gravitated to the elite circles of state power? When did Wiesel manage critical independence from power and when did he practice tactful collaboration and compromise? This chapter examines how Wiesel, so sympathetic to many victimized peoples, has fared in his relations with various "princes."

The Carter Administration and Sacred Memory

After the Vietnam War, the Watergate scandal, and Richard Nixon's resignation, Democratic President Jimmy Carter faced the difficult task of confronting a national malaise and reassuring the population that America's exceptional status in the world was not permanently diminished. Early on, his administration asserted that it would make the protection of human rights the core of its foreign policy. After the American war in Vietnam, one can see the importance of Carter's desire to assert that that policy was resuming its normal, that is, righteous, course.[6] Carter took a particular interest in the Middle East conflict, evidenced by the role he would play in persuading Israeli Prime Minister Menachem Begin and Egyptian President Anwar el-Sadat to come to a peace agreement at Camp David. At one point, the president had spoken of the need for a "Palestinian homeland," which angered the Jewish and intellectual constituency that had formed a potent Israeli lobby in the euphoric aftermath of the June 1967 war. Even in the late 1970s, a view such as Carter's—or that the Palestinians might have the same right of national self-determination as the Israelis—was considered proof of some special enmity for the Jewish state. Carter also had aroused the grave suspicion of leaders of official Jewish organizations when he used his presidential prerogative to pass through Congress a major arms deal of F-15 aircraft to Saudi Arabia. For these reasons, although there had long been a close relationship between Democratic administrations and domestic Jewish interests and organizations, Carter's administration had come to be regarded as problematic by many Jewish leaders.[7]

Although Holocaust remembrance increasingly had been the subject of attention and interest, Jimmy Carter's administration gave it major backing in the late 1970s.[8] In 1977 three of Carter's Jewish aides first conceptualized a memorial to the Jewish victims of the Holocaust; one aide in particular felt that Carter could begin to make amends for his alleged Middle East miscues by visiting a Holocaust studies center in New York. However, the memorial idea was not significantly engaged until over a year later when Jewish opposition to Carter had become more pronounced. Another aide, Ellen Goldstein, urged that some kind of memorial could "be an appropriate gesture in honor of Israel's thirtieth anniversary and a symbol of the United States's support of Israel's birth and continued life."[9] In May 1978 Carter announced that he wished to form a president's commission on remembering the Holocaust. Although some Carter aides denied that this move reflected the president's need to appease disgruntled American Jews, one Carter aide, Mark Siegel, contended that "[p]olitics obviously played a role" in this quantum leap toward increased national recognition of the Jewish tragedy.[10] Not only would the Carter administration promote a project that American citizens could recognize as a moral venture, but that project also would aid the president in a pragmatic renewal of cordial relations with the Jewish community.[11]

Carter needed a chairperson to proceed with the work of the commission. Former Supreme Court Justice Arthur Goldberg recommended Elie Wiesel for the position: "[I]n addition to his identification with the Holocaust, he also would be a 'non-political' appointment and virtually free of attack from most sources."[12] Joyce Starr, a member of Carter's White House staff, opined that Wiesel was the "one candidate who would be undisputed by the Jewish community," while other Carter aides described Wiesel as the "undisputed expert on the Holocaust period."[13] Moreover, his appointment would not be controversial even though "his political and fundraising abilities are not clearly established."[14] A requisite balance had to be struck between a chairperson's Jewish reception and broader political utility. Although Wiesel had previously enjoyed associations with major Israeli political figures such as Golda Meir, he had never before been pursued by a U.S. president. Initially, he expressed skepticism: "It is impossible not to see the public relations game involved. I tell my friends: 'This confirms my doubts: We must never use the Holocaust for political purposes.' "[15] However, his friends argued strongly for his accepting the post, but Wiesel decided to withhold a final decision until after he had met with President Carter. In their first meeting, even as the president quoted to Wiesel some of the survivor's own principles on responsible remembrance, Wiesel insisted on some preconditions for accepting the post, such as the appointed members of the commission visiting the European sites of destruction and the memorial needing a strong educational thrust.[16] With Carter in agreement, Wiesel came on board.

On 1 November 1978 Carter formally established the President's Commission on Remembering the Holocaust and requested the thirty-four citizen-nominees on the board to present recommendations on how best to remember the Holocaust. As the chair of a commission composed mostly of Jews, including several other survivors, Wiesel accepted the Carter mandate, complete with an official swearing-in.[17] In this way, Wiesel and company were charged with the responsibility of envisioning, facilitating, and building an institution to commemorate Jewish suffering in Europe under the Nazis. Whereas Wiesel already had become renowned in Jewish and Christian circles, this appointment allowed Wiesel to improve tremendously the visibility of his own cause by now being in a position of meeting, advising, and networking with a variety of politicians and other elites outside of government. Further, in his titular role of commission chairperson, he was legitimated as *the* spokesperson of Holocaust remembrance. Wiesel's growing fame was linked to the changed fortunes of American Jewry more generally, as its empowered status in American society was symbolized dramatically by the plans to establish a memorial.[18]

In February 1979 Wiesel made his opening statement as the chairman of the President's Commission on Remembering the Holocaust. He noted the immense difficulty of the task the group set for themselves in remembering the Nazi genocide. He posed the question that would haunt future discussions and debates of the project: "How does one reconcile the purely Jewish aspects of the tragedy with its inevitable universal connotations?"[19] He urged the commission to resist the temptation to form factions, which would militate against the unity this project urgently needed to fulfill its moral promise. He mentioned the likelihood of survivors on the commission being overly sensitive as they dealt with the inevitable technicalities of the project. Also, Wiesel did not mince words as he pointed out the irony of this particular commission's existence:

> While we are grateful to President Carter and his advisors for being so deeply concerned with the Holocaust now, I cannot but wonder what would have happened had the president of the United States then, and his advisors then, demonstrated the same concern.
>
> If a presidential commission had been appointed in 1942 or 1943 to prevent the Holocaust, how many victims—Jews and non-Jews—would have been saved?
>
> Well, they were forgotten while they were alive. They are dead now. Let us at least remember them and include their memory in our own.[20]

During Wiesel's first official presentation before the Congress, he highlighted the indifference of the U.S. government during the Holocaust. Even as the Carter administration had deemed the European Jewish victims now worthy of remembrance, Wiesel did not want to obscure their previous unworthy status. A present-day commitment to remember by this administration could not justify ignoring a previous administration's record of indifference.

Early on, the commission faced controversies that would continue throughout the fourteen years leading up to the museum's opening in 1993. Consonant with his earlier pleas on behalf of the dead and the survivors, Wiesel conceived of the Holocaust as an unimaginable mystery such that the commission must proceed slowly with fear and trembling. Inevitably, the commission would have to negotiate with other more pedestrian, self-interested views of institutionalizing the memory. On the playing field of politics, compromise, expedience, and quid pro quos were all part of the normal give-and-take struggle to achieve one's ends. One early issue that revealed this tension between sacred memory and political expediency was that of arriving at the proper definition of the event.[21] At the first act of national remembrance on 24 April 1979 at the Capitol Rotunda, President Carter recounted his recent visit to the Holocaust memorial in Israel, Yad Vashem, and he referred to the overwhelming enormity of the loss, the "sheer weight of its numbers—11 million innocent victims exterminated—6 million of them Jews."[22] Carter favored an inclusive definition of the number of victims killed, and his understanding was reflected in Executive Order 12169, which defined the Holocaust differently than had been proposed previously in Wiesel's commission report.[23]

Wiesel resolutely opposed President Carter's joining together Jews and non-Jews in his figure of eleven million victims of the Holocaust. This conflation endangered the sanctity of what Wiesel was interested in promoting, namely, the essential *Jewish* character of the Holocaust, for, he believed, the Jews alone were targeted for extermination, while others were murdered, for one reason or another.[24] On the same day as Carter's equation of Jewish and non-Jewish victims, Wiesel issued an anxious statement:

> Truly I must tell you when I hear certain extrapolations, I am worried. For instance, we used to speak, when we spoke—we didn't dare speak too much—about six million Jews. Then some friends, some people, began reminding us, "True, but after all there were others as well." It is true; there were others as well. So they said, "eleven million, six of whom are Jews." If this goes on, the next step will be eleven, including six, and, in a couple of years, they won't even speak of the six. They will speak only of eleven million. You see the progression: six million plus five, then eleven including six, and then only eleven.

If I were to tell you that I have an answer how to solve, how to combine
these terms, I would lie. I do not know how. For the moment I am weak. My
heart is not that large. It can barely include the figure six million.[25]

But Carter was insistent on an inclusive definition of the Holocaust,
because he had to placate other ethnic constituencies that had stepped
forward to claim representation on the council. American Poles, Ukrainians, Lithuanians, and others also wanted their suffering commemorated,
a threat to Wiesel's conviction of the project, because their peoples had
not been subjected to extermination as the Jews had been. Indeed, Wiesel
argued, sometimes they had been complicit with the Nazis in the persecution of Jews.

Wiesel pressed for a change in the executive order, which otherwise
would tie the hands of his group to a definition that Wiesel and other
Jewish survivors opposed. The solution was a grammatical one. In official literature and correspondence, the definition of the Holocaust
would read as "six million Jews—and the millions of other Nazi victims
in World War II."[26] Nevertheless, there was continued disagreement
and delay in proceeding with the work because Carter continued to hold
on to the language of the original executive order without grammatical
rectification. In consternation at this conflict, the White House can-
celed that year's Day of Remembrance event, even as officials realized
that they could not afford to permanently antagonize Wiesel, because
he was deemed indispensable to the project. In a May 1980 letter to one
of Carter's aides, Wiesel wrote in disappointment:

> In all the discussion with your staff, *the emphasis has been on politics, not loyalty*
> *to the dead.* No assurances regarding the integrity of the project have been
> kept. We have gone from frustration to frustration, from concession to
> concession and why not say it, from humiliation to humiliation. . . . What a
> sad thing it is that such a beautiful idea, announced initially by the President
> with such apparent conviction, could have come to this.[27]

Other Carter advisors, however, could not believe that Wiesel was intent
on bothering the American president with such seemingly picayune issues
as appointees and grammatical fine points. And yet, from Wiesel's point
of view, he and other Jewish survivors swallowed hard when it came to
accepting the appointment of other ethnic representatives of nations who
had a questionable record when it came to wartime relations with the Jews.
They believed that certain distinctions had to be maintained, unless the
whole project was only a degraded means of ethnic political advancement.
As Edward Linenthal noted, "linking victims together—a basic alteration

of the sacred Holocaust narrative operative in much of the Jewish community—registered, predictably, as a religious offense."[28] As a traumatized Jewish survivor with self-professed little concern for politics, Wiesel was not going to accede to political expedience without fervent resistance motivated by his "loyalty to the dead," a loyalty whose depths some members of the Carter administration could barely comprehend.[29]

It was in September 1979 that the commission presented its written report to President Carter at the White House. In his statement to the president, Wiesel recounted that the distinguished commission had visited the sites of mass death in Europe. He understood that although "all the Jews were victims, not all victims were Jews," and he reiterated his own adage: "We must also learn the dangers of indifference and neutrality. In times of evil, indifference to evil is evil. Neutrality always helps the killer, not the victim." Wiesel then handed Carter the report with an "infinite gratitude."[30] The commission presented four proposals to President Carter for consideration. First, the appropriate form of remembrance was to be a living memorial and educational center, as opposed to a monument. Second, the memorial would be built on federal land, but funded through private donations. Third, the U.S. government would designate certain days to be annual days of Holocaust remembrance, thus including the Holocaust in the American civil religion, with events to be sponsored in state capitols across the country. Fourth, the commission urged the creation of a Committee on Conscience to be composed of notable people who would serve as a monitoring group to mobilize their fellow citizens in defense of human rights wherever and whenever such abuses could be detected. This last proposal represented the logic often stressed in Wiesel's own human rights interventions: Remembrance of the Holocaust ought to inform and inspire conscientious activity in the present. However, as journalist Judith Miller pointed out, the U.S. State Department and Carter administration opposed the formation of such a committee, as "neither favored the establishment of an officially sanctioned, private group of human-rights busybodies who might offer competing assessments of various international human-rights crises and the efficacy of the U.S. government's efforts to resolve them."[31] This fourth proposal had been the brainchild of long-time activist Hyman Bookbinder, who commented that "[o]ur proposals were fine as long as they did not ask the government to extend the lessons of the Holocaust to our current foreign and national security policies."[32]

Although Wiesel claimed that he had never been involved in political activities, his acceptance of the chairmanship opened a new chapter in his public and political life. President Carter's solicitation of Wiesel and support of Holocaust remembrance is an instance of what Pierre Bourdieu calls the power of

> official naming, a symbolic act of imposition which has on its side all the strength of the collective, of the consensus, of common sense, because it is performed by a delegated agent of the state, that is, the holder of *the monopoly of legitimate symbolic violence* . . . [and there is] above all the legitimate point of view of the authorized spokesperson, the delegate of the state, the official naming, or the *title* or qualification which, like an educational qualification, is valid on all markets and which, as an official definition of one's official identity, saves its bearers from the symbolic struggle of all against all, by establishing the authorized perspective, the one recognized by all and thus universal, from which social agents are viewed.[33]

Bourdieu here built on sociologist Max Weber's formulation of the state as the holder of the monopoly on the legitimate exercise of violence by pointing out that the state also exercises a monopoly on symbolic violence, namely, those symbolic exchanges in which state power's hierarchical relations of domination tacitly are acknowledged as legitimate, both by the authorized spokesperson and by the broader collective. In this context of the U.S. government's commitment to "remembering the Holocaust," the "authorized perspective" was that of the U.S. government's concern for innocent victims and opposition to oppression.

In light of the politics of such official naming and authorizing, then, Wiesel became not only a servant of the state by virtue of his agreement to serve on this Carter-created commission, but he was also a beneficiary of the "strength of the collective" conferred by the U.S. government itself. For example, in his political-ethical interventions after 1978, Wiesel as commission chairman was able to offer his testimony "valid on all markets," from op-eds in the *Los Angeles Times* and *New York Times* to appearances before the U.S. Congress. By undertaking this unprecedented memorial venture, the U.S. government established the authorized perspective of the "worthy victims," saving Wiesel "from the symbolic struggle of all against all" in the quest for social recognition. Wiesel was all too aware of the immense practical and symbolic distance between the period when the Roosevelt administration did nothing for Europe's Jews (Jews as unworthy victims, who did not warrant military intervention, and so on) and the Carter administration's avowal of their importance (Jews as worthy victims, now deserving offi-cial commemoration).

Normally so careful not to be aligned with anything he considered political, Wiesel might have been disposed to participate in the project because he genuinely believed that the Carter administration shared his passionate, moral commitment to memory, hence, his "infinite grati-tude" to President Carter for his inauguration of the commission. By attending to the broader social and political context of this state spon-sorship of remembrance, some critical issues arise about the supposed U.S. commitment to memory and victims. For example, it is important to recall that Carter's initial impetus for the project obviously was polit-ical, given his need to pacify testy relations with the organized Jewish community. It also is worth bearing in mind that the administration refused to agree to formation of the Committee on Conscience, which, by highlighting the need for citizen awareness and mobilization, might have placed more rigorous ethical demands on U.S. foreign policy. Although it was politically pragmatic and rhetorically useful to sponsor the remembrance of a vast European atrocity, the administration wanted to ensure that the "lessons" of the Holocaust not be invoked to interfere with current foreign policy. So, at the very time Carter initi-ated the project to remember a genocide of thirty-five years earlier, his administration was continuing its diplomatic and military support of its ally Indonesia, which was at that time engaging in a brutal assault on the people of East Timor. On Western military aid to Indonesia, John G. Taylor observed that "[w]hether they were F1–11 jets, A-4 bombers or Bronco OV-10 from the United States or Hawk ground-attack planes from Britain, they all met particular military needs at specific moments in the campaign. The encirclement and annihilation operation required saturation bombing, hence the A-4 and the Hawk, both supplied in 1978."[34] Evidently, neither the administration nor the president's com-mission saw any conflict between promoting Holocaust memory and protecting a valuable U.S. ally from Holocaust-informed criticism or any other demands of conscience.[35]

In addition to the relevance of Holocaust remembrance to U.S. for-eign policy at that time, others wondered if there were not atrocities closer to home worth remembering. There was no comparable effort on the part of the U.S. government to institutionalize the memory of the suffering, oppression, and mass death of victims of the United States, whether it be the Native populations, the abducted and then enslaved

Africans, or, more recently, the Vietnamese victims of U.S. aggression in the 1960s and 1970s. Surely, it would have been unthinkable for a Carter aide to suggest a president's commission on remembering U.S. atrocities in Vietnam.[36] Peter Novick identified the useful service of evading American responsibility by focusing on German atrocities:

> The repeated assertion that whatever the United States has done to blacks, Native Americans, Vietnamese, or others pales in comparison to the Holocaust is true—and evasive. And whereas a serious and sustained encounter with the history of hundreds of years of enslavement and oppression of blacks might imply costly demands on Americans to redress the wrongs of the past, contemplating the Holocaust is virtually cost-free: a few cheap tears.[37]

Although it is understandable that Jews and their non-Jewish allies would be quite relieved that Jewish suffering be commemorated in such an official way, it also would be naive to see this U.S. effort at "preserving memory" as an ethical expression of a disinterested state power committed to alleviating the suffering of the innocent in the present or coming to terms with the suffering it caused in the past. Indeed, by its authorization of a Holocaust memorial in Washington, D.C., the U.S. government affirmed Wiesel's own lifetime project of remembering the Jewish victims. But one ought to bear in mind the operative political selectivity of the victims in the government's sponsoring of such memory.

Consider President Carter's speech on the necessity of this memorial effort on the first Day of Remembrance on 24 April 1979:

> Although the Holocaust took place in Europe, the event is of fundamental significance to Americans for three reasons. First, it was American troops who liberated many of the death camps, and who helped expose the horrible truth of what had been done there. Also, the United States became a homeland for many of those who were able to survive. Secondly, however, we must share the responsibility for not being willing to acknowledge forty years ago that this horrible event was occurring. Finally, because we are humane people, concerned with the human rights of all peoples, we feel compelled to study the systematic destruction of the Jews so that we may seek to learn how to prevent such enormities from occurring in the future.[38]

Carter's third reason was that study of the Jewish tragedy should lead to some practical difference in the prevention of other outbursts of collective victimization. Yet, at that time, the Carter administration had a major opportunity "to prevent enormities" in East Timor, not to mention Nicaragua, Iran, and Haiti. If the Carter administration had wanted an opportunity to heed the lessons of the Holocaust, it easily could have come to the aid of trapped and defenseless East Timorese but, instead, the United States supported the Indonesian killers with military, diplomatic, and economic assistance. To recall Hyman Bookbinder's words, the lessons of the Holocaust were important to remember as long as they did not apply to the United States and, moreover, as long as they could be used to score rhetorical victories over enemies, past and present.

Wiesel emphasized that he had no political agenda and that he wanted to prevent his moral perspective from being contaminated by politics. But he received a tremendous boost for his mission when he consented to participate in a project that reinforced the "authorized perspective" of state power to define and divide the social world—in the present instance, by privileging more useful, now worthy victims over other, more disturbing, unworthy victims.

The Reagan Years

In 1980 Wiesel next assumed the chairmanship of the U.S. Holocaust Memorial Council, the body that was charged with bringing to fruition the recommendations accepted by the Carter administration. The council soon engaged other vexatious, philosophical issues pertaining to the boundaries of memory as well as attended to the practical matters of fundraising and soliciting architectural designs. Politics also intruded on these discussions, often testing Wiesel's capacity of tolerance. With the coming to power of Ronald Reagan, Wiesel's council faced a different political challenge: Evidently, none of the members of the group were Republicans. In the interest of balance, a Reagan advisor told Wiesel some Republicans needed to be represented on this council, so some of the current members should resign. Wiesel threatened his own resignation from the council if this was to happen. Evidently, his resistance generated resentment among White House staff.[39] Still, during the Reagan administration, Wiesel received one public recognition after another, as he promoted Holocaust remembrance to ever-larger and more powerful audiences. In this section, I analyze his testimony on the Genocide Treaty before the U.S. Senate, his role in the 1985 Bitburg affair, and his use of the Nobel Prize to call attention to human rights issues around the world.

In March 1985 Wiesel testified before the Senate Foreign Relations Committee on the Genocide Treaty, which had long been opposed by the U.S. Congress. As the chairman of the U.S. Holocaust Memorial Council, Wiesel brought his powerful personal authority to the 99th Congress to bear on an issue central to his work as a public intellectual: the linkage of memory to morality. Wiesel's performance revealed the operative politics of consecration and moral authority in the United States.[40]

Wiesel began by citing his qualifications to speak before the dignified body of senators. Neither a law professor nor a political scientist, Wiesel was a professor of humanities who spoke "in the name of humanity" and so respectfully advised that the Senate ratify the treaty. He also spoke as an American citizen who was once stateless but who was given the freedom to pursue his vocation in America. He spoke as well as a Jew who had attempted "to do something with those memories of fire and anguish in order to reduce fire and to curtail anguish." Finally, Wiesel introduced himself as the witness "who has seen genocide at work." He understood that, of all the noteworthy people who spoke on behalf of the Genocide Treaty, he was the only one who saw genocide take place. Then, making a link between past and present suffering, he acknowledged that he also witnessed the more recent genocide of the Cambodians; in addition, he mentioned that "I have seen in a way the Miskito Indians and their suffering."[41] He did not claim that the Nicaraguan government was guilty of genocide against the Miskitos, but in juxtaposing the Miskitos with the Cambodians, Wiesel likely pleased his listeners, as the Senate was then involved in a passionate debate about the best way to "contain" the allegedly dangerous Sandinista government in Nicaragua. In these opening remarks, Wiesel's citations drew attention to the victims of the Khmer Rouge in Cambodia and the Sandinistas in Nicaragua, but he astutely did not mention the rest of the Nicaraguan civilians who were suffering from terrorist attacks by the U.S.-backed contra forces from their bases in Honduras. Wiesel did not take that opportunity to allude, even briefly, to his recent encounter with Salvadoran or Guatemalan refugees who were also the victims of loyal U.S. allies in Central America. In this presentation of self before the committee, Wiesel exhibited impressive tact and political savvy by focusing on the victims of U.S. enemies and not mentioning those of U.S. allies. He thereby insured respectable credentials before his audience and if he could be so appealing to the influential senators, perhaps they might respond favorably to his appeal regarding the Genocide Treaty.

Wiesel next recalled the ordeal of the Jews who died at Auschwitz at the rate of ten thousand a day. And then, in his distinctive lamentation, he testified:

> Mr. Chairman, I have seen the flames. I have seen the flames rising to nocturnal heavens; I have seen parents and children, teachers and their disciples, dreamers and their dreams, and woe unto me, I have seen children

thrown alive in the flames. I have seen all of them vanish in the night as part of a plan, part of a program conceived and executed by criminal minds that have corrupted the law and poisoned the hearts in their own land and the lands that they had criminally occupied.[42]

He acclaimed the American effort in fighting and winning the war against the Nazis, the practitioners of genocide. He acknowledged the thousands of Americans who gave their lives to defeat the Nazis, stating that the war of these soldiers, "our war, was not a political war. It was a moral war. And therefore, it is still being glorified and extolled by all of us with justified pride."[43] When he spoke before this chief legislative body on foreign relations, Wiesel described World War II in a way that the senators would surely appreciate, because, by characterizing the war as a moral—and not a political—war against absolute evil, he affirmed the senators' own righteous patriotism. Given that Wiesel had long been critical of the U.S. government's *inaction* during the Holocaust, this generous interpretation before the Senate committee invites some questions. If Wiesel's view was correct, why did the U.S. government not offer strong moral opposition to Nazism after, say, Kristallnacht in 1938? Why did the U.S. government not allow more Jewish refugees to come to the United States at their time of greatest need? Why did the United States wait to fight Nazism only *after* the Japanese bombed Pearl Harbor late in 1941 and after the Nazis already had a proven record of humiliating and harming Jews? Why did Wiesel claim that the war was still being "glorified and extolled" when, for years, he himself had been an adamant critic of the Roosevelt administration, which had higher priorities (political and military) than protecting Jewish life such that it had failed to bomb the railroads to the death camps?[44] Was the U.S. war "moral" when it entailed the saturation bombing of Dresden? Did the Nazi bombings of England justify the Allied bombings of German cities full of civilians? Further, were the U.S. atomic bombings of Hiroshima and Nagasaki "still being glorified and extolled by all of us"? By characterizing the war in such terms, Wiesel did not speak in the terms of early in his career—as an outraged critic and survivor—but as a discreet and solicitous advisor to American power. He realistically sought to ingratiate his memorial cause, not to antagonize his possible allies with sharp questions that he had raised on other occasions.[45]

Wiesel then assured the senators that his plea for the ratification of the Genocide Treaty was "morally inspired and not politically. I am governed by moral considerations only."[46] Also, by having voted on behalf of the treaty, the senators could take a stand against those who claimed that the genocide against the Jews did not take place. Wiesel believed that, were the Senate to pass the treaty, it would be a grand validation of his and other Jewish survivors' testimony and, as such, would be an ethical act. In addition to preserving the integrity of the past, the ratification of the treaty would also protect people in the future by its call to prevention. Wiesel claimed that "we as a moral nation whose memories are alive, we must make that statement that we are against genocide, that we cannot tolerate a world in which genocide is being perpetrated, and whoever engages in genocide, wherever that is, places himself outside the human community."[47] Certainly, very few people, senators or otherwise, could disagree with Wiesel at this level of abstract principle. Wisely, though, the Holocaust survivor was not more specific, because these views could have timely and discomfiting pertinence to such U.S. allies as Indonesian General Suharto and Guatemalan General Ríos Montt. But Wiesel was employing Holocaust remembrance before the senators not to critique the state during World War II and since but rather to affirm it, at the time of the Holocaust and then in the 1980s, as morally exemplary.

However, Wiesel did admit that he had been puzzled as to why the United States had not yet ratified the Genocide Convention. Because he was not a "political scientist," he could not explain this delay. As a witness, he was troubled by this U.S. refusal as he found "it difficult to come up with a logical answer" when his university students inquired as to why the United States has not ratified "something so simple and urgent and vital. . . ." Wiesel requested that the Senate at last provide an answer by voting on behalf of the treaty and, in so doing, "reaffirm our common belief that we have been and remain a nation governed by moral principles. When those principles were jeopardized, we had the courage to defend them." Because "murder is evil," and genocide represents "absolute evil," the United States had to go on record as having taken a stand against genocide by ratifying the treaty and making it part of the supreme law of the nation. Wiesel reminded the senators that nothing they could do would bring back the Jewish dead. But ratification would mean that at least the Jewish dead of the Nazi genocide would be remembered "without shame." And so, he concluded, ratification "would become not only an act of justice, but above all, a solemn and noble act of remembering."[48] A brief exchange between Wiesel and some senators next took place. North Carolina Senator Jesse Helms responded to Wiesel by affirming, "I have never heard a more eloquent message." But Helms asked Wiesel if he was troubled by the fact that Israel often had been accused of genocide "from the very people who do not believe that Israel should be allowed to exist," presumably Palestinians and other Arabs. Wiesel defended Israel and held that such detractions against Israel said more about the deplorable state of the world than about Israel. Also, Wiesel informed the senators that Israel previously signed the treaty.[49]

Although Wiesel typically claimed a naiveté about politics, it was not too difficult to understand why the United States had been reluctant to sign the treaty. Leo Kuper posed the issue this way: "Did [the U.S. government] fear that it might be held responsible, retrospectively, for the annihilation of Indians in the United States, or its role in the slave trade, or its contemporary support for tyrannical governments engaging in mass murder?"—historical facts that might contest a "common belief that we have been and remain a nation governed by moral principles."[50] To address such issues might have proved embarrassing not only to the Senate but also to Wiesel who had reaffirmed the "moral principles" fundamental to the U.S. government's rhetoric and self-perception. However, this was not the place for Wiesel to raise disturbing questions or make trenchant applications; rather, he claimed before the Senate that he was one proud to be "involved in our political life and who believes in our system and in our ideals," an interesting shift from two months earlier at the sanctuary conference when he professed, "I have never been involved in anything political."[51]

In this testimony on behalf of the Genocide Treaty, Wiesel self-consciously attempted to distance himself from political matters, even as the object of his advocacy—a ratified Genocide Treaty—would undoubtedly have political ramifications for the United States. By only claiming the moral status of witness and by encouraging the Senate in a most deferential manner to support this ratification, Wiesel again asserted his innocence and credibility by attempting to stand above the political fray. Whereas in his past interventions such as "A Plea for Survivors," Wiesel had spoken quite forcefully about the failure of the United States during the Holocaust, here his discourse operated along much more careful and tasteful lines, as when he lauded World War II with patriotic fervor. Wiesel's invocation of the Holocaust served to legitimate the U.S. state, past and present, in the hopes of convincing the senators to pass a piece of legislation that they had long feared might involve the United States in political and legal controversies.

Wiesel's appearance before the Senate Foreign Relations Committee imparted its own symbolic prestige to Wiesel. Both Senate members and Wiesel were engaged in reciprocal homage, inasmuch as the Senate accredited Wiesel as an honorable witness, so he, too, accredited that body with his own moral approval. In so doing, Wiesel was commending a legislative body that was not exactly the paragon of humane sensitivity to suffering. One need only consider the Senate's support of the Reagan administration's attack on Nicaragua, acts in violation of international law and ones that evidently did not place the United States itself "outside the human community."[52] It may be that Wiesel reckoned current U.S. policy toward Nicaragua and other countries irrelevant to his prior mission of securing support for the Genocide Treaty, which would also aid Jews in their struggle against Holocaust deniers.[53] In this intervention, Wiesel left behind his previous rhetoric of denouncing the bystander and enthusiastically accepted the respectable terms of American political discourse—the U.S. government as benevolent, honorable, but occasionally and bafflingly slow to act (as in ratification of the Genocide Treaty).

A short time after this testimony before the Senate Foreign Relations Committee, Wiesel became immersed in a painful issue that stunned the country and proved to be a major embarrassment to President Ronald Reagan, the "Bitburg Affair."[54] In the fall of 1984, West German Chancellor Helmut Kohl had suggested to President Reagan that, during his visit the following May to a European Summit Conference, he make a symbolic gesture of reconciliation with the West German government by lying a wreath at a German military cemetery. This obvious public relations boost to Kohl would take place, not coincidentally, on the fortieth anniversary of V-E Day. Reagan's aides had calculated that this would be an uncontroversial exercise in public relations, the forte of the former Hollywood actor. However, Reagan, his advisors, and the West German government made a series of oversights and misjudgments. It had been proposed that Reagan visit Dachau, one of the concentration camps outside of Munich, but the president begged off, preferring not to reopen the somber past but to look ahead cheerily to the future. It was then revealed that the cemetery at Bitburg contained the graves of SS officers. Jews, veterans, and church groups were shocked at the symbolism of this announced visit and they mobilized to urge Reagan not to impugn the memory of the Jewish and American dead by honoring their murderers. The members of the U.S. Holocaust

Memorial Council were greatly upset as well. One member proposed that the entire council resign in protest. They decided not to, however; in Wiesel's words, "a short and solemn resolution expressing our concern, our anguish, is passed unanimously. We appeal to the president's humanism, to his understanding of history; we shower him with praise even as we ask him to cancel his visit to the SS cemetery."[55]

The third week of April had been designated as the National Days of Remembrance of the Holocaust, sponsored by the U.S. Holocaust Memorial Council. Having earlier refused to visit Dachau to pay his respects, Reagan now declared that he would also place a commemorative wreath at a death camp to be announced. Then, on April 18, the Day of Holocaust Remembrance, Reagan said in response to press questions about his Bitburg visit: "I think that there's nothing wrong with visiting that cemetery where those young men are victims of Nazism, also, even though they were fighting in the German uniform, drafted into service to carry out the hateful wishes of the Nazis. They were victims, just as surely as the victims in the concentration camps."[56]

Such an equation precipitated more protests. The U.S. Holocaust Memorial Council considered once again the issue of resignation, this time strongly favored by Wiesel, who stated,

> I cannot quite see how we can continue to serve a president who has just insulted the memory of our dead. Since we have been appointed by him, we have only one option: to signify our disagreement by resigning. Otherwise we lose the moral right to defend that memory. Our resignation will leave only a small trace, but a trace nevertheless: Two or three phrases in this document will recall that we were able to resist the temptations of cowardice.[57]

Yet again, the council opposed resignation and instead sent another telegram to the president expressing outrage at his nonchalant linkage of victims and killers. Soon thereafter, Wiesel met with Reagan personally and told him that there was still time for him to make the right choice. But Reagan remained firm in his commitment to Kohl, which made Wiesel feel sorry for the seemingly passive U.S. president: "I know he feels trapped, and that if it depended solely on him, he would decide differently. The threesome of Regan, Deaver, and Buchanan have in fact made the decision in his place."[58]

On the next day, April 19, Reagan added further insult to injury by stating that he would visit the German concentration camp at Bergen-Belsen, as if to say that this concession should soothe the sensibilities of his detractors. At this point of increasingly indignant criticism and damage control, April 19 was the day that Elie Wiesel was scheduled to receive the Congressional Gold Medal, which honored him for his lifetime achievement.[59] The bestowing of the Congressional Medal during the Bitburg crisis ironically constituted the apex of Wiesel's "consecration" by the state. Pierre Bourdieu argued that such "[c]ultural consecration does indeed confer on the objects, persons, and situations it touches a sort of ontological promotion akin to a transubstantiation."[60] By receiving the congressional medal in the context of the Bitburg publicity, Wiesel would have become even more "transubstantiated" as a national moral icon.

And as if April 19 was not already saturated in memories, it was also part of National Jewish Heritage Week, as well as the forty-second anniversary of the Warsaw Ghetto Revolt. Reagan's aides decided to play down the ceremony honoring Wiesel by moving the event from the much larger East Room to the Roosevelt Room. With the ceremony televised nationally by NBC and CNN, President Reagan recalled the immense tragedy of the Holocaust, the miraculous Jewish rebirth of the State of Israel, and the continuing persecution of Jews in the Soviet Union, thus affirming as his own agenda three major concerns of Wiesel's own public mission. Reagan's accolade concluded:

> As the people of Europe rebuilt their shattered lands, the survivors rebuilt their shattered lives, and they did so despite the searing pain. And we who are their fellow citizens have taken up their memories and tried to learn from them what we must do.
>
> No one has taught us more than Elie Wiesel.
>
> His life stands as a symbol; his life is testimony that the human spirit endures and prevails. Memory can fail us, for it can fade as the generations change. But Elie Wiesel has helped make the memory of the Holocaust eternal by preserving the story of the 6 million Jews in his works. Like the Prophets whose words guide us to this day, his words will teach humanity timeless lessons. He teaches about despair but also about hope. He teaches about our capacity to do evil but also about the possibility of courage and resistance and about our capacity to sacrifice for a higher good. He teaches about death. But in the end, he teaches about life.
>
> Elie, we present you with this medal as an expression of our gratitude for your life's work.[61]

In serving as a representative for the Jewish dead and survivors, reminding U.S. citizens of his people's suffering, and urging contemporary "courage and resistance," Wiesel's lifetime achievement was then recognized as an inspiringly ethical one. Thus, the nation's highest elected official encouraged citizens to look upon this public servant with respect and gratitude for his many contributions to the commonwealth.

With a nationwide audience looking on, Reagan handed Wiesel the medal with Wiesel's own words inscribed on it, "Indifference to evil is evil." Wiesel's acceptance speech was full of themes he had sounded in the previous three decades as a witness. He began by noting that he was interested in conciliation. He felt that he and President Reagan were never on two different sides: "We were on the same side. We were always on the side of justice, always on the side of memory, against the SS and against what they represent."[62] Given the Reagan administration's support of governments with some of the world's worst human rights records (from South Africa to El Salvador), one wonders what side it was that Wiesel saw himself and Reagan as sharing. Perhaps here Wiesel was referring only to Holocaust remembrance and not to the lessons of the Holocaust, which surely would have been pertinent to U.S. policy in Central America and elsewhere.[63]

Wiesel then poignantly added that the medal was not exclusively his; rather, in a pointed reference to Bitburg, it belonged as well to all those Jews that the SS murdered. One of the lessons he learned since his own time in Auschwitz was that "in extreme situations when human lives and dignity are at stake, neutrality is a sin. It helps the killers, not the victims."[64] He invoked the heroism of the Warsaw Ghetto fighters and here reminded his audience that the Allies did nothing to save the Jews from ongoing genocide. Wiesel gratefully acknowledged the U.S. Army liberators of the death camps. He also showed no hesitation in expressing his enthusiasm for his adopted country and for Israel:

> We are grateful to this country, the greatest democracy in the world, the freest nation in the world, the moral nation, the authority in the world. And we are grateful, especially, to this country for having offered us haven and refuge, and grateful to its leadership for being so friendly to Israel. . . . And we are grateful, of course, to Israel. We are eternally grateful to Israel for existing. We needed Israel in 1948 as we need it now. And we are grateful to Congress for its continuous philosophy of humanism and compassion for the underprivileged.[65]

Wiesel then mentioned his appreciation for President Reagan's support of the Soviet Jews as well as his advocacy for Israel. But, having enumerated these causes for his thankfulness and shown himself to be a loyal ally to the President, Wiesel admitted feeling not indignation at

Reagan's recurrent insensitivity, but rather "sadness." Still, as one who took seriously his Jewish heritage being honored that very week, Wiesel felt compelled to "speak truth to power," in a prophetic manner.

Speaking to the president "with respect and admiration," Wiesel recounted previous meetings with President Reagan and stated that he had left those exchanges "enriched, for I know of your commitment to humanity." Wiesel politely excused Reagan for originally not knowing that members of the SS had been buried in the Bitburg cemetery. Then, in words that would become famous, Wiesel uttered the following supplication:

> May I, Mr. President, if it's possible, implore you to do something else, to find a way, to find another way, another site? That place, Mr. President, is not your place. Your place is with the victims of the SS.
>
> Oh, we know there are political and strategic reasons, but this issue, as all issues related to that awesome event, transcends politics and diplomacy.
>
> The issue here is not politics, but good and evil. And we must never confuse them.
>
> For I have seen the SS at work. And I have seen their victims. They were my friends. They were my parents.
>
> Mr. President, there was a degree of suffering and loneliness in the concentration camps that defies imagination. Cut off from the world with no refuge anywhere, sons watched helplessly their fathers being beaten to death. Mothers watched their children die of hunger. And then there was Mengele and his selections. Terror, fear, isolation, torture, gas chambers, flames, flames rising to the heavens.[66]

At the moment Wiesel received the nation's highest honor, he issued a moral challenge to the president, begging Reagan to follow the same duty of remembrance for which he had just extolled Wiesel. Remembrance of the innocent Jewish dead necessitated refusing to debase their suffering by giving even the slightest, retrospective legitimation to their Nazi murderers. Throughout his speech, Wiesel reaffirmed the moral stature of the president's office, for, as leader of "the moral nation, the authority in the world," Reagan ought not deviate from his assumed path of habitual rectitude and compassionate proximity to victims. On this issue, Wiesel deployed his state-conferred consecration to challenge Reagan's realpolitik and his administration's insouciance toward sacred Holocaust memory, thus exhibiting some critical independence from American power.[67] Although he did so for what he considered purely moral reasons, Wiesel nevertheless found himself in the middle of a political tempest. Although his pleading to Reagan did not dissuade the president from making the trip to the Bitburg cemetery, Wiesel's intervention did much to confirm in the public mind his own status as a moral hero.[68] Similar to his testimony on the Genocide Treaty, Wiesel's speech was another demonstration of his skill at playing the political game, as he balanced moralistic precepts with deferential graciousness. In his memoirs, Wiesel reported that, after the ceremony, Reagan Chief of Staff Donald Regan "thanks me for my courteous and respectful tone. After all, I could have said anything I chose. I could have, with the whole country listening, flaunted my disappointment. 'We appreciate your moderation,' Regan tells me."[69]

Wiesel's acceptance speech revealed how he had produced a message that came to be recognized, even celebrated, by American power. As Wiesel rose to the rank of a nationally approved moral luminary, he often raised critical questions about U.S. policy vis-à-vis the Jews during the Holocaust, but rarely did he interrogate postwar U.S. foreign policy and certainly not with any critical appreciation of that policy's contribution to human rights violations.[70] According to Wiesel, the only problematic issue with Ronald Reagan's presidency was Bitburg. In a later interview with Bob Costas, Wiesel affirmed,

> I have a soft spot for Reagan, too. He was a warm person, really. Except he relied too much on his advisors, and they told him to go [to Bitburg]. . . . I feel sorry for him because [Bitburg] was the lowest point of his Presidency. And he could have avoided it. He deserves better than that, really, to remain in history linked to Bitburg.[71]

Outside of Reagan's Bitburg lapse, then, Wiesel evidently found nothing troubling about Mr. Reagan's record. For anyone committed to the consistent linkage of memory to justice, Wiesel's earnest pleading to Reagan could be framed differently: Why did he assert President Reagan's place was with the victims when his administration had been aiding and abetting the governments of El Salvador, Guatemala, and the Nicaraguan contras, the victimizers of tens of thousands of innocent civilians? Or Reagan's "constructive engagement" with the South African apartheid regime? Wiesel was correct in challenging Reagan's de facto indifference to the dictates of Holocaust remembrance, yet outside of issues pertaining to that remembrance, Wiesel rarely addressed contemporary "political" issues that put him at odds with established power, Democratic or Republican. Recall Wiesel's intervention at the sanctuary conference a few months earlier, at which he said nothing about the political causes of Central Americans' suffering, which had roots in U.S. policy. This neutrality allowed Wiesel to present himself as moral only, and so unimpeachable for not being contaminated by partisanship and controversy. The linkage of the Bitburg imbroglio to the Congressional Medal tribute confirmed how the once unworthy Jewish victims had become the worthiest of victims, symbolized that very day by Wiesel.[72] In his celebration of Elie Wiesel, President Reagan pontificated about the U.S. commitment to Jewish victims, past and present, even while his administration funded, supported, lauded, and presided over extensive terrorism, repression, and slaughter in Central America.

Increasingly aware of his own lack of managerial and organizational skills, Elie Wiesel finally resigned from the U.S. Holocaust Memorial Council in late 1986.[73] He had become distressed by the growing "politicization" in the council, as evidenced by the bickering and jockeying for status in the council as well as the decision to honor large donors to the memorial by naming sections of the complex after them.[74] Wiesel still believed in preserving the purity of the project, regardless of the dictates of schedules and fund-raising: "I was not in a hurry. So what if it takes another year? We're dealing with a monument for centuries. We have to be sure of what we are doing rather than go fast in the wrong direction."[75] Wiesel and his colleagues faced the classic dilemma of how to preserve the charisma of the first-generation prophets/witnesses as it was channeled into necessary, but possibly distorting, institutionalization for future generations. Wiesel the survivor was acutely concerned that the purity of memory be safeguarded, even as that precious memory had to be shaped into bricks, mortar, and exhibits.

Although the Congressional Medal demonstrated Wiesel's ascendancy in the United States, he was to receive an even greater international tribute when he received the 1986 Nobel Peace Prize, for which he had been nominated for several years. The Nobel Peace Prize confers on its recipients inestimable symbolic and moral renown the world over, even though increasingly it has come under more critical scrutiny for its own politics of consecration.[76] For example, one official contended that the year Wiesel received the prize was the year that the Nobel Committee felt it had to make an uncontroversial, unabashedly pro-Western selection.[77] The Nobel Committee was all too aware of its own power not only to honor outstanding individuals but also to call attention to troubling issues about which not everyone would be grateful.[78] Wiesel was awarded the prize for his work as a moral guardian. Egil Aarvik, the Nobel Committee Chairman, declared, "Elie Wiesel is not only the man who survived, he is also the spirit which has triumphed. In him we see a man who has gone from utter humiliation to become one of our most important spiritual leaders and guides. . . . It is vital that we have such guides in an age when terror, repression and racial discrimination still exist in the world."[79] The Nobel Committee thus joined Jewish leaders, Christian theologians, and Presidents Carter and Reagan in recognizing Wiesel's amazing journey from Sighet through Auschwitz to New York.

Upon receiving the famous prize, Wiesel gave an address that reiterated his abiding commitments to the Jewish people, Holocaust memory, and the State of Israel. There, he returned to his enduring theme and motivation:

> [T]he world did know and remained silent. And that is why I swore never to be silent whenever and wherever human beings endure suffering and humiliation. We must always take sides. Neutrality helps the oppressor, never the tormented. Sometimes we must interfere. When human lives are endangered, when human dignity is in jeopardy, national borders and sensitivities become irrelevant.[80]

Wiesel asserted that Jewish interests and causes ranked first with him, but then immediately he stated that other peoples' causes also were important, specifying the abominable nature of South African apartheid. He also invoked such dissidents as Joseph Begun, Andrei Sakharov, Lech Walesa, and Nelson Mandela. He noted the universality of human rights violations by left-wing and right-wing governments. And he cited the truism: "Human suffering anywhere concerns men and women everywhere."[81]

Wiesel also addressed the contentious Israeli–Palestinian issue and granted the applicability of his truism above to the Palestinians, "to whose plight I am sensitive, but whose methods I deplore when they lead to violence." Recall that Wiesel was so sensitive to Israel's plight that he never publicly deplored Israel's violent methods, from collective punishment, house demolitions, torture, and illegal settlements. He considered that "[t]errorism is the most dangerous of answers" (his assumption here being that only Palestinians commit terrorism, never Israel) but that something must be done to relieve the Palestinians of their frustration. He regretted that both peoples had lost too many people to violence. He insisted that this violence must stop and that

> Israel will cooperate, I am sure of that. I trust Israel, for I have faith in the Jewish people. Let Israel be given a chance, let hatred and danger be removed from her horizons, and there will be peace in and around the Holy

Land. Please understand my deep and total commitment to Israel: if you could remember what I remember, you *would* understand. Israel is the only nation in the world whose very existence is threatened.[82]

Wiesel's "deep and total commitment" to his favorite state prevented him from commenting on Israel's refusal—under both Labor and Likud governments—to abide by the international consensus toward a two-state peace settlement. Also, that uncompromising commitment rendered him unable to evaluate the Israeli government's solidarity, not with Nelson Mandela, but with the South African apartheid regime over many years.[83]

The Nobel Prize magnified Wiesel's international reputation, and he continued to transmit his testimony and deliver his strictures against silence, indifference, and neutrality in both elite and popular circles.[84] He put his economic, symbolic, cultural, and social resources to work in support of his mission as a cosmopolitan intellectual and witness. With the $210,000 Nobel Prize money, he and his wife created the nonprofit institution, the Elie Wiesel Foundation for Humanity, to support various projects of reconciliation and public understanding. He undertook to sponsor a series of international forums on "The Anatomy of Hate," involving respected figures such as Václav Havel, Lech Walesa, and François Mitterand. Some of the themes Wiesel and his allies explored included "The Anatomy of Hate and Conflict Resolution" (1990), "To Save Our Children" (1992), "The Leaders of Tomorrow" (1995), and "The Future of Hope" (1995). In 1993 he helped institute the Universal Academy of Cultures, which would gather "men and women professionally dedicated to the service of truth and beauty who are also committed to the pursuit of good."[85] Eminent writers and thinkers would address a theme each year (such as "intervention"), and generate discussions, books, and even encyclopedias that would engage the broader public. He also published dialogues with John Cardinal O'Connor of New York and with French President François Mitterand.[86]

As a Nobel Peace laureate, Wiesel had the visibility and reputation to gather fellow laureates to devote their intellectual savvy and ethical vision to address a series of pressing world problems. A gathering of seventy-five laureates from eighteen nations participated in Wiesel's first meeting in Paris in 1988 to discuss "Facing the 21st Century: Threats and Promises." It is clear that Wiesel did not want to rest on his laurels: He wanted other fellow Nobel laureates to serve as a kind of ethical elite. He joined several other Nobel laureates in calling for the release of Aung San Suu Kyi, the Burmese dissident leader who had been under house arrest for several years.[87] Because of their own prestige, the Nobel winners could call attention to such current crises and urge civic solidarity. However, this was easier to envision than to implement, as Wiesel confessed: "I feel guilty that since 1988 we have not been able to overcome the financial difficulties and create an association of Nobel laureates. It could have intervened in Bosnia, sounded the alarm, saved some children, helped their mothers. We could have given the victims human and moral support and testified on their behalf."[88]

Bosnia, Kosovo, and Clinton

In the early 1990s, Wiesel turned his attention to the crisis unfolding in Europe. The end of the Soviet Union had immense ramifications for Europe, one of which was the breakup of Yugoslavia. For decades, Premier Josip Tito had maintained peace in Yugoslavia, but ethnic aspirations and enmities came to the surface as Communism disintegrated. Slovenia and Croatia declared independence in 1991, but Serbia was intent on maintaining control of Yugoslavia as Serbian President Slobodan Milosevic aimed for a "greater Serbia," which would include Serbian populations from the other republics. When Bosnia-Herzegovina opted for independence in 1992, Serbian forces invaded and expelled Croats and Muslims, established concentration camps, and perpetrated mass rapes against Muslim women. Croatia retaliated in kind, and an escalation of atrocities fueled a bloody cycle, leaving the international community puzzled as to how to respond: Lift a 1991 arms embargo that could benefit the Bosnians? Send U.S. bombers to repel the Serb attacks on Sarajevo? Recognize the Serbian partition and conquest of Bosnia?[89] The Bush and Clinton administrations were reluctant to become involved and, moreover, offered no clear objective for intervention. The specter of Vietnam loomed; U.S. officials were cautious before the possibility of U.S. military casualties resulting from a Balkan quagmire. Although innocents were being slaughtered, this time in Europe, there were evidently no U.S. vital interests at stake (unlike Iraq's invasion of Kuwait in 1990, where regaining control of the oil-rich region warranted prompt and immediate intervention).

In his 1999 memoirs, Wiesel recounted how he came to make a personal investment in the Balkans. It began with a communication from Israel Singer and Elan Steinberg of the World Jewish Congress. Wiesel had been invited by the President of the Federal Republic of Yugoslavia, Dobrica Cosic, to serve as the head of an investigative mission on the infamous prison camps of Yugoslavia. There was a certain poetic justice in Wiesel being summoned to inspect such camps. Consistent with his previous discourse and practice, he described the situation:

> The world media are talking about these [prison] camps. The televised images arouse indignation everywhere. Systematic humiliations, rapes, arbitrary arrests, deportations, summary executions—all are part of a policy of "ethnic cleansing." Everybody is accusing the Serbs. Some people do not hesitate to use the words "concentration camps," "genocide," and even . . . "Auschwitz." I do not. I have never wavered in my affirmation that Auschwitz is unique and will remain so.[90]

With Singer and Steinberg, Wiesel met President Cosic in London at an international conference on Yugoslavia. Also present were Serbian Slobodan Milosevic, Bosnian Serb leader Radovan Karadjic, and Bosnian President Alija Izetbegovic. Croatian President Franjo Tudjman, known for anti-Semitic views, was not invited.

The leaders welcomed Wiesel's intervention, assuring him of freedom of movement and action, even as they protested media distortion about what was happening. They admitted that unfortunate incidents had occurred, but they promised Wiesel that all such camps would be closed in Yugoslavian territory. The leaders agreed publicly to this as well. But later, in November, Wiesel was invited on Ted Koppel's *Nightline* program to comment on reports about the ongoing bloodshed. From that point on, Wiesel decided he must witness the situation firsthand and he soon left on a four-day mission. But he was concerned about two issues as he and his group made their way to Belgrade. First, he did not want to be used as an instrument of propaganda and, second, reflecting his awareness of his own "celebrity," he did not want to attend state dinners or receptions; he had come to see prisoners and speak to the victims. Yet, after a press conference on the first day, Wiesel was ushered into a room with an extravagant meal, contrary to his wishes. As it was Friday evening, Wiesel excused himself: "I am a Jew, and this is Friday evening; my place is not here but in the synagogue. . . ."[91] The next day, Wiesel was disheartened to learn that his delegation's presence had already been grist for the Serbian propaganda mill, as if they had come, not to seek the truth, but to improve the Serbs' tarnished international image. Wiesel protested, but to no avail. After a tour in the city of places that emphasized Serbs' historical suffering, Wiesel and the delegation faced more foot-dragging about their visits to the prison camps. Threatening to return to the United States unless they were granted freedom of movement, Wiesel was taken to the prison camp of Maniaca.

There Wiesel met the camp commander Bozidar Popovic, who promised his famous international visitor that he could choose to interview any fifteen prisoners he wanted and to inquire about their lives under incarceration. Wiesel agreed but only on the solemn promise of Popovic that no harm would come to the men on account of his interview. The commander gave Wiesel his word. Wiesel discovered that the conditions of food, shelter, and warmth were not all that satisfactory. But mostly the prisoners objected to being cut off from their neighbors and the outside world, as they endured anxiety about what the future would bring. Reminiscent of his visit to the Soviet Jews in the mid-1960s, Wiesel related: "Looking at them, we feel guilty. We are a different species: free. How can we best help them? How can we express our solidarity? In this place 'solidarity' is a word that rings empty."[92] After his delegation's visit, he later received word that the camp had been closed on the order of Karadzic and the prisoners had been given over to the care of the International Committee of the Red Cross. But Wiesel also learned that several hundred of the prisoners were not accounted for, and that the specific individuals he had interviewed had been relocated to an even harsher camp. Because they had talked to Wiesel, they endured punitive consequences. He lamented that the people he had come to assist were the very people who paid a heavy price at the hands of the Serbian leaders.

Wiesel next traveled to Sarajevo, where French General Phillippe Morillon served as his guide. He visited another prison where he saw someone who made him sensitive to imminent analogies to the Holocaust: "His name is Borislav Herak. He had confessed to having assassinated thirty-five men and having raped thirteen women, all Muslims. His acts are an abomination, but why call them genocide? (He will be condemned to death and executed.)"[93] Next, President Izetbegovic pointed out to Wiesel where Archduke Francis-Ferdinand had been assassinated in 1914, precipitating World War I. Wiesel also visited the National Library in Sarajevo and met a local writer who pressed him to inquire of the authorities why it had been necessary to burn the library. Wiesel agreed to do so and soon found himself across from Radovan Karadjic, the leader of the Bosnian Serbs, who protested his innocence.

Wiesel disputed Karadjic's interpretation and Karadjic retorted that Wiesel did not know what he was talking about.

Wiesel finished his tense visit with a trip to Belgrade, where he met again with President Cosic of the Federal Yugoslav Republic. He attempted to persuade the president to cease the terror against the Bosnians. But the president made his case for ethnic exclusion of Muslims and noted that the State of Israel itself would soon face a similar problem. Wiesel explained to him that he was mistaken, because Jews had long coexisted with many peoples for centuries. Wiesel's remark may have been accurate but somewhat beside the point, for President Cosic was speaking about the State of Israel's Palestinian problem and Wiesel's response seemed to be about the Jewish people more generally. Reminiscent of Wiesel's remarks to Reagan during the Bitburg Affair, he persisted in pleading with the president to close all the camps and appealed to his vanity: "But at least you will have earned a few lines in the history books. And I don't think you would be taking much of a chance. No one will dare attack you. You will be the hero of the day. You will be applauded by the whole world. You will have the support of all free men."[94] But Cosic remained noncommittal.

Wiesel wrote about this trip in an op-ed for the *New York Times* in February 1993. As with his intervention regarding Cambodia, he asked how the bloodshed in the Balkans and how the attacks on Sarajevo might be stopped. He supported the UN Security Council's determination to establish an international war crimes tribunal, even as he realized that some time would be necessary before it could fully and effectively function. He believed that "only an imaginative, spectacular gesture from the international community could be effective."[95] President Bill Clinton ought to call for a summit meeting in Sarajevo of the leaders of the former Yugoslav republics. Clinton and the other hosts of the conference then ought to appropriate Jimmy Carter's method with Egypt's Anwar el-Sadat and Israel's Menachem Begin at Camp David: The squabbling leaders should not be allowed to leave until they have come to peaceful terms.[96] In addition to President Clinton, Wiesel's appeal went to John Major of Great Britain, Boris Yeltsin of Russia, François Mitterand of France, and Helmut Kohl of Germany. As it turned out, only Mitterand, Wiesel's personal friend, traveled to Sarajevo to lobby for peace.

Wiesel continued to make other entreaties to respond to the killing and misery in the former Yugoslavia. In April 1993 the U.S. Holocaust

Memorial Museum opened after many years of planning, debate, and design. The original chairman and visionary of the project, Wiesel was a featured speaker at the opening ceremonies. As the museum was dedicated, he took this highly public opportunity to remind President Bill Clinton of the terrors in Bosnia: "As a Jew, I am saying that we must do something to stop the bloodshed in that country! People fight each other and children die. Why? Something, anything must be done."[97] Wiesel's plaintive remarks were reported widely in the media and he was interpreted as favoring military intervention, though he himself did not specify any particular course of action. Perhaps thinking of Wiesel's own earlier statements about never using the Holocaust for political purposes, political commentator Charles Krauthammer challenged Wiesel on the timing and place of his advocacy. Wiesel's own justification was twofold: First, a museum was not a sacred site, and, second, "when men are dying, when innocent people are subjected to rape and torture, when cities are being transformed into cemeteries, Jews do not have the right to be silent."[98]

But at the opening of the museum, Wiesel was not alone in using in the rhetoric of memory. President Bill Clinton also embraced Wiesel's views about the importance of keeping memory alive and he acknowledged the brutality in the former Yugoslavia. But, in the concrete case of Bosnia, nothing came of Clinton's concern. In his account of those years of the "slaughterhouse," critic David Rieff commented sharply:

> To utter words like "Never again," as Clinton did at the opening of the Holocaust Museum, was to take vacuity over the border into obscenity as long as the genocide in Bosnia was going on and Clinton was doing nothing to stop it. His words were literally meaningless. For if there was to be no intervention to stop a genocide that was taking place, then the phrase "Never again" meant nothing more than: Never again would Germans kill Jews in Europe in the 1940s.[99]

In the case of Bosnia, Wiesel spoke out as a Jew who identified all too quickly with those people who had suffered imprisonment, torture, hunger, and the destruction of their homes. Yet, from the vantage point of the U.S. government, the victims in Bosnia were not so important as to warrant some American intervention until more than two hundred thousand people had been killed and two million people made refugees. The political and military risks were too great for the United States to intervene at an early stage of the conflict, and so the Bosnians were expendable. Unlike the excuse given after the Holocaust, people knew what was happening in Bosnia, but no serious response was forthcoming until well after destruction and barbarism had been in force for years.[100]

Wiesel had challenged Clinton to "do something, anything," but it took more than two years before the U.S. president finally did, when, after the Dayton Peace Accords, he sent U.S. forces as part of a UN peacekeeping mission. Having decided at last to engage more forcefully with the Bosnian crisis, Clinton shrewdly invited Elie Wiesel to the White House. Although their time together was rather brief, the Clinton and Wiesel tête-à-tête disclosed the operative mutual recognition of moral authority between the witness and the president. Having discussed his administration's policy with Wiesel, the U.S. president complimented his visitor: "Throughout his life, he has been an advocate for peace and human dignity and the duty we owe to one another, and I'd like to ask him to say just a few words about the decisions that are before our country and the work of peace in Bosnia."[101] Wiesel exuded confidence in Clinton's decision to send U.S. troops to intervene and he recalled their earlier remarks at the Holocaust Memorial opening when, Wiesel said, "I left my prepared remarks and appealed to you, to your humanity, which I know is profound, to do something, anything, to stop the killing, the bloodshed, the violence, the hatred, the massacre in former Yugoslavia." As he gave Ronald Reagan the benefit of the doubt regarding Bitburg, so, too, Wiesel believed that Clinton had been seriously concerned about Bosnia and had tried, to no avail, to influence American allies in Europe and the United Nations. But in December 1995, Clinton intervened, according to Wiesel, "on the highest level and in its most noble form." And the future would be kind to Bill Clinton because it was Clinton who helped to stop the killing in the Balkans. At this point, Wiesel gushed effusively before the American leader: "I know of no other world figure today who has done so much in the field of foreign affairs as you have, Mr. President." For Clinton's intervention was "an act of morality," which is why Wiesel was pleased to give his blessing to the president's policy.

After making further remarks on the U.S. determination to give Bosnia a future, Clinton expressed his gratitude to Elie Wiesel, "for being a conscience of this terrible conflict for the last four years." And then in an exchange with the press, Clinton affirmed that the United States traditionally had been reluctant to intervene militarily overseas because "we have not been a country that has sought the gains of empire. We have not been a country that has sought to tell other people how they must live their lives. But that we are fundamentally a good people and when we understand our duty, historically, we nearly always do it." Over the years, Wiesel correctly had been quick to challenge other people who whitewashed their own history when it came to Jewish suffering and the Holocaust. For example, in 1979 when Wiesel traveled to the Ukraine with a delegation of the President's Commission on the Holocaust, he was scandalized about the historical engineering that characterized the monument to the dead at Babi Yar, where a revolting mass murder of Jews had taken place in 1941:

> I can and must reproach [the Ukrainians] for their lack of decency and honesty, their distortion of historical truth, for the word "Jew" does not appear on the monument. The inscription describes the victims as Soviet citizens assassinated by the Fascists. . . . I ask [Ukrainian officials] how they dare deal so shabbily with the truth. I ask who gave them permission, who ordered them to commit this sacrilege.[102]

But at this time of mutual moral cheerleading with President Clinton, there is no record of Wiesel disputing Clinton's amazingly sanitized version of U.S. history, which many peoples in the Western hemisphere alone might likewise find a "sacrilege" and "distortion of historical truth."[103]

Wiesel had served Clinton earlier that year in January when he acted as the president's representative to attend the ceremonies of the fiftieth anniversary of the liberation of Auschwitz. A couple of years later in a *Jerusalem Post* interview, Wiesel remarked, "I came here for [prime minister Yitzhak] Rabin's funeral. [U.S. President Bill] Clinton took me in his plane. It was a special experience. Clinton's a good president for us, a very good president."[104] He also came to Clinton's defense at the time of impeachment proceedings in the aftermath of the Lewinsky affair.[105] This steadfast support was not forgotten by Clinton. In 1998 Wiesel was invited by Hilary Clinton to give a special millennial speech at the White House and a year later, on 12 April 1999, Wiesel addressed a White House audience of dignitaries on the subject, "The Perils of Indifference: Lessons Learned from a Violent Century."[106]

In her introduction of Wiesel, Mrs. Clinton noted the current political context of Wiesel's speech: "children in Kosovo crowded into trains, separated from families, separated from their homes, robbed of their childhoods, their memories, their humanity." She went on to assert that the United States was committed to work against indifference, which is why the United States was in Kosovo. In his short address, Wiesel raised questions about the indifference of people during the Holocaust. He recalled the fate of the Saint Louis, a ship with a thousand Jews that was turned away from the United States after Kristallnacht and sent back to Germany. He expressed incomprehension as to how U.S. businesses continued to have working relations with Germany until 1942. And yet, the simple conclusion to be drawn was that the businesses had higher priorities—profit—than showing solidarity with oppressed Jews, an institutional feature of capitalist enterprises that did not disappear with the end of World War II. Wiesel also addressed the current Kosovo crisis in light of his maxims against indifference and how that situation was so different from World War II: "the joint decision of the United States and NATO to intervene in Kosovo and save those victims, those refugees, those who were uprooted by a man whom I believe that because of his crimes, should be charged with crimes against humanity. But this time, the world was not silent. This time, we do respond. This time, we intervene." Wiesel wondered if this intervention signaled a new era: "Is today's justified intervention in Kosovo, led by you, Mr. President, a lasting warning that never again will the deportation, the terrorization of children and their parents be allowed anywhere in the world?"

The intervention to which Wiesel referred with such approbation was the seventy-eight-day NATO bombing raid on Yugoslavia, undertaken after the breakdown of the negotiations at Rambouillet in March 1999.[107] In an interview in *Tikkun* magazine, Wiesel further explained his support for the NATO war. Once again, he asserted that the moral response was "to show compassion and take the side of the victims," which necessitated the NATO bombing. Wiesel's interviewer raised the issue, though, of the bombing of innocent civilians by NATO and Wiesel asked what alternative there was, given Milosevic's determination to engage in "ethnic cleansing." He believed that the NATO intervention sent a message to Milosevic's victims that "there are people in this world who do care about the victims" in Kosovo. He acknowledged that civilians had been killed by NATO and he expressed his desire that NATO have "better precision in its bombing and a better map of Belgrade. I wish the bombs would only fall on military equipment and not on people." But then he treated from further comment on such matters: "But who am I to give advice to military people? I've never seen a tank from the inside!" Wiesel also believed that it was only a set of moral motivations that dictated U.S. policy and he mused that, after the 1994

Rwandan bloodbath when the United States did not intervene, "[t]here is a kind of regret or remorse that has set into the minds of our decision-makers."[108] There was no evidence, however, that such "regret or remorse" had been so powerful as to dictate current U.S. policy when it came to Turkey: At the very time of time of Milosevic's outrages against the ethnic Albanians, the U.S. government was offering bountiful support to its Turkish ally (and NATO member) then engaged in ethnic cleansing of its own troublesome Kurdish minority, which had resulted in the deaths of thirty thousand people and the creation of three million refugees.[109]

In Wiesel's eyes, the United States had a moral responsibility to intervene whenever countries were engaged in mass murder; it was this ethical drive that made a "superpower" "super." There were times, he believed, that the United States should have intervened in some cases, even if it could not get UN backing or, in the case of the NATO war, congressional authorization to wage war. In other words, Wiesel championed unilateral action by the United States, an option expressly in violation of international law, because the UN Charter forbids the use of threat of force, except in self-defense to armed attack or in authorization by the UN Security Council. Wiesel seemed ignorant here of the many precedents of U.S. intervention that had taken place throughout the world with far from noble intentions, a fact that underscored the importance of supporting respect for international law rather than its dismissal.[110]

Wiesel believed that President Clinton acted morally both in the previous case of Bosnia when he sent the U.S. military and in the current case of NATO's war, which resulted in the destruction of the civilian infrastructure of Serbia. It should be noted that Clinton's ethical agenda included dealing with the brutal Milosevic at the 1995 Dayton Accords, even as the U.S. president ignored Kosovar Ibrahim Rugova's nonviolent resistance movement to Serbia. Unequivocally on the side of the NATO victors, Wiesel attempted to show sensitivity to the Albanian victims by making a mission to the refugee camps in Macedonia and Albania to listen to their stories and make a report back to President Clinton. He met with refugees who were jubilant about the NATO attack, even though they realized that the air attacks "may have accelerated Milosevic's program of destroying their grounds and their lives."[111] Indeed, according to NATO Commander Wesley Clark, it was "predictable" that the bombing would unleash huge refugees and ethnic retaliation by the Serbs against the Albanians.[112]

Wiesel's sincerity and personal concern for the suffering of the ethnic Albanians is not in doubt. But beyond such sympathies, however, the Kosovo crisis highlighted Wiesel's role as a respected moralist for the Establishment. Evening television appearances, millennial addresses at the White House, a state-sponsored visit to refugee camps, all are forthcoming as long as one adheres to the administration's line, that is, that the United States is concerned, rhetorically anyway, about the suffering of this politically useful group of innocent people. From the U.S. government's perspective, the ethnic Albanians were the current worthy victims in a battle against the recalcitrant Milosevic; while the Serbs, whose electrical infrastructure, water systems, bridges, factories, and medical facilities were being bombed, resulting in well over $100 billion in damages, were unworthy victims. Not incidentally, such attacks on civilians constituted a war crime, a fact missed by the Nobel laureate. This U.S. concern for the ethnic Albanians was utterly cynical, if only taking into account the fact that many other innocent people were then being murdered by U.S. allies; consider, for example, how the United States did so little to interfere with Indonesia's rampage in East Timor after the August 1999 referendum when the Timorese voted for independence from Indonesia. There was no humanitarian intervention to stop that bloodbath that left the country in ruins.

Wiesel's responses to the latest European bloodbaths of the 1990s had all the marks of his previous interventions: his empathetic identification with the victims, his assertion of the Holocaust's singularity, his lament about the world's silence, and, increasingly, his willingness to directly serve the aims of U.S. power in its crusades against unadulterated evil. As with Bosnia in 1995, so with Kosovo in 1999, Wiesel lined up solidly behind U.S. power and his own voice—of sensitivity and anguish—became merged with that of his presidential supporter in the White House. Whereas in 1965 he went to Soviet Russia determined that his reportage not be used for propaganda purposes, in the case of the Balkans, Wiesel enthusiastically contributed his signature witness to the propaganda about U.S. intervention and war aims.

Since the late 1970s, Elie Wiesel became a welcomed guest in Washington, D.C., by Presidents Carter, Reagan, and Clinton. Quite often supporting their own foreign policy agenda as his own (except when it clashed with Holocaust remembrance), Wiesel consciously celebrated the morality of U.S. power as he became a trusted confidante and advisor. Inasmuch as Wiesel has used his social and political contacts to promote his product of Holocaust remembrance on the U.S. cultural and political market, he, as an intellectual producer of that Holocaust memory, also had been promoted to a position of great prominence by these representatives of U.S. power. Whereas Wiesel had once spoken of a criminal political silence in 1971 with an imprecise reference to the Vietnam War, he had come to see the United States as *the* moral force in the world. Beyond the American scene, Wiesel the Nobel Peace laureate had become part of an international network of venerable spokespersons on human rights, speaking on issues from Tibet to Burma.

In one of the epigraphs to this chapter, Czech dissident Václav Havel stressed the intellectual's role as a doubter of power, its incantations, and its deceit. Havel also makes clear the role of bearing witness to misery to which Elie Wiesel has gravitated much more readily. He has spoken out on mass dislocation, starvation, concentration camps, and ethnic cleansing. Contrary to the kind of critical, rational discourse that social theorist Alvin Gouldner deemed the stock-in-trade resource of the modern intellectual class, Wiesel suspended such speech in favor of a more moralizing, at times mystical discourse that derived its authority from the traumatized experience of enduring and surviving the Nazi horrors.[113] It is such discourse that characterized Wiesel as a sensitive witness, moral spokesperson, and spiritual guide and this, coupled with his avoidance of penetrating political critique, made him especially useful—regardless of his own conscious intentions—to U.S. state power. For Wiesel esteemed American and Israeli power with no evident recognition of the roles each government played in the kind of victimization he denounced when it was sponsored or committed by official enemies—governments or organizations—of the United States and Israel. Patronage by the state conferred enormous benefits, to be sure; but Wiesel's accommodation to and compromises with power brought him into very close proximity with those philosopher Walter Benjamin once warily described as follows: "And all rulers are the heirs of those who conquered before them. Hence, empathy with the victor invariably benefits the rulers. Historical materialists know what that means. Whoever has emerged victorious participates to this day in the triumphal procession in which present rulers step over those who are lying prostrate."[114] Wiesel's own moral authority to testify about past victimization was embraced and honored by those U.S. rulers whose own triumphal procession continues and who have seen fit to include, at this late date, some formerly unworthy victims in their ranks.[115]

6

The Unfinished Project
of Solidarity
If We Remain Silent

I am obsessed with silence because of the silence of the world.
I do not understand why the world was silent when we
needed its outcry. I always come back to that problem. Where
were the humanists, the leaders, the liberals, the spokesmen
for mankind? The victims needed them. If they had spoken up,
the slaughterer would not have succeeded in his task.

—Elie Wiesel, *Against Silence: The Voice and Vision of Elie Wiesel*

The Holocaust might serve a powerful purpose if it led us to
think of the world today as wartime Germany—where
millions die while the rest of the population obediently goes
about its business. It is a frightening thought that the Nazis, in
defeat, were victorious: today Germany, tomorrow the world.
That is, until we withdraw our obedience.

—Howard Zinn, "A Larger Consciousness," *ZNet Daily Commentaries*

To deepen his solidarity with Soviet Jewry in the early 1970s,
Elie Wiesel wrote a play drawn in part from his own experiences during his two missions to Russia in 1965 and 1966.
The result was *Zalmen, or the Madness of God.* In addition to
Zalmen, one of Wiesel's celebrated madmen, the play focuses
on the plight of a rabbi who is so old, weary, and resigned that

he can no longer muster the courage to speak out against the chilling repression his people endure. To further ensure his woes, the rabbi's daughter has married a defiant atheist, with the likelihood that their son will know nothing of the Judaic heritage to which the rabbi has devoted his life. Also playing a key role is the chairman of the synagogue, who is a savvy collaborator with the state authorities. When an international group of actors visit the area and want to attend services on Yom Kippur, the chairman wants to make sure that all goes smoothly, that there is no "trouble" during the services. However, Zalmen, the rabbi's assistant, incites and encourages the rabbi to speak out against the intimidation and encroachments of the Soviet state. At the end of the first act, the rabbi, having envisioned a horrible future of assimilation and the end of Jewish religiosity, overcomes his hesitations, silence, and prudence to speak out loudly and courageously on behalf of his people. The second act explores the consequences of this bold stand not only for the rabbi himself, but also for his family and the Jewish community. During his own visits to the Soviet Union, Wiesel had encountered a similar rabbi who would not speak out. Wiesel kept hoping he would do so and rally and comfort his people. In writing the play, Wiesel created a different outcome to the one that so disappointed him in real life: a rabbi speaking out in solidarity and in defiance of state power.[1] Philosopher Jürgen Habermas has spoken of the "unfinished project of modernity," that is, the need to continue to seek greater self-determination and self-realization, despite many betrayals in the recent past.[2] From his solidarity on behalf of Soviet Jews to his own silence before dispossessed Palestinians, the journey of Elie Wiesel reveals how demanding and difficult is the unfinished—and unfinishable—project of solidarity with suffering people. In this last chapter, I draw on and go beyond Elie Wiesel's work to privilege three themes that are informing the contemporary project of solidarity of religious believers and citizens in the struggle against silence.

Dangerous Remembrance

German theologian Johann Baptist Metz is one of the preeminent Christian theologians who insisted that Christians can only move forward into the future if they act in solidarity with the Jewish victims of the Holocaust.[3] In addition to remembering Christian complicity and Jewish agony, Metz also maintained that Christianity ought to be based on the dangerous memory of Jesus. If this memory were taken seriously by his followers, the results could prove disruptive to imperial arrangements in the current era. Metz believed that this

> memory of suffering, on the other hand, brings a new moral imagination into political life, a new vision of others' suffering that should mature into a generous, uncalculating partisanship on behalf of the weak and unrepresented. Hence, the Christian memory of suffering can become, alongside many other often subversive innovative factors in our society, the ferment for that new political life we are seeking on behalf of our future.[4]

One of Elie Wiesel's major contributions to American public life has been to propagate the dangerous remembrance of the Holocaust. I believe a confrontation with his work can help ward off retrospective and current self-congratulation, a consistent mode of triumphal powers of both church and state. Although Wiesel's work has come out of an undeniable Jewish particularity, his memorial message has had universal relevance. By reminding Jews, Christians, and other Americans of the Holocaust, he points to the urgent need for "partisanship on behalf of the weak," principally but not exclusively with Jewish victims. And with the zeal of an Émile Zola, Wiesel continues to issue his own "*J'accuse*'s" to people indifferent, insensitive, and hostile toward past and present Jewish suffering. As a witness to incredible crimes, Wiesel promotes the memory of his own people's suffering in the Holocaust and challenges the non-Jewish world to include Jewish suffering in our own collective memory. In his 1986 Nobel lecture, Wiesel affirmed about this reckoning with the Holocaust: "There are no theological answers, there are no psychological answers, there are no literary answers, there are no philosophical answers, there are no religious answers. The only conceivable answer is a *moral* answer."[5] Wiesel's work aims to force a confrontation with this unsettling and disorienting chapter of recent history in the hope that the present may be different from the past.

In many of his social and ethical interventions, Wiesel consciously acted as a guardian of memory. For example, in 1987 he visited Hiroshima, where he spoke strongly and sympathetically to his Japanese hosts: "At a meeting with high Japanese officials I feel compelled to say: 'I shall never forget Hiroshima, but you in turn must never forget Pearl Harbor.' Our hosts are clearly unsettled by this remark."[6] It was in that unsettling spirit of working against a selective and self-serving memory that Daniel McGowan, an American university professor, organized Palestinians and Jews to serve on a board to plan and implement a

memorial to the 254 Palestinian civilians who were murdered by Menachem Begin's Irgun in the spring of 1948. This project, Deir Yassin
Remembered, calls to mind various memorials in Israel, Europe, and the
United States intended to commemorate Jewish suffering during the
Holocaust.[7] McGowan is clear that, although this memorial should
highlight the human dimensions of this particular atrocity, it should also
stand as a reminder of the far more extensive suffering—exile, dispossession, and death—that the Palestinians have endured over the last
decades and that has too often been downplayed in the United States. In
its early stages, McGowan sought the participation of Elie Wiesel, given
the Nobel laureate's well-known commitment to memory, testimony,
and solidarity with victims. McGowan had politely contacted Wiesel
over a period of years yet did not receive an answer to his join the board.
Frustrated by Wiesel's distance, McGowan criticized the Jewish writer
for his silence not only in general terms on the Palestinian issue but also
for never condemning the Irgun massacre at Deir Yassin. McGowan juxtaposed Wiesel's silence with the position taken by the noted Jewish
scholar Martin Buber, who denounced the brazen Jewish terrorism at
Deir Yassin.[8] Yet, as the analysis in Chapter 4 should make clear, it is not
so surprising that McGowan's letters and calls were not returned. In a
recent interview on Kosovo in *Tikkun* magazine, Wiesel was asked about
Jewish sensitivity, not just to the suffering of ethnic Albanians, but also
to the Palestinians under Israeli rule. His response: "There were reasons
in the past to see some Palestinians as victims. There is no doubt about
it. But now at this moment, after Oslo and after Barak's victory [in 1999],
we should not think in those terms. We should be more hopeful."[9]
Wiesel's refusal to acknowledge the Deir Yassin Remembered project as
well as his willingness to "not think in those terms" point to a variation
of the major theme of this study, that of worthy and unworthy memories: The remembrance of Jewish suffering is mandatory and crucial to
any civilized people, but the narrative of Palestinian suffering—and its
causes in Zionist and Israeli policies—is divisive, and is best ought not
be brought up, all in the spirit of "hope."[10]

As Wiesel's own practice shows, consistent cultivation of dangerous
remembrance is an arduous ethical practice. In the spirit of Wiesel's
own commitment to remembering the Holocaust, some other groups
have been attempting to confront the difficult past and seek a new religious and political life in the present. I want to briefly mention three
cases of such self-critical remembrance in the Christian community.

A first example of dangerous remembrance is the development of Christian liturgies for Yom HaShoah Day, or Holocaust Remembrance Day. This date, derived from the Jewish religious calendar, is on the fifth day after the eighth day of Passover each spring. Since the early 1970s, Christian ministers, pastors, and lay people have devised liturgies which focus on the suffering of the Jews during the Holocaust and the Christian Church's complicity then and responsibility since to remember. These rituals may have many goals, according to Alice Eckhardt:

> to educate; to share the suffering vicariously (as on Good Friday); to become sensitized to the consequences of hatred and idolatries; to remember the victims; to see the broader implications on moral issues; to help us understand our Jewish neighbors and the State of Israel; to become more aware of the past persecutions of Jews and of our own attitudes; to comprehend Christian failure to respond adequately to the needs of desperate people; to see where our teachings need changing, along with our rituals; to dedicate ourselves to Never Again; to raise theological questions.[11]

Some of those Christians who have made grappling with the Holocaust central to their own work have contributed to these liturgies, such as Eugene Fisher, Franklin Littell, and Harry James Cargas. In Cargas's liturgy, he has the narrator of the service utter a line that would surely have Elie Wiesel's assent: "For if the Holocaust is forgotten, the way will be paved for another, perhaps final destruction of all humanity."[12] The commemoration goes on to include a poem by Israeli poet Dan Pagis, a recitation of Psalm 79, a poem by Nelly Sachs, a famous passage from Elie Wiesel's *Night*, a reflection on the Jews' salvific centrality by Karl Barth, and a working ethical principle by Holocaust theologian Irving Greenberg. Candles are then lit and extinguished as the assembly offers prayer, before the members leave in silence. By confronting their own history marked by contempt for and violence against Jews, such Christians are determined to repent of their past and seek a new relationship with the Jewish people based on respect and solidarity. Franklin Littell believes that such liturgies may ultimately contribute to a "healing between the peoples and to the mending of the world."[13] Although these kinds of disturbing liturgies are far from being a commonplace in mainstream U.S. Christian churches today, they do give witness to some Christians' refusal to carry on religious "business as usual."

A second example of incorporating dangerous remembrance into ritual is the recent addition to the American Christian calendar of events that pertain to the Central American martyrs. The dates of these rituals include March 24 (the assassination of El Salvadoran Archbishop Oscar Romero), November 16 (the murder of 6 El Salvadoran Jesuit intellectuals, their housekeeper, and her daughter), and December 2 (the rape and murder of U.S. missionaries Maura Clark, Ita Ford, Dorothy Kazel, and Jean Donovan).[14] Typically these gatherings include dramatic readings from the martyrs as well as testimonies from those who knew them, worked with them, or struggled for justice and peace in their country under horrendous conditions. Margaret Swedish identified a central motivation in such commemorations:

> Romero's memory, incarnated in the poor of El Salvador and all of Latin America, is a call to us and an invitation to join the poor on this faith journey, to be converted, to accompany them as they struggle for the fulfillment of their hope. That's why the international community also celebrates the anniversary of his death each year, to acknowledge that in Oscar Romero, a prophet did indeed come into the world and that hearing him, accepting his judgment on the world, his pronouncement of what sin is and the causes of that sin, and allowing ourselves to be converted and changed by it, has become critical to the authenticity of our own faith.[15]

The rituals on such dates remind participants of the formative events of persecution of the Central American Church since the late 1970s. Moreover, given the predominant role of the U.S. government in sponsoring and funding this persecution by aiding the executioners, U.S. Christians resolve to offer continued engagement with Christians in Central America. It should be noted, however, that these few men and women who are being celebrated are but the famous symbols of the tens of thousands who were slaughtered in recent decades. And by these commemorations and commitment, Christians are attempting to respond to the challenge posed by Jesuit Father Jose Maria Tojeira in the aftermath of the Jesuit murders in 1989: "The developed world's solidarity will not be authentic as long as it is limited to supporting us, the Jesuits, . . . while alienation, poverty and injustice continue to batter the disenfranchised."[16]

A third example outside of the United States of a people's attempt to come to terms with its own painful history is the Recovery of Historical Memory (REMHI) project of the Human Rights Office of the Guatemalan Archdiocese.[17] In a four-volume work, the Church interviewed rural Mayan survivors of the Guatemalan civil war and documented in meticulous, heart-breaking fashion the systematic campaigns of murder and destruction undertaken by the Guatemalan government over the last four decades. The Church believes that confronting the truth of what happened in Guatemala is indispensable to any serious social reconstruction in the future. The Church's work preceded the Guatemalan Historical Clarification Commission, a goal of the 1994 Peace Accords between the Guatemalan government and the guerrilla forces (URNG). In both cases, the Guatemalan governments were assigned the overwhelming responsibility for the atrocities against the civilian population.[18] The REMHI report gives extensive testimony from the victims on the violence used against children, the massive displacement of the rural population, the role of the civil patrols in militarizing daily life, mass rapes, as well as the method and techniques of torture. Bishop Juan Gerardi released the REMHI report at the Metropolitan Cathedral in Guatemala City on 24 April 1998. In his speech, he noted that the project hoped to break the silence of those long traumatized by decades of state-sponsored horror. He described the centrality of the search for truth in this strenuous process:

> REMHI's work has been an astonishing endeavor of discovery, exploration, and appropriation of our personal and collective history. It has been an open door for people to breathe and speak in freedom and for the creation of communities with hope. Peace is possible—a peace that is born from the truth that comes from each one of us and from all of us. It is a painful truth, full of memories of the country's deep and bloody wounds. It is a liberating and humanizing truth that makes it possible for all men and women to come to terms with themselves and their life stories. It is a truth that challenges each one of us to recognize our individual and collective responsibility and to commit ourselves to action so that those abominable acts never happen again.[19]

Johann Baptist Metz has emphasized the memory of suffering as contributing to the ferment of a new political life; the REMHI report concurs: "Historical memory has an important role to play in dismantling the mechanisms that made state terrorism possible and in exposing the role terrorism plays in an exclusive political and economic system."[20] Indeed, such memory can be dangerous: It is widely assumed that Bishop Juan Gerardi's assassination on 26 April 1998 was linked to his releasing the report just two days earlier.

In his early work, American Jewish theologian Marc Ellis affirmed the need to incorporate the perilous memories of the Holocaust into contemporary Jewish life. He referred to the work of Rabbi Irving Greenberg, a preeminent Holocaust theologian, who had this grim conviction:

> The Scriptures of the new era are hidden. They do not present themselves as
> Scripture but as history, fact, and sometimes, as anti-Scripture. . . . They are
> the accounts that tell and retell the event, draw its conclusions and orient the
> living. In the Warsaw Ghetto, Chaim Kaplan wrote in his journal: "I will
> write a scroll of agony in order to remember the past in the future."[21]

Because of his own growing commitment to the Palestinian people,
remembrance of the European Holocaust was not and could not be
enough for Ellis. He expanded Greenberg's view by stating that "If it is
true that the new scriptures, the scrolls of agony written with bitterness
and hope, come from the ghettos of eastern Europe, are not similar
scrolls being written today by Lebanese and South African women and
men and their 'burning children'?"[22] I would add: Given the U.S.
responsibility for supporting the Guatemalan death machine over many
decades, *Guatemala: Never Again* may rightly assume a place alongside
earlier Holocaust "scrolls of agony" and so help "orient the living"
today.

From Bystanders to Resisters

Elie Wiesel would agree that it is not enough simply to remember and
lament past agony; such remembrance should inspire action to relieve
suffering today. And yet, such engagement is what elite groups typically consider to be, not the essence of democracy, but its very crisis.
Edward Herman and Noam Chomsky's many studies of the American
propaganda system show how elites want the population to be passive
before or diverted from issues of actual policy formation. The ideological system seeks to increase the likelihood of citizens being
bystanders, both in regards to domestic issues and foreign affairs.
With people concerned more about private life and personal consumption, elites will be free to pursue their agenda, which is framed
as "the national interest."[23]

Paul Ricoeur once characterized Marx, Nietzsche, and Freud as three
"masters of suspicion" of the modern age.[24] Wiesel might feel a kinship
with these critical intellectuals, at least given his own profound suspicion and critique of anti-Semitism at the heart of Western civilization
and Christianity. He frequently has issued an unforgiving critique of the
Roosevelt administration as well as the American Jewish community for
its indifference to Hitler's increasingly systematic genocidal attack on
European Jewry. He also has been quite cutting of Christianity:

How is one to explain that neither Hitler nor Himmler was ever excommunicated by the church? That Pius XII never thought it necessary, not to say indispensable, to condemn Auschwitz and Treblinka? That among the S.S. a large proportion were believers who remained faithful to their Christian ties to the end? That there were killers who went to confession between massacres? And that they all were from Christian families and had received a Christian education? . . . As surely as the victims are a problem for the Jews, the killers are a problem for the Christians.[25]

Not only the killers but the bystanders are a problem for the Christians as well. Because of his own experiences, Wiesel made a personal decision to refuse to be such a spectator when others were suffering. Over many decades, Wiesel has placed himself in close proximity to those who were suffering and abandoned, from Soviet Jews to Cambodian refugees. He has testified as to their misery in books, articles, op-eds, and speeches, and made an emotive, ethical linkage between then and now: As the Jews were then sacrificed, so we must not allow people today to be sacrificed.

By his own work on behalf of different peoples, Wiesel also has reminded his readers of the need to consider ourselves as global citizens or, in the words of international law scholar Richard Falk, "citizen pilgrims" whom he describes this way:

The pilgrim is on a journey in space and time, seeking a better country, a heavenly one. There are no illusions that the present is an embodiment of what is possible. The citizen pilgrim is loyal to this quest and is not bound by any sense of duty to carry out the destructive missions of a given territorial state to which she or he owes temporary secular allegiance.[26]

Given the analysis in Chapter 4, Wiesel's total allegiance to and uncritical acceptance of Israel is problematic in this respect. But it is important to note that some Israelis have chosen not to carry out the "destructive mission" of the Israeli occupation. For example, a group of Israeli reservists, Yesh Gvul (Hebrew, "There is a border/limit"), refused to serve in the Israeli military invasion of Lebanon in 1982 and later to serve in the Occupied Territories during the intifada. The organization issued a declaration on 1 January 1988:

The Palestinian people is in revolt against Israeli occupation. Over 20 years of occupation and repression have not checked the Palestinian struggle for national liberation. The uprising in the Occupied Territories, and its brutal suppression by IDF [Israeli Defense Force] forces, graphically illustrate the terrible price of occupation and the absence of a political solution.

> As IDF reservists, we declare that we can no longer bear the burden of shared responsibility for this moral and political depravation.
>
> We hereby proclaim that we shall refuse to take part in suppressing the uprising and insurrection in the Occupied Territories.[27]

These Israelis chose to serve jail time and face incomprehension if not obloquy rather than remain indifferent to the suffering of the Palestinians.

Another example of this refusal to remain calm about injustice that ought to be better known involves a great American hero. On the third Monday of each January, American citizens are encouraged to remember and celebrate the life and "dream" of civil rights leader Martin Luther King, Jr. King's dream, of course, was that the scourge of White supremacy might be overcome so that all Americans would be able to live in dignity and security, North and South. Similar to Elie Wiesel, King was a Nobel Peace Prize winner (1964). Since his death by assassination in April 1968, gradually King has come to be an honored figure, a symbol of the promise of America and an advocate of its ideals. Indeed, at many King Day speeches by American government officials, one gets the sense that King has become posthumously respectable: The King who is remembered is the minister who championed nonviolence, integration, and Christian values. This is no doubt true, but there is another side to King that began to emerge in the post–Nobel Prize years, when his view of America as a "dream" was challenged by seemingly intractable urban poverty, White liberals' wavering on racial justice, and the U.S. war in Vietnam.[28] King had been concerned about U.S. engagement in the war as early as 1965. And yet his response evolved quite gradually. That summer he proposed a negotiated settlement of the Vietnam conflict on a CBS television program; however, Johnson administration officials as well as prominent White allies and Black leaders in the civil rights movement urged King to tone down his views, which he did.

It was only in early 1967 while in Jamaica that King read a moving article on the children suffering in Vietnam; and he then resolved to speak out against the war. At a retreat with his staff, King confessed:

> I want you to know that my mind is made up. I backed up a little when I came out in 1965. My name then wouldn't have been written in any book called *Profiles in Courage*. But now I have decided. I will not be intimidated. I will not be harassed. I will not be silent and I will be heard.[29]

Some advisors in the civil rights movement were strongly opposed to King's growing defiance of U.S. policy in Vietnam: There were the risks of a loss of liberal financial support as well as increased governmental antagonism. And yet King was not swayed. In a famous speech at New York's Riverside Church in April 1967, he described the United States as the "greatest purveyor of violence in the world today," a description not readily invoked by patriotic speechmakers on the King holiday. Throughout the last year of his life, he devoted many sermons to denouncing the war in Vietnam. At the Ebenezer Church, he proclaimed, "It is just as evil to kill Vietnamese as it is to kill Americans, because they are all God's children."[30] King found a prophetic voice to speak on behalf of America's Vietnamese victims, even though such commitment might cost his own people's movement for civil rights. He was determined to put solidarity with the suffering before a respectable silence.

King's struggle on Vietnam may be but a dramatic instance of what many people face in their own personal, professional, and civic lives: the difficulty of facing injustice, overcoming silence, and keeping in mind and heart the suffering of other people, near and far. One more recent example of American citizens refusing to be complicit in the atrocities sanctioned by U.S. foreign policy is the grassroots effort to close the U.S. Army School of the Americas at Fort Benning, Georgia. The School of the Americas has trained Latin American military officers and soldiers in techniques of torture, assassination, and terrorism; some of its graduates have been found responsible for the murder of Salvadoran Archbishop Oscar Romero, the six Salvadoran Jesuit intellectuals, and the four U.S. missionaries mentioned above.[31] Combining lobbying pressure on Congress, public education, fasting, nonviolent civil disobedience, and liturgical commemorations of the Latin American victims and martyrs, this movement to shut down this "school of assassins" has confronted the Army and government's righteous propaganda with the appalling record of the school's graduates and has undermined claims that the School of the Americas promotes democracy and human rights.[32] More than eleven thousand people arrived at Fort Benning in late November 1999 for a peaceful demonstration in support of closing the school. More than four thousand people risked arrest as they "crossed the line" into Fort Benning to indicate their resolve that such atrocities not be committed in the name of American citizens. Repeat offenders of such civil disobedience have spent many months in federal prisons for their willingness to speak the truth about U.S. support for some of the worst human rights violators in this hemisphere.

In a famous essay, "The Power of the Powerless," Czech playwright

Václav Havel begins by echoing Karl Marx and Friedrich Engels: "A spectre is haunting eastern Europe: the spectre of what in the West is called 'dissent.' "[33] This essay clarifies the emergent "dissident" movements that agitated the Communist rulers and captured the attention and esteem of the West in the 1970s and 1980s.[34] Havel suggests that what the Czechoslovakian citizens faced was not a classical dictatorial regime, but a "post-totalitarian system" in which ideology, manipulation, conformity, and obedience combined to form a "secularized religion." This system, he asserts, was based on "living with the lie":

> Because the regime is captive to its own lies, it must falsify everything. It falsifies the past. It falsifies the present, and it falsifies the future. It falsifies statistics. It pretends not to possess an omnipotent and unprincipled police apparatus. It pretends to respect human rights. It pretends to persecute no one.[35]

Individuals reinforced this system of lies by passively accepting and participating in the rituals, automatism, and "world of appearances" of daily life, in other words, by playing it safe as bystanders.

Throughout the essay, Havel uses the example of a greengrocer who is expected to display a sign with conformist political slogans in his shop window. Once, however, the greengrocer resists and refuses to follow social expectations, he steps out of living in the lie and begins "living within the truth." Havel proposes that "[i]f the main pillar of the system is living a lie, then it is not surprising that the fundamental threat to it is living the truth. This is why it must be suppressed more severely than anything else."[36] Havel emphasizes that the more famous dissidents could only be fully understood by acknowledging the more extensive number of ordinary people who found ways to live in truth and so further the "aims of life" over against the system. These people did not set out to become full-time dissidents; often, it was simply their desire to safeguard their dignity and do their work that brought them into confrontation with the punitive system. Elsewhere, Havel describes the dissident this way:

> The dissident does not operate in the realm of genuine power at all. He is not seeking power. He has no desire for office and does not gather votes. He does not attempt to charm the public, he offers nothing and promises nothing. He can offer, if anything, only his own skin—and he offers it solely because he has no other way of affirming the truth he stands for. His actions simply articulate his dignity as a citizen, regardless of the cost.[37]

Living within the truth was grounded within prepolitical spheres and dimensions of life, but such conscientious activity nevertheless constituted a threat to the political system based on lies. As more people who chose living in truth communicated their experiences and engaged with others, they became more overtly political insofar as the state repressed and punished them for their disobedience. These citizens also began to create a series of alternative structures, institutions, and means of extending living in truth, in effect, a "parallel polis."[38] Initially, Havel contends, the "power of the powerless" was not so much political as it was moral and existential. That power appealed to those citizens still submerged in the "hidden spaces" of a society based on deceit and mystification. In the specific examples cited above, Yesh Gvul, Dr. King, and the movement to close the School of the Americas all rejected versions of "living with the lie" as they became more engaged with the fates of those people deemed dispensable by the dominant system.[39]

A Preferential Option for Unworthy Victims

On the Jewish feast of Purim in the spring of 1967, several Jewish thinkers assembled to participate in a symposium on "Jewish Values in the Post-Holocaust Future." Among the featured speakers were Elie Wiesel, philosopher Emil Fackenheim, and literary critic George Steiner. Later endowed with chairs at Oxford and Geneva, Steiner was a brilliant scholar, polymath, and polyglot, as well as an unapologetic elite when it came to the privileging the best that has been thought in Western culture.[40] In addition to his scholarly work on the modern Russian novel, Greek tragedy, and the theory of translation (to name but three of his interests), Steiner also has made the Holocaust a central part of his broader cultural criticism. In doing so, he has raised questions that go to the heart of the humanist enterprise in literature, philosophy, theology, and politics. In one of his most famous passages, which summarizes his own critique of the humanities vis-à-vis political inhumanity, Steiner writes, "We know now that a man can read Goethe or Rilke in the evening, that he can play Bach and Schubert, and go to his day's work at Auschwitz in the morning."[41] Steiner reckoned sooner than did many intellectuals with the ramifications of the Holocaust, as he himself was "a kind of survivor."[42]

At the symposium, Steiner agreed with Wiesel that there was something absolute about the Holocaust. But he went on to remind his colleagues that at the very time they were convening, an immense mass murder had been proceeding apace in Indonesia, and without U.S.

concern, as those who were being murdered were Communists. Steiner made a link between the lack of prompt response to Jewish suffering during the Nazi reign and that of these contemporary atrocities:

> Massacres are also going on right now, and, if I cannot comprehend how men in this room did not move in 1940 or 1941, I am not sure I can comprehend why I do not move now when certain things are going on in Asia, at the very moment when I'm speaking. This evening we'll go to our friends, to our dinners, to our good sleep, while torture is going on and many human beings are being burned alive. And the great difference is this: it is at least conceivable that when the first news got through about Auschwitz—and there is some evidence on this—there was not actually in the minds of those who heard it the possibility of believing it; it seemed outside the categories of understanding. *We who come after* know that whatever the news is, it may be so. Whatever the massacre, the torture, the children being burned now in our name—it may be so. . . . I think it is our job as Jews, if anywhere in the world human beings are being burned alive, to ask ourselves: How can we sit still?[43]

For Steiner, the Jew should never become a "good German" who tolerates the torture or murder of innocent people. He proposed that the Jewish vocation in the post-Holocaust world ought to be that of agitating witnesses not only to the crimes against the Jews in the 1930s and 1940s, but also against the crimes being perpetrated against victims and tolerated by so many citizens today. Since the Holocaust represented a fundamental rupture of Western civilization, as Steiner contended, then vigilance of the most exacting kind was demanded in its aftermath, a vigilance that had been noticeably absent in such renowned intellectuals as philosopher Martin Heidegger.[44] Those who come after the Holocaust have few excuses to justify inaction when it comes to offering aid and comfort to the victims of state-sponsored oppression and violence.

In his "Theses on the Philosophy of History," philosopher Walter Benjamin wrote, "In every era the attempt must be made anew to wrest tradition away from a conformism that is about to overpower it."[45] Even Holocaust remembrance can constitute a tradition able to be wed to a conformism with American state power, and then be overpowered, as the examples of Bitburg and Bosnia showed. Particularly since the late 1970s, Elie Wiesel has not been so much a dissident toward U.S. power as much as a devoted ally and consequent beneficiary of it. In the case of Israel, he glorified the Jewish state and ignored its own systematic violations of Palestinian human and national rights. By such leaders as Ronald Reagan, Wiesel was acclaimed as a prophet, but it is worth keeping in mind that Wiesel rarely criticized U.S. power except the failure of the United States to come to the aid of victims, a seemingly incomprehensible repetition from the Holocaust era. In these later years, one could see Wiesel as a kind of "worthy prophet" who was honored by the state for his principal concern for the worthy victims. Were Wiesel—or anyone else favorably received by U.S. power—to raise critical questions about the unworthy victims of the United States (and its allies)—the Palestinians, say, or the Kurds under Turkey—he or she would likely not be invited back to the White House to speak against the danger of indifference.[46]

The Brazilian Archbishop Helder Câmara once remarked, "When I give food to the poor, they call me a saint. When I ask why the poor are hungry, they call me a Communist." In Brazil, to do charity work was admirable; to question the status quo of a National Security State, however, was to warrant the label "Communist" and to be considered a subversive. One of the things that such an unworthy prophet will do is to engage in critical and systematic analysis of his or her own government's power and history of victimization. It was because of Wiesel's reluctance to challenge the State of Israel that Rabbi Arthur Hertzberg wrote an eloquent "open letter to Elie Wiesel" in the *New York Review of Books* in August 1988.[47] Hertzberg pleaded with Wiesel to speak out against the Israeli occupation of the West Bank and Gaza Strip. He began this letter by recalling his friendship with Wiesel in the 1950s when they were just starting their careers; the young men both shared the Yiddish language and the inconsolable loss of so many relatives in the Holocaust. But when it came to the contemporary Middle East issue, Hertzberg noticed that Wiesel had the proclivity to issue moralistic apothegms rather than to take clear political stands: "For all the nuances in your statements, and the distress that you feel as a Jew and as a moral human being, your position amounts to an elegant defense of the Likud hard line. When it comes to policy, you have said little that Yitzhak Shamir could not countersign."[48] His pointed letter, full of anguish but free of acrimony, issued the challenge to the public intellectual acclaimed by the U.S. government and Nobel committee alike: "In the memory of the Holocaust we have been reminded by you that silence is a sin. You have spoken out against indifference and injustice. Why are you making a special exception of Israel?"[49] Hertzberg called Wiesel to accountability and, in so doing, referred to the biblical patrimony that he shared with Wiesel:

The prophets Amos, Elijah, Isaiah, and Jeremiah, and all the rest, were
opposed, generation after generation, by prophets who belonged to the royal
courts, who assured the king that his conduct was beyond reproach. The
biblical prophets were harassed as traitors who weakened the resolve of a
small people—but it is their "treason" and not the prudence of the court
prophets, that is our unique Jewish tradition.[50]

One of the characteristics, it seems, of those men and women who commit such "treason" year in and year out is their predilection for the marginalized, the despised, the forgotten—the unworthy victims of their
culture and government.

In recent decades, Wiesel often has raised his own voice to speak out
against the politics of hatred and fanaticism, phenomena that have
shown no sign of dissipating, from the reciprocal violence in the Balkans
to the genocide in Rwanda. He claims, "I have been fighting against
[fanaticism] for years, wherever it appears. Be it religious or political,
fanaticism is the real danger threatening the twenty-first century.
Those who sow it today are provoking tomorrow's catastrophes."[51]
Wiesel has done a public service in speaking and writing about the evils
of hatred, but there are other "real dangers" worth attending to that do
not involve frightening outbursts of murderous hatred. It is the case that
much avoidable human suffering takes place not because of fanaticism
but because of the predictable consequences of rational policies devised
and carried out by individuals devoted to the aims of their corporations,
organizations, and governments. One glaring example is the case of Iraq
and the hundreds of thousands of Iraqi children who have died as a
result of U.S.–UN-backed sanctions since the Iraqi invasion of Kuwait
in 1990.[52] The U.S. government had supported Saddam Hussein
throughout the 1980s, even when he was gassing Kurds in 1988. But
when Hussein dared to invade Kuwait in August 1990, he became a ver-
itable demon and was seen as a successor to Hitler. After the U.S.-led
Gulf War pulverized Iraq, the United States insisted on keeping economic sanctions, which have wreaked havoc on the Iraqi people and
have done nothing to dislodge Hussein from power.[53] Approximately
five thousand children die each month as a result of these sanctions.
When challenged about this suffering of the innocent Iraqis on a
national television program, U.S. Ambassador to the UN Madeline
Albright noted that the policy "was a very hard choice." Nevertheless,
she went on to affirm "but the price—we think the price is worth it."[54]

Some American citizens have refused to sit still, though, while the sanctions were imposed and the Clinton administration continued to bomb Iraq. Voices in the Wilderness, a faith-based group from Chicago, has committed itself to taking medical and humanitarian supplies to Iraq in defiance of U.S. law.[55] These men and women, "who come after" the Holocaust, know that children are being denied essential food and medicines, as the Iraqi infrastructure crumbles around them. In addition to traveling to Iraq and risking long prison sentences, these grassroots activists confront U.S. officials and do educational work in schools and in their communities to put a human face on the Iraqis. Surely, Madeline Albright has no hatred for the Iraqi people; but hatred is not the issue here. Rather, it is public policy that is justified by intelligent people who, in their positions of power, have more important considerations than hundreds of thousands of Iraqi deaths, the responsibility for which can be avoided by blaming Saddam Hussein. Other people, though, have been in a position to observe the workings of the United Nations on this issue and they have resigned in disgust. Two include Denis Halliday and Hans von Sponek, both of whom headed up the UN humanitarian aid program for Iraq. Their firsthand observation of the devastating consequences of the UN sanctions appalled them. Halliday has taken to using the term genocide to describe what is happening. An interviewer wondered about its validity in the Iraq context, to which Halliday responded as follows:

> It certainly is a valid word in my view when you have a situation where we see thousands of deaths per month, a possible total of 1 million to 1.5 million over the last nine years. If that is not genocide, then I don't know quite what is.
>
> There's no better word I can think of. Genocide is taking place right now, every day, in Iraq's cities. To say it's a passive thing is not correct. It's an active policy of continuing sanctions. The member states know full well what they're doing and what the impact is. To hide behind Saddam Hussein is a cop-out. It's not acceptable to me. We have got to take responsibility, we the Europeans, the North Americans, the members of the Security Council. It's our responsibility.[56]

Perhaps this is what Howard Zinn had in mind when he wrote about "today Germany, tomorrow the world"—"Business as usual" for the United States and mass death for the Iraqis.

While Voices in the Wilderness attends to the specific policy of the United States in Iraq, other grassroots groups—churches, labor, environmentalists, human rights workers, feminists—have been focusing their attention on the millions of people who are suffering and dying, again, not from vicious hatred, but by the normal, operating policies of such International Financial Institutions as the World Bank, the International Monetary Fund, and the World Trade Organization.[57] Surely, Nobel laureates and other groups would be welcome to sponsor conferences on the "anatomy of the global economy," which could shed light on how decisions are being made that will continue to result in profits for the few and misery for the many. Basic questions for such an agenda quickly come to mind: What are the vital interests of the United States? Are they assumed to be strictly those of the vital interests of U.S. corporations? Or are they the vital interests of the citizens—affordable health care, decent education, safe neighborhoods, and jobs that pay a living wage? Must the quest for profit subordinate every other human or ecological value?[58] It may be assumed that those who resist such corporate-based globalization will be considered another group of unworthy victims, ungrateful for the salvific spread of "free markets." But since the economy is being globalized, so, too, "citizen pilgrims" need to start and strengthen networks of solidarity across transnational civil society.

In a set of cogent lectures, Edward Said has enunciated a normative role for the intellectual as one who makes her representations to an audience more as an amateur than as a professional, who works as a critic speaking truth to power instead of as a flatterer of established authority, and who positions herself as an exile rather than as an insider. Said champions a job description of the intellectual that is not at all likely to endear her to the dispensers of conventional wisdom and to the guardians of the status quo. He identifies a fundamental option that intellectuals from Émile Zola to Václav Havel had to face:

> I think the major choice faced by the intellectual is whether to be allied with the stability of the victors and rulers or—the more difficult path—to consider that stability as a state of emergency threatening the less fortunate with the danger of complete extinction, and take into account the experience of subordination itself.[59]

Today, the stability of the victors—state and private corporate power—needs not reinforcement but critical interrogation by intellectuals seeking to be responsible to today's victims. Intellectuals ought to take the more difficult path by critiquing U.S. power and finding practical ways to support domestic and international grassroots movements for democratic social change. Further, we ought to engage those who continue to be marginalized by the much more developed modes of modernity more than five hundred years after the European conquest, particularly the U.S. hegemony in the global economy.[60]

Richard Falk has retrieved and applied to contemporary issues the postwar Nuremberg Obligation of citizens to oppose their government when it is engaged in heinous crimes. On this question of who remembers, and when, how, and why, Falk made this comment:

> It is certainly a sign of ethical sensitivity or more astutely of political cynicism (the legacy of Bitburg) for American leaders to visit the carnal [*sic*] houses of the Holocaust, as George Bush did a few years back, perceptively writing in the Visitors' Book at Birkenau: "In remembrance lies redemption." But truly, to remember the atrocities of others is not redemptive at all. To visit the diseased survivors of Hiroshima might be redemptive for George Bush, if this occasion of the first atomic attack on a human settlement were then and there acknowledged without qualification as a crime against humanity.[61]

As noted in Chapter 5, the U.S. government saw fit to sponsor the institutionalization of memory of the victims of an official (former) enemy. A few years ago, Robert McNamara's retrospective admission of U.S. "wrongdoing" in Vietnam reopened the debate about U.S. policy in Indochina.[62] But, as James Young noted in reference to Holocaust memorials in Germany, the Germans were forced by the triumphant Allied powers to remember and repent their crimes against the Jews and humanity; there has been no such external pressure on the United States to remember and repent its crimes against the Vietnamese people.[63] Those in the antiwar movement, however, remember the violence and deceit of those years and continue to oppose devastating U.S. intervention in other countries around the world.[64] One major task of popular, grassroots groups and religious communities is to keep up the vigilance and the pressure on U.S. foreign policy, as they did in Central America during the 1980s. In such ways, they can serve in the same capacity as that was intended by the proposed yet rejected Committee on Conscience from the President's Commission on the Holocaust in 1979. A deliberate focus of these groups ought to be on the extent to which the U.S. government is not merely a "guilty bystander" (as with Bosnia) but a complicitous ally or an active perpetrator in violence and repression.

President Bill Clinton once rightly observed that the Holocaust should be "ever a sharp thorn in every national memory."[65] The same ought to be said of the U.S. bombings of Hiroshima and Nagasaki, not to mention the long-standing U.S. support for oppression and repression in Central America. Wiesel's critique in the opening epigraph to this chapter retains a timely pertinence to our situation today: "Where were the humanists, the leaders, the liberals, the spokesmen for man-kind?" Indeed, the Holocaust may be one of many sharp thorns in our national memory. But citizens and religious believers today ought not simply denounce Nazi crimes, horrific and unforgettable as they were, but also contest U.S. policies that victimize innocent people today. Such grassroots communities, nongovernmental organizations, and ever-growing networks of concerned citizens certainly can see the connec-tions between the Holocaust victims with the past and present suffering of Japanese, Vietnamese, Timorese, Salvadorans, and Palestinians and thus subvert the self-serving rhetoric of state power by practicing a self-critical solidarity with our victims.[66]

In his 1995 memoir, Elie Wiesel recalled the ending of his first book, the 1956 Yiddish volume, *And the World Stayed Silent*. He printed the ending of the original Yiddish version, which differs from the version that appeared in the subsequently edited and translated volume, *Night*. In that first volume, Wiesel noted that when the American soldiers lib-erated Buchenwald in the spring of 1945, he began writing notes about his experiences in the camps. He then offered this acerbic commentary on the civilized West for its indifference to the monstrous crime the Nazis inflicted upon the Jewish people:

> Today, ten years after Buchenwald, I realize that the world forgets. Germany is a sovereign state. The German army has been reborn. Ilse Koch, the sadist of Buchenwald, is a happy wife and mother. War criminals stroll in the streets of Hamburg and Munich. The past has been erased, buried.
>
> Germans and anti-Semites tell the world that the story of six million Jewish victims is but a myth, and the world, in its naïveté, will believe it, if not today, then tomorrow or the next day.
>
> So it occurred to me that it might be useful to publish in book form these notes taken down in Buchenwald.
>
> I am not so naïve as to believe that this work will change the course of history or shake the conscience of humanity.
>
> Books no longer command the power they once did.
>
> Those who yesterday held their tongues will keep their silence tomorrow.[67]

Despite this seeming despairing tone, since the mid-1950s, Wiesel has helped to "shake the conscience of humanity" with his insistent call to remember the Holocaust, respect its victims, and assail its perpetrators and bystanders. And still, the world today forgets the crimes of today and more recent years. The past of victims typically is erased and buried by the powerful who do not wish their crimes to receive attention, much less accountability.

Liberation theologies have emphasized the importance of making a preferential option for the poor. This option has earned the Christian churches much ill repute, if not persecution, in many places. In Europe before and during the World War II, for Christians to act in solidarity with Europe's historically unworthy victims, the Jews, certainly would have exacted a cost, from defamation to harassment to execution. While "the world remained silent," in Wiesel's earliest formulation, Europe's Jews were exterminated. There was no ecclesial preferential option for the European Jews during the Holocaust. The tremendous suffering of those unworthy Jewish victims still ought to compel us to ask questions so rarely raised in the U.S. intellectual community: Who are our unworthy victims in this moment, how can we assist them in surviving, and how can we resist the temptations of silence and respectable status? For if we remain silent, if U.S. power goes unchallenged by its own citizens, if the elite manufacture of consent proceeds without citizen interference, far too many innocent people alive today will join the ranks of the Jewish abandoned, damned, and dead, still so mourned by Elie Wiesel.

Notes

Notes to the Preface

1. Elie Wiesel, *Night*, trans. Stella Rodway (New York: Bantam Edition, 1982).
2. See Marc H. Ellis, *Toward a Jewish Theology of Liberation: The Uprising and Beyond*, upd. ed. (Maryknoll, NY: Orbis, 1989); idem, *Beyond Innocence and Redemption: Confronting the Holocaust and Israeli Power—Creating a Moral Future for the Jewish People* (San Francisco: HarperCollins, 1990); idem, *Ending Auschwitz: The Future of Jewish and Christian Life* (Louisville, KY: Westminister/John Knox, 1994); idem, *Unholy Alliance: Religion and Atrocity in Our Time* (Minneapolis: Fortress, 1997); and idem, *O, Jerusalem: The Contested Future of the Jewish Covenant* (Minneapolis: Fortress, 1999). See also Otto Maduro, ed., *Judaism, Christianity, and Liberation: An Agenda for Dialogue* (Maryknoll, NY: Orbis, 1991).
3. Harry James Cargas, *Reflections of a Post-Auschwitz Christian* (Detroit, MI: Wayne State University Press, 1989).
4. John K. Roth, *A Consuming Fire: Encounters with Elie Wiesel and the Holocaust* (Atlanta, GA: John Knox, 1979).
5. Robert McAfee Brown, *Elie Wiesel: Messenger to All Humanity*, 2d. upd. ed. (Notre Dame, IN: University of Notre Dame Press, 1989).
6. See Michael Lerner, *Jewish Renewal: A Path to Healing and Transformation* (New York: Grosset/Putnam, 1994).
7. See Naim S. Ateek, Marc H. Ellis, and Rosemary Radford Ruether, eds., *Faith and the Intifada: Palestinian Christian Voices* (Maryknoll, NY: Orbis, 1992).
8. Rosemary Radford Ruether, "Theological and Ethical Reflections on the Shoah: Getting Beyond the Victim-Victimizer Relationship," in *Contemporary Christian Religious Responses to the Shoah*, ed. Steven L. Jacobs (Lanham, MD: University Press of America, 1993), 193. See her earlier works: Rosemary Radford Ruether, *Faith and Fratricide: The Theological Roots of Anti-Semitism* (New York: Seabury, 1974); idem, *Disputed Questions: On Being a Christian* (Maryknoll, NY: Orbis, 1989); and idem and Herman J. Ruether, *The Wrath of Jonah: The Crisis of Religious Nationalism in the Israeli-Palestinian Conflict* (San Francisco: HarperCollins, 1989).

Notes to Chapter One

1. See, for example, Elie Wiesel, "An Interview Unlike Any Other" in idem, *A Jew Today*, trans. Marion Wiesel (New York: Vintage, 1979), 17–23.

2. Quoted in Ilya Levkov, ed., *Bitburg and Beyond: Encounters in American, German and Jewish History* (New York: Shapolsky, 1987), 41.

3. See Elie Wiesel, *All Rivers Run to the Sea: Memoirs*, trans. Marion Wiesel (New York: Alfred A. Knopf, 1995), and idem, *And the Sea Is Never Full: Memoirs 1969–*, trans. Marion Wiesel (New York: Alfred A. Knopf, 1999). A third volume entitled *My Masters and My Friends* was announced in Wiesel, *And the Sea Is Never Full*, 6.

4. Robert N. Bellah, Richard Madsen, William M. Sullivan, Ann Swidler, and Steven M. Tipton, *Habits of the Heart: Individualism and Commitment in American Life* (San Francisco: Perennial, 1986).

5. Edward Shils, *Tradition* (Chicago: University of Chicago Press, 1981), 21.

6. See Robert Alter, *Hebrew and Modernity* (Bloomington: Indiana University Press, 1994).

7. Wiesel, *All Rivers Run to the Sea*, 22.

8. Ibid., 13.

9. Ibid., 292.

10. Moshe Rosman, *Founder of Hasidism: A Quest for the Historical Ba'al Shem Tov* (Berkeley and Los Angeles: University of California Press, 1996), 210.

11. Wiesel, *And the Sea Is Never Full*, 29.

12. Wiesel, *All Rivers Run to the Sea*, 42. In 1974, Wiesel claimed, "I'm still a Hasid. That means I still believe in what I believed as a child. I still love to sing and tell stories. I still love whatever characterized the Hasidic movement in its early stages—a longing fervor, passion and compassion, doing things together with other people. The Hasidic movement was a movement of friendship. That is why it has always had such a strong appeal to me." See Gene Koppel and Henry Kaufman, *Elie Wiesel: A Small Measure of Victory* (Tucson: The University of Arizona, 1974), 19. Wiesel did qualify his enthusiasm for Hasidism in its "early stages." In their study of Jewish fundamentalism in the State of Israel, Israel Shahak and Norton Mezvinsky reported from an Israeli Hebrew historical article by David Asaf: "[there was a riot] in Uman in the Ukraine, where one of the more famous Hassidic rabbis, Nahman of Braslaw, was buried and where his followers who came on pilgrimage to his tomb on the Jewish New Year were attacked and beaten year after year for decades by other Hassids. The annual beatings finally culminated in 1863 in an especially nasty attack by a coalition of Hassidic sects that was described by a contemporary Jewish writer in the Hebrew press of that time. The writer of the article noted the similarity between this Hassidic 'pogrom' and those committed by the anti-Semites." Israel Shahak and Norton Mezvinsky, *Jewish Fundamentalism in Israel* (London: Pluto, 1999), 133.

13. In a 1993 interview, Wiesel admitted, "I would not say that I am a Kabbalist, but just a student of Kabbalah. I love the Kabbalah. I love it for its beauty and find in it a great deal of beauty and truth. . . . The Kabbalist is not wrapped up in history; on the contrary, he wants to overcome history." Ekkehard Schuster and Reinhold Boschert-Kimming, *Hope against Hope: Johann-Baptist Metz & Elie Wiesel Speak Out on the Holocaust*, trans. J. Matthew Ashley (Mahwah, NJ: Paulist, 1999), 71.

14. For an elaboration on his mystical interests, see Wiesel, *All Rivers Run to the Sea*, 34.

15. Koppel and Kaufman, *Elie Wiesel*, 5.

16. Wiesel, *All Rivers Run to the Sea*, 26.

17. For an illuminating comparison between Wiesel's ingrained sense of mystery and mystification and Holocaust theologian Richard Rubenstein's critical, demystifying stance, see Michael Berenbaum, *Elie Wiesel: God, the Holocaust, and the Children of Israel* (West Orange, NJ: Behrman House, 1994), 160–171.

18. Quoted in François Mitterand and Elie Wiesel, *Memoir in Two Voices*, trans. Richard Seaver and Timothy Bent (New York: Arcade, 1996), 21.

19. Wiesel, *All Rivers Run to the Sea*, 78.

20. Elie Wiesel, *A Passover Haggadah* (New York: Touchstone, 1993), 6.

21. Elie Wiesel, *Night*, trans. Stella Rodway (New York: Bantam, 1982), 6.

22. Wiesel, *All Rivers Run to the Sea*, 66.

23. Ibid., 78.

24. Ibid., 113.

25. Ibid., 128.

26. Harry James Cargas, *Conversations with Elie Wiesel*, 2d rev. enl. ed. (South Bend, IN: Justice, 1992), 65–66.

27. On French literary influences on Wiesel, see Rosette C. Lamont, "Elie Wiesel: In Search of a Tongue," in *Confronting the Holocaust: The Impact of Elie Wiesel*, eds. Alvin H. Rosenfeld and Irving Greenberg (Bloomington: Indiana University Press, 1978), 80–98.

28. Elie Wiesel, *Against Silence: The Voice and Vision of Elie Wiesel*, ed. Irving Abrahamson (New York: Holocaust Library, 1985), 3: 312. For a wide-ranging collection of essays on the ongoing issues and debates concerning the Holocaust, see Michael Berenbaum and Abraham J. Peck, eds., *The Holocaust and History: The Known, the Unknown, the Disputed, and the Reexamined* (Bloomington: Indiana University Press, 1998).

29. Berenbaum, *Elie Wiesel*, 6.

30. Wiesel, *All Rivers Run to the Sea*, 84.

31. Wiesel, *And the Sea Is Never Full*, 70.

32. Wiesel, "An Interview Unlike Any Other," 23.

33. Naomi Seidman, "Elie Wiesel and the Scandal of Jewish Rage," *Jewish Social Studies* 2:3 (Fall 1996): 3–4.

34. Wiesel, *All Rivers Run to the Sea*, 267.

35. See Seidman, "Elie Wiesel," for an analysis of the important differences between the original Yiddish narrative and the French and English versions. Years before Seidman's essay appeared, noted Yiddish scholar David Roskies commented that "[t]he original Yiddish version of Elie Wiesel's *Night* is not only four times longer and less unified than its French (and later English) version, but it has a different message. Themes of madness and existential despair are not as highlighted in the Yiddish narrative, which ends with the *engagé* writer's appeal to fight the Germans and anti-Semites who would consign the Holocaust to oblivion. Since no one in the literary establishment was ready to be preached to by a Holocaust survivor, existentialist doubt became the better part of valor." See David G. Roskies, *Against*

the Apocalypse: Responses to Catastrophe in Modern Jewish Culture (Cambridge, MA: Harvard University Press, 1984), 301. Seidman's essay more fully delineates Wiesel's negotiations with his narrative and with Mauriac.

36. Elie Wiesel, "The Reporter," in idem, *Against Silence*, 3: 45. Elsewhere, Wiesel remarked on his work as a journalist: "Someone made a survey and found that the *Daily News* never used more than 800 words, *The New York Times* maybe 2,000. Poor and unexciting, it can be destructive. Fortunately, I was never politically minded and I don't understand much about politics. I don't know how I managed to file political cables without betraying my ignorance. Oh, I know how, really: I copied *The New York Times*—we all did. We took from the city edition and we simply quoted from the *Times*." Quoted in Cargas, *Conversations with Elie Wiesel*, 90.

37. Elie Wiesel, *Dawn*, trans. Frances Frenaye (New York: Bantam, 1982); idem, *The Accident*, trans. Anne Borchardt, new pref. (New York: Hill and Wang, 1985); idem, *The Town beyond the Wall*, trans. Stephen Becker (New York: Schocken, 1982); and idem, *The Gates of the Forest*, trans. Frances Frenaye (New York: Schocken, 1982).

38. Elie Wiesel, *The Jews of Silence: A Personal Report on Soviet Jewry*, trans. Neal Kozodoy, exp. ed. (New York: Schocken, 1987).

39. See Elie Wiesel, *Souls on Fire: Portraits and Legends of Hasidic Masters*, trans. Marion Wiesel (New York: Random House, 1972); idem, *Somewhere a Master: Further Hasidic Portraits and Legends*, trans. Marion Wiesel (New York: Summit, 1982); idem, *Four Hasidic Masters and Their Struggle against Melancholy* (Notre Dame, IN: University of Notre Dame Press, 1982); and idem, *Sages and Dreamers: Biblical, Talmudic, and Hasidic Portraits and Legends*, trans. Marion Wiesel (New York: Summit, 1991).

40. On the decisive influence of his grandfather on Wiesel's commitment to the Hasidic Masters, see Wiesel, *All Rivers Run to the Sea*, 42.

41. See Wiesel, *And the Sea Is Never Full*, 16.

42. Elie Wiesel, *One Generation After*, trans. Lily Edelman (New York: Bard, 1972).

43. See Wiesel, *And the Sea Is Never Full*, 43.

44. On these hermeneutic tasks vis-à-vis religious classics in the context of history's radical ambiguity, see David Tracy, *Plurality and Ambiguity: Hermeneutics, Religion, and Hope* (San Francisco: Harper and Row, 1987), 79.

45. For a radically different perspective on the Jewish tradition, see the work by a formerly Orthodox Polish Jew, survivor of the death camps, and Israeli dissident, Israel Shahak, *Jewish History, Jewish Religion: The Weight of Three Thousand Years* (London: Pluto, 1994). In this work, Shahak exposed the antigentile bias in Jewish texts and tradition and claimed that this bias has been kept from Western audiences by such Jewish thinkers as Gerschom Scholem and Martin Buber. One does not get the sense from Wiesel's heartfelt rhapsodies to the Hasidic masters, past and present, that there might be anything problematic about their attitude toward non-Jews. Shahak wrote, "Let us take the famous *Hatanya*, fundamental book of the Habbad movement, one of the most important branches of Hassidism. According to this book, all non-Jews are totally satanic creatures 'in whom there is absolutely nothing good.' Even a non-Jewish embryo is qualitatively different from a Jewish one. The very existence of a non-Jew is 'inessential', whereas all of creation was creates solely for the sake of the Jews." Shahak, *Jewish History, Jewish Religion*, 26–27.

46. Elie Wiesel, *Messengers of God: Biblical Portraits and Legends,* trans. Marion Wiesel (New York: Touchstone, 1994), xiv. In another collection of his lectures, he commented on the prophet Ezekiel: "From his exile, Ezekiel speaks to all generations, and particularly to ours, for, more than his own contemporaries, we have witnessed the frailty of social structures and the irresistible power of spiritual courage and dreams. For once upon a time some of us did see a deserted land covered with dry bones. And yes, we could testify to man's ability to transform memories of tragedy into necessary hope. Indeed, no generation can understand Ezekiel as well—as profoundly—as ours." Wiesel, *Sages and Dreamers,* 82.

47. See the representative authors in Steven L. Jacobs, ed., *Contemporary Christian Religious Responses to the Shoah* (Lanham, MD: University Press of America, 1993) and Carol Rittner and John K. Roth, eds., *From the Unthinkable to the Unavoidable: American Christian and Jewish Scholars Encounter the Holocaust* (Westport, CT: Greenwood, 1997).

48. Harry James Cargas, ed., *Responses to Elie Wiesel: Critical Essays by Major Jewish and Christian Scholars* (New York: Persea, 1978); Alvin H. Rosenfeld and Irving Greenberg, eds., *Confronting the Holocaust: The Impact of Elie Wiesel* (Bloomington: Indiana University Press, 1978).

49. John K. Roth, *A Consuming Fire: Encounters with Elie Wiesel and the Holocaust* (Atlanta, GA: John Knox, 1979).

50. Robert McAfee Brown, *Elie Wiesel: Messenger to All Humanity,* 2d. upd. ed. (Notre Dame, IN: University of Notre Dame Press, 1989).

51. See also Carol Rittner, R.S.M., ed., *Elie Wiesel: Between Memory and Hope* (New York: New York University Press, 1990); Harry James Cargas, ed., *Telling the Tale: A Tribute to Elie Wiesel on the Occasion of His 65th Birthday—Essays, Reflections, and Poems* (St. Louis: Time Being, 1993); and Alan Rosen, ed., *Celebrating Elie Wiesel: Stories, Essays, Reflections* (Notre Dame, IN: University of Notre Dame Press, 1998).

52. See Edward T. Linenthal, *Preserving Memory: The Struggle to Create America's Holocaust Museum* (New York: Viking, 1995) and Judith Miller, *One, by One, by One: Facing the Holocaust* (New York: Touchstone, 1990).

53. See Wiesel, *And the Sea Is Never Full,* 369–383.

54. Elie Wiesel, *The Fifth Son,* trans. Marion Wiesel (New York: Summit, 1985); idem, *Twilight,* trans. Marion Wiesel (New York: Summit, 1988); and idem, *The Forgotten,* trans. Stephen Becker (New York: Summit, 1992).

55. For a critical study of a comparable human rights icon and Nobel laureate, see David Stoll, *Rigoberta Menchú and All Poor Guatemalans* (Boulder, CO: Westview, 1999).

56. Some wonder about this American mainstreaming of Wiesel and, by extension, Holocaust remembrance. For example, Ilene Flanzbaum asked, "What does it mean, for instance, when Elie Wiesel receives the honor of throwing the ceremonial first pitch of the New York Mets' 1988 home season? Is it a tribute to Wiesel's suffering? Or does it naturalize the Holocaust in an absurd fashion? What does Daddy answer when his five-year-old son asks who that is throwing the ball, or why he is famous—that is, if Daddy even knows? What words from announcers should precede such an appearance? How, in the beginning of a baseball game, could they satisfactorily describe the Holocaust?" See Ilene Flanzbaum, "The Americanization

of the Holocaust," in *The Americanization of the Holocaust*, ed. Ilene Flanzbaum (Baltimore: Johns Hopkins University Press, 1999), 5–6.

57. On Wiesel's mesmerizing effect on a Midwestern university audience, see Alan E. Steinweis, "Reflections on the Holocaust from Nebraska," in Flanzbaum, *The Americanization of the Holocaust*, 167–168.

58. Peter Novick, *The Holocaust in American Life* (Boston: Houghton Mifflin, 1999), 351.

59. Elie Wiesel, "Why I Write," in idem, *From the Kingdom of Memory: Reminiscences* (New York: Summit, 1990), 16.

60. See Graham B. Walker, Jr., *Elie Wiesel: A Challenge to Theology* (Jefferson, NC: McFarland, 1987); Maurice Friedman, *Abraham Joshua Heschel and Elie Wiesel: You Are My Witnesses* (New York: Farrar, Straus and Giroux, 1987); Ellen S. Fine, *Legacy of Night: The Literary Universe of Elie Wiesel* (Albany: State University of New York Press, 1982); Colin Davis, *Elie Wiesel's Secretive Texts* (Gainesville: University Press of Florida, 1994); and Simon P. Sibelman, *Silence in the Novels of Elie Wiesel* (New York: St. Martin's, 1995). It is interesting to note, however, that Wiesel's fictional works did not make the cut in literary critic Harold Bloom's canonical choices for the contemporary "Chaotic Age." See Harold Bloom, *The Western Canon: The Books and School of the Ages* (New York: Harcourt Brace, 1994).

61. Davis, *Elie Wiesel's Secretive Texts*, 119.

62. Joe Holland and Peter Henriot, S.J., *Social Analysis: Linking Faith and Justice*, rev. enl. ed. (Maryknoll, NY: Orbis, 1983), 87.

63. See, for example, the essays collected in Beverly Wildung Harrison, *Making the Connections: Essays in Feminist Social Ethics*, ed. Carol S. Robb (Boston: Beacon, 1985).

64. For a balanced discussion, see Arthur McGovern, *Liberation Theology and Its Critics* (Maryknoll, NY: Orbis, 1990).

65. For a sample of the variety of issues explored in an explicitly Christian framework, see Rebecca Chopp and Mark Lewis Taylor, eds., *Reconstructing Christian Theology* (Minneapolis: Fortress, 1996).

66. Beverly Wildung Harrison, "The Role of Social Theory in Religious Social Ethics: Reconsidering the Case for Marxian Political Economy," in idem, *Making the Connections*, 67.

67. Among Chomsky's many works, see especially Noam Chomsky, *American Power and the New Mandarins* (New York: Pantheon, 1969); idem, *For Reasons of State* (New York: Pantheon, 1973); idem, *Towards a New Cold War: Essays on the Current Crisis and How We Got There* (New York: Pantheon, 1982); idem, *On Power and Ideology: The Managua Lectures* (Boston: South End, 1987); idem, *The Culture of Terrorism* (Boston: South End, 1988); idem, *Necessary Illusions: Thought Control in Democratic Societies* (Boston: South End, 1989); idem, *Deterring Democracy*, 2d ed. (New York: Hill and Wang, 1993); idem, *Year 501: The Conquest Continues* (Boston: South End, 1993); idem, *World Orders Old and New*, 2d ed. (New York: Columbia University Press, 1996); idem, *Powers and Prospects: Reflections on Human Nature and the Social Order* (Boston: South End, 1996); and idem, *Profit Over People: Neoliberalism and Global Order* (New York: Seven Stories, 1999). Among Herman's works, see Edward S. Herman, *The Real Terror Network: Terrorism in Fact and Propaganda* (Boston: South End, 1982); idem, *Beyond Hypocrisy: Decoding the News in an Age of Propaganda* (Boston: South End, 1992); idem, *Triumph of the Market: Essays in Eco-*

nomics, Politics, and the Media (Boston: South End, 1995); idem, *The Myth of the Liberal Media: An Edward Herman Reader* (New York: Peter Lang, 2000); and idem with Robert W. McChesney, *The Global Media: The New Missionaries of Corporate Capitalism* (London: Cassell, 1997).

68. See Noam Chomsky, *Chronicles of Dissent: Interviews with David Barsamian* (Monroe, ME: Common Courage, 1992), 82–83. For an expansive study reflecting this view from the underside, see Howard Zinn, *A People's History of the United States, 1492-Present*, rev. upd. ed. (New York: New Press, 1997).

69. See Noam Chomsky and Edward S. Herman, *The Washington Connection and Third World Fascism*, v. 1 *The Political Economy of Human Rights* (Boston: South End, 1979) and idem, *After the Cataclysm: Postwar Indochina and the Reconstruction of Imperial Ideology*, v. 2 *The Political Economy of Human Rights* (Boston: South End, 1979). For a series of incisive responses, see "Seven Reviews of Chomsky and Herman, *The Political Economy of Human Rights* (1979)," in *Noam Chomsky: Critical Assessments*, ed. C. P. Otero (New York: Routledge, 1994), v.3, t.2, 199–231.

70. Chomsky and Herman, *The Washington Connection and Third World Fascism*, 3–4.

71. Quoted in Noam Chomsky, *Turning the Tide: U.S. Intervention in Central America and the Struggle for Peace* (Boston: South End, 1985), 48.

72. Chomsky and Herman, *The Washington Connection and Third World Fascism*, 82–83.

73. Ibid., 67.

74. For a critical appraisal of the Indonesian dictator, see Edward S. Herman, "Suharto: The Fall of a Good Genocidist" in idem, *The Myth of the Liberal Media*, 207–229.

75. Edward S. Herman and Noam Chomsky, *Manufacturing Consent: The Political Economy of the Mass Media* (New York: Pantheon, 1988). See Herman's response to the work's critics in Edward S. Herman, "The Propaganda Model Revisited" in *Capitalism and the Information Age: The Political Economy of the Global Communication Revolution*, eds. Robert W. McChesney, Ellen Meiksins Wood, and John Bellamy Foster (New York: Monthly Review, 1998), 191–205. See also Chomsky's response in Noam Chomsky, "The Propaganda Model: Some Methodological Considerations," in idem, *Necessary Illusions*, 137–159.

76. Herman, "The Propaganda Model Revisited," 194.

77. Herman and Chomsky, *Manufacturing Consent*, 37–86.

78. Herman, "The Propaganda Model Revisited," 193.

79. Herman and Chomsky, *Manufacturing Consent*, xv.

80. Edward Herman's apt comment: "The later attention and indignation [regarding the Holocaust] were associated with the growth in affluence, confidence and power of Jewish communities in the United States and other great Western powers, and the increasing importance of Israel as a U.S. surrogate in the Middle East. In short, Jews became worthy victims in retrospect." Edward S. Herman, "Politically Correct Holocausts," in idem, *Triumph of the Market*, 107.

81. Harry James Cargas, "Can We Bring the Messiah?: An Interview with Elie Wiesel" in Cargas, *Telling the Tale*, 38.

82. Chomsky, *On Power and Ideology*, 51. See also Chomsky and Herman, *The Washington Connection and Third World Fascism*, 38.

Notes to Chapter Two

1. See the French edition of Wiesel's second volume of memoirs, Elie Wiesel, . . . *Et La Mer N'est Pas Remplie* (Paris: Seuil, 1996), 172.

2. Quoted in Harry James Cargas, *Conversations with Elie Wiesel*, 2d upd. rev. ed. (South Bend, IN: Justice, 1992), 33.

3. Agnes Heller and Ferenc Fehér, "Citizen Ethics and Civic Virtues," in idem, *The Postmodern Political Condition* (New York: Columbia University Press, 1988), 84–86.

4. Heller and Fehér, "Citizen Ethics and Civic Virtues," 84.

5. Dostoevsky referred to this sensibility in *The Brothers Karamazov* when the Elder Zosima describes a doctor he once met: " 'I love mankind,' he said, 'but I am amazed at myself: the more I love mankind in general, the less I love people in particular, that is, individually, as separate persons. In my dreams,' he said, 'I often went so far as to think passionately of serving mankind, and, it may be, would really have gone to the cross for people if it were somehow suddenly necessary, and yet I am incapable of living in the same room with anyone for even two days, this I know from experience. As soon as someone is there, close to me, his personality oppresses my self-esteem and restricts my freedom.' " Fyodor Dostoevsky, *The Brothers Karamazov*, trans. Richard Pevear and Larissa Volokhonsky (New York: Everyman's Library, 1992), 57.

6. Heller and Fehér, "Citizen Ethics and Civic Virtues," 85.

7. For one of the rare examples to the contrary of solidarity with European Jews, see Philip P. Hallie, *Lest Innocent Blood Be Shed* (New York: Harper Torchbooks, 1985).

8. For earlier interpretations of Wiesel's practice of solidarity, see Michael Berenbaum, *Elie Wiesel: God, the Holocaust, and the Children of Israel* (West Orange, NJ: Behrman House, 1994), 133–141 and Dow Marmur, "Silence—Survival—Solidarity: Reflections on Reading Elie Wiesel," in *Elie Wiesel: Between Memory and Hope*, ed. Carol Rittner, R.S.M. (New York: New York University Press, 1990), 50–60.

9. For background, see the penetrating study by Tom Segev, *The Seventh Million: The Israelis and the Holocaust*, trans. Haim Watzman (New York: Hill and Wang, 1993).

10. Hannah Arendt, *Eichmann in Jerusalem: A Report on the Banality of Evil*, rev. enl. ed. (New York: Penguin, 1977).

11. For a suggestive application of Arendt's thesis to American history—slavery, nuclear weaponry, and the Persian Gulf War—see Edward S. Herman, "The Banality of Evil," in idem, *Triumph of the Market: Essays on Economics, Politics, and the Media* (Boston: South End, 1995), 97–101.

12. On Hannah Arendt's relation to Jewry, see Richard J. Bernstein, *Hannah Arendt and the Jewish Question* (Cambridge, MA: MIT Press, 1996).

13. In addition to Segev, for background on the trial and its controversies, see Peter Novick, *The Holocaust in American Life* (Boston: Houghton Mifflin, 1999), 127–145.

14. Elie Wiesel, "A Plea for the Dead," in idem, *Legends of Our Time* (New York: Schocken, 1982), 174–197. The article was published originally in the *Jewish Chronicle* (London) in 1964 and reprinted in *Hadassah Magazine* in 1968.

15. Ibid., 176.
16. Ibid.
17. Ibid., 177–178.
18. Ibid., 178.
19. In addition to Arendt being part of the backdrop to Wiesel's plea, so, too, was historian Raul Hilberg who recounted, "I had included the behavior of the Jewish community in my description because I saw Jewish institutions as an extension of the German bureaucratic machine. I was driven by force of logic to take account of the considerable reliance placed by the Germans on Jewish cooperation. I had to examine the Jewish tradition of trusting God, princes, laws, and contracts. Ultimately I had to ponder the Jewish calculation that the persecutor would not destroy what he could economically exploit. It was precisely this strategy that dictated accommodation and precluded resistance." Raul Hilberg, *The Politics of Memory: The Journey of a Holocaust Historian* (Chicago: Ivan R. Dee, 1996), 126–127.
20. Wiesel, "A Plea for the Dead," 179.
21. Ibid., 180. In his memoirs thirty years later, Wiesel was more forthcoming in his estimation of Hannah Arendt; see Elie Wiesel, *All Rivers Run to the Sea: Memoirs*, trans. Marion Wiesel (New York: Alfred A. Knopf, 1995), 347–348. Arendt was recently the subject of another controversy, the publication of a book by Elzbieta Ettinger about Arendt's relationship with German philosopher Martin Heidegger. Wiesel did not refrain from issuing another dismissal of Arendt: "The book shows that Arendt was so arrogant that she thought she alone could decide who should be forgiven and who should not. I'm not so sure her moral stature will remain intact." Quoted in William H. Honan, "Book on Philosopher's Life Stirs Scholarly Debate Over Her Legacy," *New York Times*, 5 November 1996, A26.
22. See Wiesel's later reflection, "Job: Our Contemporary" in Elie Wiesel, *Messengers of God: Biblical Portraits and Legends*, trans. Marion Wiesel (New York: Simon and Schuster, 1994), 211–235.
23. Wiesel, "A Plea for the Dead," 181. Emphasis Wiesel's.
24. Ibid.
25. Pierre Bourdieu, "Delegation and Political Fetishism," in idem, *Language and Symbolic Power*, ed. John B. Thompson, trans. Gino Raymond and Matthew Adamson (Cambridge, MA: Harvard University Press, 1991), 211. Emphasis Bourdieu's. In terms similar to this "priestly humility" described by Bourdieu, Michael Goldberg commented: "In ancient times, the cultic shrine was superintended by priests. Local shrines had local priests while national shrines, for example, the Temple in Jerusalem, had high priests. Without a doubt, the Holocaust cult's High Priest is Elie Wiesel. His blessing is sought for every Holocaust museum and memorial, from the local *bamot* to the central *hechal* in Washington. Whether his name appears on a letter-head or whether he himself appears at a dedication, any effort to consecrate a site as a Holocaust memorial is almost unthinkable without at least his tacit approval." Michael Goldberg, *Why Should Jews Survive? Looking Past the Holocaust toward a Jewish Future* (New York: Oxford University Press, 1995), 59. Long before Wiesel's recent popularity, he was advocating a view of the Holocaust as sacred mystery.
26. Wiesel, "A Plea for the Dead," 182.

27. Ibid., 185.

28. Ibid., 185–186.

29. Ibid., 186–187. On U.S. press coverage, see Deborah E. Lipstadt, *Beyond Belief: The American Press and the Coming of the Holocaust 1933–1945* (New York: Free Press, 1986). Essentially in accordance with Wiesel's view, Lipstadt remarked, "One is loath to accept that as true, but it must be acknowledged that many government officials, members of the press, and leaders of other religions behaved as if Jewish lives were a cheap commodity." Lipstadt, *Beyond Belief*, 276.

30. Ibid., 187.

31. Ibid., 188.

32. Ibid., 191–192. For a different appraisal of Allied behavior, see Novick, *The Holocaust in American Life*, 19–29.

33. Ibid., 193.

34. Ibid., 195. However, Raul Hilberg offerred a critical perspective on this tendency to focus a great deal on armed Jewish resistance: "Active, armed acts of self-defense within the destructive arena have nevertheless remained the centerpiece of a historiography and celebration. That these acts have been magnified and popularized should not be surprising. The image of a resister with gun in hand is comforting. Something that is uplifting can be salvaged from the catastrophe. To resist is not to cooperate with the perpetrator, not to follow his orders, not to be meek in the face of death. In Israel such an elevation of the ghetto Jew has been especially important. . . . Needless to say I had a problem with this campaign of exaltation. When relatively isolated or episodic acts of resistance are represented as typical, a basic characteristic of the German measures is obscured. The destruction of the Jews can no longer be visualized as a process. Instead the drastic actuality of a relentless killing of men, women, and children is mentally transformed into a more familiar picture of a struggle—however unequal—between combatants." Hilberg, *The Politics of Memory*, 134–135.

35. Ibid., 196.

36. Ibid., 197.

37. Werner Weinberg surfaced some limitations of thinking of oneself as a Holocaust "survivor." For example: "I feel 'survivor' to be a temporary designation. One survives an earthquake, a shipwreck, but after a while one returns to one's former identity, despite possible scars left by the calamity. However, Holocaust-survivorship is terminal. Especially now that 'The Holocaust' has become a separate academic discipline, with a perfect right to its own terminology I have been categorized for the remainder of my natural life. I have been set apart for having been in the Holocaust, while in my own sight I am a person who lived before and who is living after. True, I am essentially changed; but I do not feel that I have joined a club. The ones to be set apart are the nonsurvivors. To be categorized for having survived adds to the damage I have suffered; it is like wearing a tiny new Yellow Star." Werner Weinberg, *Self-Portrait of a Holocaust Survivor* (Jefferson, NC: McFarland, 1985), 151.

38. For one account of Wiesenthal's sharp differences with Wiesel on the interpretation of the Holocaust, see Alan Levy, *The Wiesenthal File* (Grand Rapids, MI: William B. Eerdmans, 1993), 435–437. For Wiesel's critique of Wiesenthal, see

Elie Wiesel, *And the Sea Is Never Full: Memoirs, 1969–*, trans. Marion Wiesel (New York: Alfred A. Knopf, 1999), 127–131.

39. See Berenbaum, *Elie Wiesel*, 198. Berenbaum rightly noted, "For Wiesel the Holocaust is a mystery that should be protected from the process of demystification. The analytic writings of the historian, the critical tone that assimilates and evaluates facts, threaten to destroy the mystery and rob it of its power." Ibid., 193.

40. Many years later, Wiesel will address this issue of speaking and authority; see Wiesel, *And the Sea Is Never Full*, 123.

41. Elie Wiesel, "Holocaust: Twenty-Five Years Later," *Hadassah Magazine* LII (September 1970), 8–9, 42–43; reprinted as "One Generation After," in idem, *One Generation After* (New York: Bard, 1972).

42. Wiesel, "One Generation After," 17.

43. For a wide range of Wiesel's speeches and writings on the Holocaust era, see Elie Wiesel, *Against Silence: The Voice and Vision of Elie Wiesel*, ed. Irving Abrahamson (New York: Holocaust Library, 1985), 1: 89–240.

44. Elie Wiesel, "Art and Literature after the Holocaust," in *Auschwitz: Beginning of a New Era?*, ed. Eva Fleischner (New York: KTAV, 1977), 403–415.

45. Elie Wiesel, "A Plea for the Survivors," in idem, *A Jew Today*, trans. Marion Wiesel (New York: Vintage, 1979), 218–247.

46. Ibid., 219.

47. See Wiesel's reminiscences of Primo Levi, Jerzy Kozinski, and Piotr Rawicz in the chapter entitled "Three Suicides," in Wiesel, *And the Sea Is Never Full*, 345–351.

48. Wiesel, "A Plea for the Survivors," 220.

49. Ibid., 221.

50. Ibid., 222.

51. Ibid., 223. For a study of the arduous demands facing the survivor who bears witness, see Lawrence L. Langer, *Holocaust Testimonies: The Ruins of Memory* (New Haven, CT: Yale University Press, 1991).

52. Ibid., 224.

53. Ibid., 225.

54. Ibid.

55. Ibid., 226.

56. Ibid.

57. Ibid., 227.

58. Ibid., 229.

59. See Gil Loescher and John A. Scanlan, *Calculated Kindness: Refugees and America's Half-Open Door, 1945 to the Present* (New York: Free Press, 1986), 1–24.

60. Wiesel, "A Plea for the Survivors," 231.

61. Ibid., 232.

62. Ibid., 233.

63. Ibid., 234.

64. Ibid.

65. Ibid., 237–238.

66. Ibid., 241.

67. Ibid., 244.

68. Ibid., 245.

69. Ibid., 247.

70. Alvin H. Rosenfeld, "The Problematics of Holocaust Literature," in *Confronting the Holocaust: The Impact of Elie Wiesel*, eds. Alvin H. Rosenfeld and Irving Greenberg (Bloomington: Indiana University Press, 1978), 26. Emphasis Rosenfeld's.

71. Abraham Joshua Heschel, *The Prophets: An Introduction* (New York: Harper Colophon, 1969), 1: 7.

72. Otto Maduro, *Religion and Social Conflicts*, trans. Robert R. Barr (Maryknoll, NY: Orbis, 1982), 107.

73. According to Peter Novick, "By the 1980s and 1990s many Jews, for various reasons, wanted to establish that they too were members of a 'victim community.' Their contemporary situation offered little in the way of credentials. American Jews were by far the wealthiest, best-educated, most influential, in-every-way-most-successful group in American society—a group that, compared to most other identifiable minority groups, suffered no measurable discrimination and no disadvantages on account of that minority status. But insofar as Jewish identity could be anchored in the agony of European Jewry, certification as (vicarious) victims could be claimed, with all the moral privilege accompanying such certification." Peter Novick, *The Holocaust in American Life*, 8–9. Israeli novelist A. B. Yehoshua offered a contrary view of moral privilege via such certification: "we must bear in mind that our having been victims does not accord us any special moral standing. The victim does not become virtuous for having been a victim. Although the Holocaust inflicted a horrible injustice upon us, it did not grant us a certificate of everlasting righteousness. The murderers were amoral; the victims were not made moral. To be moral you must behave ethically. The test of that is daily and constant." Quoted in Michael Bernstein, *Foregone Conclusions: Against Apocalyptic History* (Berkeley and Los Angeles: University of California Press, 1994), 87.

74. Henry Greenspan, *On Listening to Holocaust Survivors: Recounting and Life History* (Westport, CT: Praeger, 1998), 29–56.

75. Alvin H. Rosenfeld, "The Americanization of the Holocaust," in *Thinking about the Holocaust: After Half a Century*, ed. Alvin H. Rosenfeld (Bloomington: Indiana University Press, 1997), 136–137.

76. See Elie Wiesel, "Trivializing the Holocaust: Semi-Fact and Semi-Fiction," in idem, *Against Silence*, 1: 155–158.

77. This success was mirrored by recognition of individuals' accomplishments in the United States; see William Helmreich, *Against All Odds: Holocaust Survivors and the Successful Lives They Made in America* (New York: Simon and Schuster, 1992).

78. At the beginning of the 1990s, Wiesel mused, "There was a time when many of us—friends and anonymous, faceless, ageless Jews—declared that if, by a miracle, by the grace of the almighty God, we should be spared, we would dedicate our lives to telling the story of our agony and the agony of the human multitudes engulfed by the kingdom of night. If we survive, we said to each other and to ourselves, we should make each day a monument and each night a prayer so that, upon the ruins of Creation, new hope would arise for future generations. . . . Now we ask

ourselves: Have *we* kept our promise? In the grip of daily worries, locked into circumstances filled with temptations, with fears, with challenges, we do so many things—too many things—we find so many pretexts, so many reasons. . . . Who among us can say that he or she has kept the pledge given to the dead?" Elie Wiesel, *Sages and Dreamers: Biblical, Talmudic, and Hasidic Portraits and Legends*, trans. Marion Wiesel (New York: Summit, 1991), 384–385. Emphasis Wiesel's.

79. For background, see Zvi Gitelman, *A Century of Ambivalence: The Jews of Russia and the Soviet Union, 1881 to the Present* (New York: Schocken, 1988); Benjamin Pinkus, *The Jews of the Soviet Union: The History of a National Minority* (Cambridge, U.K.: Cambridge University Press, 1988); Ilya Ehrenburg and Vasily Grossman, eds., *The Black Book: The Ruthless Murder of Jews by German-Fascist Invaders throughout the Temporarily-Occupied Regions of the Soviet Union and in the Death Camps of Poland during the War of 1941–1945*, trans. John Glad and James S. Levine (New York: Holocaust Library, 1981); Yehoshua A. Gilboa, *A Language Silenced: The Suppression of Hebrew Literature and Culture in the Soviet Union* (New York: Herzl, 1982); and Louis Rapoport, *Stalin's War against the Jews: The Doctors' Plot and the Soviet Solution* (New York: Free Press, 1990).

80. Elie Wiesel, *The Jews of Silence: A Personal Report on Soviet Jewry*, trans. Neal Kozodoy, exp. ed. (New York: Schocken, 1987).

81. Ibid., xi.

82. Ibid., 6–7.

83. Ibid., 49.

84. Ibid., 61.

85. Quoted in Molly Abramowitz, comp., *Elie Wiesel: A Bibliography* (Metuchen, NJ: Scarecrow, 1974), 100.

86. Wiesel, *The Jews of Silence*, 54.

87. Ibid., 5.

88. Ibid., 55.

89. Ibid., 75.

90. See William W. Orbach, *The American Movement to Aid Soviet Jews* (Amherst, MA: University of Massachusetts Press, 1979).

91. See Abraham Joshua Heschel, "The Plight of Russian Jews," in idem, *Moral Grandeur and Spiritual Audacity: Essays*, ed. Susannah Heschel (New York: Noonday, 1996), 213–215.

92. Wiesel, *All Rivers Run to the Sea*, 377.

93. Wiesel, *The Jews of Silence*, 76.

94. See Wiesel's report on this trip in "Moscow Revisited," in Wiesel, *Legends of Our Time*, 143–160.

95. Ibid., 159.

96. Elie Wiesel, "The Jews of Silence," in idem, *Against Silence*, 2: 221–222.

97. For a revealing exchange with Israeli Prime Minister Levi Eshkol, see Wiesel, *All Rivers Run to the Sea*, 377.

98. Wiesel, *All Rivers Run to the Sea*, 370.

99. For background, see Joshua Rubenstein, *Soviet Dissidents: Their Struggle for Human Rights*, rev. ed. (Boston: Beacon, 1985).

100. Elie Wiesel, "To a Young Jew in Soviet Russia," in idem, *A Jew Today*, 139.

101. Historian Martin Gilbert noted, "Hundreds of thousands of Jews were electrified by Israel's victory in the 1967 war. But it was the shrill Soviet propaganda about Israel's imminent and total defeat that ignited the fuse of national identity. Some recall that this propaganda was so gloating in tone as to heighten to its limit the sense of affinity with the apparently doomed State. From that moment, many Soviet Jews regarded Israel as their nation, and emigration to Israel as their national purpose." Martin Gilbert, *The Jews of Hope* (New York: Elisabeth Sifton/Viking, 1985), 109.

102. Wiesel, "To a Young Jew in Soviet Russia," 146.

103. Elie Wiesel, *Zalmen or The Madness of God*, trans. Nathan Edelman (New York: Schocken, 1985). Wiesel explained the contretemps involving the play and his no longer amicable relations with some Israelis in *All Rivers Run to the Sea*, 411–415.

104. Elie Wiesel, *The Testament*, trans. Marion Wiesel (New York: Summit, 1981).

105. See Elie Wiesel, "Peretz Markish," in idem, *From the Kingdom of Memory: Reminiscences* (New York: Summit, 1990), 93.

106. Gitelman, *A Century of Ambivalence*, 276–277.

107. In an address in New York in 1974, Wiesel spoke admiringly of Senator Jackson: "A couple of years ago, I asked [Senator Jackson] why he is so much a friend of the Jewish people. I do not trust politicians. Very few are humane. They are so caught up in their personal mystique, in their own party machinery, and in who knows what else that I do not trust them. I asked him, 'Why *are* you such a friend of Israel?'. . . Since then we have become good friends, and thanks to him I have more faith in politicians and more faith in man." Elie Wiesel, "Blessed be the Madmen—and Their Friends," in idem, *Against Silence*, 1: 304. Emphasis Wiesel's. For a critical interpretation of Jackson's friendship with Israel, see Alfred M. Lilienthal, *The Zionist Connection II: What Price Peace?* (New Brunswick, NJ: North American, 1982), 248–252.

108. Noam Chomsky and Edward S. Herman, *The Washington Connection and Third World Fascism*, v. 1 *The Political Economy of Human Rights* (Boston: South End, 1979), 262. Emphasis Chomsky and Herman's.

109. Quoted in Edward Drachman, *Challenging the Kremlin: The Soviet Jewish Movement for Freedom, 1967–1990* (New York: Paragon House, 1992), 466–468. On differential press coverage of Communist as compared with Western victims, see "Jerzy Popieluszko versus a Hundred Religious Victims in Latin America," in Edward S. Herman and Noam Chomsky, *Manufacturing Consent: The Political Economy of the Mass Media* (New York: Pantheon, 1988), 37–86.

110. Quoted in John S. Friedman, "The Art of Fiction LXXIX: Elie Wiesel," *Paris Review* 26 (1984), 151. Wiesel did not have patience with the earlier ostrich-like approach of the major Jewish organizations: "After I returned from the USSR, Nahum Goldmann asked me to speak at a plenary session of the World Jewish Congress. I thought he wanted me to share my recent experiences with the delegates. Instead, I was asked to speak about the German problem. When I refused, on the grounds that the most pressing problem of the Jewish world today is that of Russian Jewry, I was very candidly informed that this problem was not on the agenda." Wiesel, "The Jews of Silence," 221.

111. See Martin Gilbert, *Shcharansky: Hero of Our Time* (New York: Elisabeth Sifton/Viking, 1989).

112. Elie Wiesel, "What Shcharansky Means to the World," *New York Times*, 19 February 1986, A23.

113. Ibid.

114. Ibid. Such a march eventually took place, with more than two-hundred thousand people showing up. For Wiesel's sober, then enthused, reaction, see Wiesel, *And the Sea Is Never Full*, 153.

115. Martin Gilbert wrote, "Thanks to Elie Wiesel's own writing and the work of hundreds of campaigners for Soviet Jewry throughout the free world, that Western silence is no longer what it was, a pitiful gap in Jewish unity." See Gilbert, "Afterword," in Wiesel, *The Jews of Silence*, 115.

116. Elie Wiesel, "The Nobel Lecture," in idem, *From the Kingdom of Memory*, 247.

117. Orbach, *The American Movement to Aid Soviet Jews*, 161. Earlier in this work, Orbach commented that "in November 1977, Carter administration officials requested that Congress consider altering the Jackson-Valik Amendment to remove the need for Soviet emigration assurances and instead allow Carter to extend tariff benefits annually if emigration levels were adequate. Inasmuch as only 16,737 Soviet Jews emigrated in 1977, approximately half the 1973 total, it would seem that President Cater had decided to bury human rights in favor of Soviet-American trade." Ibid., 153–154.

118. Don Peretz noted in 1993 that "[p]rospects for major improvement of the economy in the Occupied Territories are not bright, especially considering the difficult problems facing Israel during the next decade. One of the most daunting Israeli priorities at present is to absorb about one million new Russian Jewish immigrants by the end of the decade. Neither Israel nor its supporters abroad are likely to make the investments necessary to improve the Palestinian economy." Don Peretz, *Palestinians, Refugees, and the Middle East Peace Process* (Washington, D.C.: United States Institute of Peace, 1993), 78. See also Edward W. Said, "On Nelson Mandela, and Others," in idem, *The Politics of Dispossession: The Struggle for Palestinian Self-Determination, 1969–1994* (New York: Pantheon, 1994), 370; and Petrus Buwalda, *They Did Not Dwell Alone: Jewish Emigration from the Soviet Union 1967–1990* (Baltimore: Johns Hopkins University Press, 1997).

119. For an overview of issues raised here, such as Israeli settlements and U.S. aid to Israel, see Noam Chomsky, *Fateful Triangle: The United States, Israel, and the Palestinians*, upd. ed. (Cambridge, MA: South End, 1999); Paul Findley, *Deliberate Deceptions: Facing the Facts about the U.S.-Israeli Relationship* (New York: Lawrence Hill, 1995); and Edward W. Said, *The Question of Palestine*, upd. ed. (New York: Vintage, 1992).

120. Elie Wiesel, "The Plight of the Falashas," in idem, *Against Silence*, 1: 388; idem, "A Response to a Letter from the Falashas," in idem, *Against Silence*, 2: 132; idem, "To Our Falasha Brothers and Sisters," in idem, *Against Silence*, 2: 135.

121. Elie Wiesel, "The Tale of Arab Jewry," in idem, *Against Silence*, 2: 139–140.

122. Lawrence Langer remarked, "Having survived, one learns that one's fate

might have been prevented by the outrage and protest of others; and it is to an understanding of these 'others' that Wiesel directs our attention and so much of his imaginative energy. One studies the Holocaust less to explain the murder of six million than to comprehend the six hundred million who permitted or encouraged it. We learn less from how men die than from why others let—or cause them—to die so." Lawrence L. Langer, "The Divided Voice: Elie Wiesel and the Challenge of the Holocaust," in Rosenfeld and Greenberg, *Confronting the Holocaust*, 36.

123. Gene Koppel and Henry Kaufman, *Elie Wiesel: A Small Measure of Victory: An Interview* (Tucson: University of Arizona Press, 1974), 12.

Notes to Chapter Three

1. Robert McAfee Brown, "Elie Wiesel: Writer as Peacemaker," in idem, *Elie Wiesel: Messenger to All Humanity*, 2d upd. ed. (Notre Dame, IN: University of Notre Dame Press, 1989), 253.

2. Ibid. Emphasis Brown's.

3. Alexander Cockburn, "Double Your Standard," *The Nation*, 8 November 1986, 478.

4. Elie Wiesel, *And the Sea Is Never Full: Memoirs, 1969–*, trans. Marion Wiesel (New York: Alfred A. Knopf, 1999), 88.

5. See Elie Wiesel, "Biafra, the End," in idem, *A Jew Today*, trans. Marion Wiesel (New York: Vintage, 1979), 35–37.

6. See Richard Arens, ed., *Genocide in Paraguay* (Philadelphia: Temple University Press, 1976). Wiesel's epilogue, "Now We Know," was reprinted in Wiesel, *Against Silence: The Voice and Vision of Elie Wiesel*, ed. Irving Abrahamson (New York: Holocaust Library, 1985), 2: 371–372. I quote from the *Against Silence* text. A modified version was also included in Wiesel, *A Jew Today*, 38–40.

7. Wiesel, "Now We Know," 371.

8. Ibid.

9. In a volume of essays dedicated to Wiesel, Steven T. Katz reviewed the case of the Aché Indians and claimed that what happened, while deplorable, was not genocide: "The Paraguayan leadership has certainly strained the legal and ethical limits of state behavior in regard to the Aché but it has not denied or transcended these limits altogether. It has committed serious crimes of commission and omission against the Aché (and other indigenous peoples), but both the individual and collective nature of these many crimes falls far short of a program of extermination." Along these lines, Katz has made several criticisms of articles in Arens's volume. See Steven T. Katz, "The Aché: A Re-Evaluation," in *Celebrating Elie Wiesel: Stories, Essays, Reflections*, ed. Alan Rosen (Notre Dame, IN: University of Notre Dame Press, 1998), 243. This essay is part of Katz's ongoing project to show the phenomenological uniqueness of the Holocaust; see Steven T. Katz, *The Holocaust in Historical Context*, v.1 *The Holocaust and Mass Death before the Modern Age* (New York: Oxford University Press, 1994). For a critical appraisal of Katz's project,which denies that genocide is an applicable category to any group but the European Jews during the Holocaust, see Ward Churchill, *A Little Matter of Genocide: Holocaust and*

Denial in the Americas 1492 to the Present (San Francisco: City Lights, 1998). My focus here is not on the debates of genocide semantics, but on Wiesel's concern for and attention to a group of unworthy victims, or, to use Herman and Chomsky's terminology, the victims of a "benign bloodbath."

10. Wiesel, "Now We Know," 371.

11. Ibid.

12. Ibid., 372.

13. See Christopher Simpson, *Blowback: America's Recruitment of Nazis and Its Effect on the Cold War* (New York: Weidenfeld and Nicolson, 1988).

14. Churchill, *A Little Matter of Genocide*, 110–111.

15. David E. Stannard, "Uniqueness as Denial: The Politics of Genocide Scholarship," in *Is the Holocaust Unique? Perspectives on Comparative Genocide*, ed. Alan S. Rosenbaum (Boulder, CO: Westview, 1996), 198. See also David E. Stannard, *American Holocaust: Columbus and the Conquest of the New World* (New York: Oxford University Press, 1992).

16. In his "Editor's Afterword," Richard Arens noted that "the failure to protest the Indian tragedy in Paraguay is also in part a product of a tragically misconceived American foreign policy, predicated upon the assumption that the anti-Communist leader of any foreign state—in particular if it is a state within a 'sphere of influence'—is deserving of our unstinted support, regardless of the means by which he maintains power in his country. The policy is not only flagrantly immoral, but equally impractical as well as counterproductive. Although bruised in its encounter with the realities of Indochina, it continues to dominate official action and provides the sole explanation of our tolerance and, indeed, cover-up of Paraguayan atrocities. It is a tolerance which today has become indistinguishable from oral, and indeed legal, complicity." Arens, *Genocide in Paraguay*, 169.

17. On press coverage, see Noam Chomsky and Edward S. Herman, *The Washington Connection and Third World Fascism*, v.1 *The Political Economy of Human Rights* (Boston: South End, 1979), 117–119.

18. For background, see Marvin E. Gettleman, Jane Franklin, Marilyn Young, and H. Bruce Franklin, eds., *Vietnam and America: A Documentary History* (New York: Grove, 1985); William Appleman Williams, Thomas McCormick, Lloyd Gardner, and Walker La Feber, eds., *America in Vietnam: A Documentary History* (Garden City, NY: Anchor, 1985); Douglas Allen and Ngô Vĩnh Long, eds., *Coming To Terms: Indochina, the United States, and the War* (Boulder, CO: Westview, 1991); and Marilyn B. Young, *The Vietnam Wars: 1945–1990* (New York: Harper-Perennial, 1991).

19. See Noam Chomsky and Edward S. Herman, *After the Cataclysm: Postwar Indochina and the Reconstruction of Imperial Ideology*, v.2 *The Political Economy of Human Rights* (Boston: South End, 1979).

20. Bertrand Russell, "Opening Statement to the First Tribunal Session" in *Against the Crime of Silence, Proceedings of the International War Crimes Tribunal*, ed. John Duffett (New York: Simon and Schuster, 1968), 51. See also Seymour Melman, Mervyn Baron, Dodge Ely, and Edward Connely, *In the Name of America* (New York: E.P. Dutton, 1968).

21. Quoted in Judith Miller, *One, by One, by One: Facing the Holocaust* (New

York, Touchstone, 1990), 223–224. See similar views by another participant of the anti-war movement in Michael Albert, *Stop the Killing Train: Radical Visions for Radical Change* (Boston: South End, 1994), 5.

22. Abraham Joshua Heschel, "A Prayer for Peace," in idem, *Moral Grandeur and Spiritual Audacity: Essays*, ed. Susannah Heschel (New York: Noonday, 1996), 231. See also Heschel, "The Reasons for My Involvement in the Peace Movement," ibid., 224–226.

23. Elie Wiesel, *All Rivers Run to the Sea: Memoirs*, trans. Marion Wiesel (New York: Alfred A. Knopf, 1995), 353–354.

24. Harry James Cargas, "What Is a Jew? Interview of Elie Wiesel," in *Responses to Elie Wiesel: Critical Essays by Major Jewish and Christian Scholars*, ed. Harry James Cargas (New York: Persea, 1978), 155.

25. In his 1999 memoir, Wiesel recalled the tumult of the early 1970s, including his disbelief over the tragedy of the My Lai massacre. See Wiesel, *And the Sea Is Never Full*, 15. Journalist John Pilger offers a different interpretation of this "tragedy": "My Lai eventually made the cover of *Newsweek* under the headline 'An American Tragedy'. This invited sympathy for America and deflected from the truth: that the massacre was, above all, a Vietnamese tragedy and that, far from being an 'aberration', as the army claimed, it accurately reflected the criminal and racist nature of the war. That the war was a series of 'blunders', or a 'quagmire' into which naïve politicians and generals were somehow 'drawn', even 'dragged', was the preferred media version, and still is." John Pilger, "Still a Noble Cause," in idem, *Hidden Agendas* (London: Vintage, 1998), 559.

26. Concerning my own direct contact with the boat people issue, I had the privilege to serve as an English tutor for a Vietnamese family of five girls and one boy from 1983 to 1988.

27. Elie Wiesel, "Plea for the Boat People," in idem, *Against Silence*, 3: 158. On the supposed indifference to the Vietnamese boat people, see David Dellinger, *Vietnam Revisited: From Covert Action to Invasion to Reconstruction* (Boston: South End, 1986), 162–171. For further background, see Gil Loescher and John A. Scanlon, *Calculated Kindness: Refugees and America's Half-Open Door, 1945 to the Present* (New York: Free Press, 1986), 120–146.

28. Wiesel, "Plea for the Boat People," 158. For a study of such divisions, see Raul Hilberg, *Perpetrators Victims Bystanders: The Jewish Catastrophe, 1933–1945* (New York: HarperCollins, 1992).

29. Wiesel, "Plea for the Boat People," 158.

30. Dellinger, *Vietnam Revisited*, 88.

31. Elie Wiesel, "The Victims of Injustice Must Be Cared For," in idem, *Against Silence*, 3: 144.

32. Ibid., 144–145.

33. Ibid., 145.

34. Ibid.

35. Ibid.

36. Elie Wiesel, "For the Sake of History and Justice," in idem, *Against Silence*, 3: 159.

37. Ibid.

38. For background, see Michael Vickery, *Cambodia, 1975–1982* (Boston: South End, 1983); Kimmo Kiljunen, ed., *Kampuchea: Decade of the Genocide* (London: Zed, 1986); David P. Chandler, *The Tragedy of Cambodian History: Politics, War, and Revolution since 1945* (New Haven, CT: Yale University Press, 1991); Ben Kiernan, *The Pol Pot Regime: Race, Power, and Genocide in Cambodia under the Khmer Rouge, 1975–1979* (New Haven, CT: Yale University Press, 1996); and Ben Kiernan, ed., *Genocide and Democracy in Cambodia: The Khmer Rouge, the United Nations and the International Community* (New Haven, CT: Yale University Southeast Asia Studies, 1993). On Western press coverage of Cambodia, see Chomsky and Herman, *After the Cataclysm*, 135–294 and Edward S. Herman and Noam Chomsky, *Manufacturing Consent: The Political Economy of the Mass Media* (New York: Pantheon, 1988), 260–296.

39. Elie Wiesel, "*A Jew Today* and Its Author," in idem, *Against Silence*, 3: 107–108.

40. In his history of recent Cambodia, David Chandler noted that "American bombing of Cambodian targets—'the only game in town,' as CIA director William Colby called it later—had turned much of Cambodia into a free-fire zone under Operation Freedom Deal. The campaign killed thousands of people not at war with the United States. It also had the effect of digging a fire trench around the capital, providing a breathing spell to the Cambodian army, and slowing down the advance of the [Communist Party] forces. Some of the raids struck enemy positions less than a dozen miles from Phnom Penh. Until the bombing was halted at this insistence of the U.S. Congress in August 1973, U.S. planes, secretly and openly, dropped half a million tons of bombs on Cambodia. The tonnage was more than three times the amount dropped on Japan in the closing stages of World War II. Casualties, although certainly high, are impossible to estimate." Chandler, *The Tragedy of Cambodian History*, 225.

41. Elie Wiesel, "Cambodia: How Can an Entire People Wither and Die," *Los Angeles Times*, 13 April 1980, V, 3.

42. Ibid. Emphasis Wiesel's.

43. Ibid. Emphasis Wiesel's.

44. Ibid.

45. Ibid., 6.

46. Elie Wiesel, "Kaddish for Cambodia," in idem, *From the Kingdom of Memory: Reminiscences* (New York: Summit, 1990), 133. See William Shawcross, *The Quality of Mercy: Cambodia, Holocaust, and Modern Conscience* (New York: Simon and Schuster, 1984).

47. It is worth bearing in mind that Pol Pot was supported by the United States after the 1979 Vietnamese invasion of Cambodia, as he could be used as another means to apply pressure on Vietnam, the primary U.S. enemy. On the selectivity of indignation toward war criminals (a topic still of interest in light of indictments against Serbian leaders), see Edward S. Herman, "Pol Pot and Kissinger: On War Criminality and Impunity," *Z Magazine* (September 1997), www.zmag.org/zmag/articles/hermansept97.htm.

48. Wiesel, "Cambodia: How Can an Entire People Wither and Die," 6.

49. Ibid.

50. Wiesel, "Kaddish for Cambodia," 134.

51. Chomsky and Herman, *After the Cataclysm*, 54–57.

52. See John G. Taylor, *Indonesia's Forgotten War: The Hidden History of East Timor* (London: Zed, 1991); Constâncio Pinto and Matthew Jardine, *East Timor's Unfinished Struggle: Inside the Timorese Resistance* (Boston: South End, 1997); and Chomsky and Herman, *The Washington Connection and Third World Fascism*, 129–204.

53. For a helpful overview, see Tom Barry, *Central America Inside Out: The Essential Guide to Its Societies, Politics, and Economics* (New York: Grove Weidenfeld, 1991).

54. See Michael T. Klare, *Beyond the "Vietnam Syndrome": U.S. Interventionism in the 1980s* (Washington, D.C.: Institute for Policy Studies, 1981).

55. See Martin Diskin, ed., *Trouble in Our Backyard: Central America and the United States in the Eighties* (New York: Pantheon, 1983); Noam Chomsky, *Turning the Tide: U.S. Intervention in Central America and the Struggle for Peace* (Boston: South End, 1985); and Walter LaFeber, *Inevitable Revolutions: The United States in Central America*, 2d upd. rev. ed. (New York: W.W. Norton, 1993).

56. See James McGinnis, *Solidarity with the People of Nicaragua* (Maryknoll, NY: Orbis, 1985) and Jon Sobrino, S.J., and Juan Hernández Pico, S.J., *Theology of Christian Solidarity*, trans. Phillip Berryman (Maryknoll, NY: Orbis, 1985). See also the extensive treatment of citizen initiative and activism by Christian Smith, *Resisting Reagan: The U.S. Central American Peace Movement* (Chicago: University of Chicago Press, 1996).

57. Decades before, President Franklin Roosevelt had declared of an earlier Somoza, "He may be a son-of-a-bitch, but he's our son-of-a-bitch." Cited by Penny Lernoux, *Cry of the People: The Struggle for Human Rights in Latin America—The Catholic Church in Conflict with U.S. Policy* (New York: Penguin, 1983), 81.

58. See E. Bradford Burns, *At War in Nicaragua: The Reagan Doctrine and the Politics of Nostalgia* (New York: Harper and Row, 1987); Peter Kornbluh, *Nicaragua, The Price of Intervention: Reagan's Wars against The Sandinistas* (Washington, D.C.: Institute for Policy Studies, 1987); Morris Morley and James Petras, *The Reagan Administration and Nicaragua: How Washington Constructs Its Case for Counterrevolution in Central America* (New York: The Institute for Media Analysis, Inc., 1987); Thomas W. Walker, ed., *Reagan versus the Sandinistas: The Undeclared War on Nicaragua* (Boulder, CO: Westview, 1987); and Holly Sklar, *Washington's War on Nicaragua* (Boston: South End, 1988).

59. See Reed Brody, *Contra Terror in Nicaragua: A Report of a Fact-Finding Mission, September 1984-January 1985* (Boston: South End, 1985) and Noam Chomsky, *The Culture of Terrorism* (Boston: South End, 1988).

60. On the social and political connections among Wiesel, Maître, Boston University president John Silber (Wiesel's employer), and the Reagan war against Nicaragua, see Alexander Cockburn, "Four Men in North's Safe: The Uses of Intellectuals," *The Nation*, 21 March 1987, 350–351, 363–364. Given such a context, one wonders how Wiesel can possibly claim to be above politics and be taken seriously.

61. Elie Wiesel, "Miskitos Try to Recapture Way of Life," *Los Angeles Times*, 5 February 1984, IV, 2.

62. Ibid.

63. Ibid.
64. Ibid.
65. Ibid.
66. Quoted in Cynthia Brown, ed. *With Friends Like These: The Americas Watch Report on Human Rights & U.S. Policy in Latin America* (New York: Pantheon, 1985), 164.
67. Quoted in Chomsky, *Turning the Tide*, 75.
68. Quoted in Sklar, *Washington's War on Nicaragua*, 103–104.
69. For a detailed study of this issue of the political selectivity of victims, see Martin Diskin, "The Manipulation of Indigenous Struggles," in Walker, *Reagan versus the Sandinistas*, 80–96.
70. Such cordiality was tested by the Bitburg Affair in 1985; see chapter 5 below.
71. See Burns, *At War in Nicaragua*, 42–43, 180–181.
72. See Sklar, *Washington's War on Nicaragua* and Marlene Dixon, ed., *On Trial: Reagan's War against Nicaragua: Testimony of the Permanent People's Tribunal* (San Francisco: Synthesis, 1985).
73. Wiesel, *And the Sea Is Never Full*, 92.
74. On Guatemala, see Jean-Marie Simon, *Guatemala: Eternal Spring, Eternal Tyranny* (New York: W.W. Norton, 1987); Susanne Jonas, *The Battle for Guatemala: Rebels, Death Squads and U.S. Power* (Boulder, CO: Westview, 1991); Tom Barry, *Inside Guatemala* (Albuquerque, NM: The Inter-Hemispheric Education Resource Center, 1992); and Victor Perera, *Unfinished Conquest: The Guatemalan Tragedy* (Berkeley and Los Angeles: University of California Press, 1993). On El Salvador, see Raymond Bonner, *Weakness and Deceit: U.S. Policy and El Salvador* (New York: Times Books, 1984); Michael McClintok, *The American Connection*, v. 1 *State Terror and Popular Resistance in El Salvador* (London: Zed, 1985); Americas Watch, *A Year of Reckoning: El Salvador a Decade after the Assassination of Archbishop Romero* (New York: Americas Watch Committee, 1990); Anjali Sundaram and George Gelber, eds., *A Decade of War: El Salvador Confronts the Future* (New York: Monthly Review, 1991); and Scott Wright, *Promised Land: Death and War in El Salvador* (Maryknoll, NY: Orbis, 1994).
75. At the time, President Reagan declared that Ríos Montt was getting a "bum rap" from human rights groups. See Chomsky, *Turning the Tide*, 31. On Israel's contributions, see Jane Hunter, *Israeli Foreign Policy: South Africa and Central America* (Boston: South End, 1987), 111–135.
76. Barry, *Central America Inside Out*, 194, 264.
77. See Gary MacEoin, ed., *Sanctuary: A Resource Guide for Understanding and Participating in the Central American Refugees' Struggle* (San Francisco: Harper and Row, 1985). See also Rennie Golden and Michael McConnell, *Sanctuary: The New Underground Railroad* (Maryknoll, NY: Orbis, 1986).
78. Elie Wiesel, "The Refugee," *Cross Currents* 34 (Winter 1984–1985), 385–390.
79. Ibid., 386.
80. Ibid.
81. Ibid., 387.
82. Ibid., 388.
83. Ibid.

84. Ibid., 389.
85. Ibid.
86. Ibid., 390.
87. Quoted in Armando Durazo, "Author Calls for Study of Threats to Refugees," *Tucson Citizen*, 23 January 1985, c, 1, 3.
88. For powerful testimonies, see Jennifer Harbury, *Bridge of Courage: Life Stories of the Guatemalan Compañeros and Compañeras* (Monroe, ME: Common Courage, 1994), and Maria Teresa Tula, *Hear My Testimony: Maria Teresa Tula, Human Rights Activist of El Salvador*, ed. and trans. Lynn Stephen (Boston: South End, 1994).
89. Wiesel, *And the Sea Is Never Full*, 398.
90. Elie Wiesel, "Reviewing Jacobo Timerman," in idem, *Against Silence*, 2: 343–344.
91. See Elie Wiesel, "Dateline: Johannesburg," in idem, *A Jew Today*, 61–65; idem, "Apartheid's So-Called Law," *New York Times*, 22 May 1985, A31.
92. See Elie Wiesel, "Epilogue," in Phil Borges, *Tibetan Portrait: The Power of Compassion* (New York: Rizzoli International, 1996), n.p., and Wiesel, "Biafra, the End," 35–37.

Notes to Chapter Four

1. Elie Wiesel, *All Rivers Run to the Sea*, trans. Marion Wiesel (New York: Alfred A. Knopf, 1995), 149.
2. Wiesel, *All Rivers Run to the Sea*, 163. On Wiesel's romantic satisfaction with his participation, see ibid., 162, 164–165.
3. Ibid., 183–184, 207–208.
4. See Donald Neff, *Warriors for Jerusalem: The Six Days that Changed the Middle East* (New York: Linden Press/Simon and Schuster, 1984). For recent commentary on this watershed period, see Haim Gordon, ed., *Looking Back at the June 1967 War* (Westport, CT: Praeger, 1999) and William W. Haddad, Ghada H. Talhami, and Janice J. Terry, eds., *The June 1967 War after Three Decades* (Washington, D.C.: Association of Arab-American University Graduates, 1999).
5. See John Quigley, *Palestine and Israel: A Challenge to Justice* (Durham, NC: Duke University Press, 1990), 158.
6. For examples, see Neff, *Warriors for Jerusalem*, 138–139, 181.
7. Ibid., 140. For further background, see Norman G. Finkelstein, *Image and Reality in the Israel-Palestine Conflict* (London: Verso, 1995), 126–130.
8. Wiesel, *All Rivers Run to the Sea*, 386.
9. Ibid., 388.
10. Ibid., 389.
11. See, for example, how Wiesel could not resist a mystical reframing of General Mordechai Gur's conquest of Jerusalem in his report "Motta Gur" in Elie Wiesel, *One Generation After*, trans. Lily Edelman and Elie Wiesel (New York: Bard, 1972), 180–188. Gur, a secular Sabra, was uncomfortable with Wiesel's leading questions. Still, Wiesel persisted, "No, Motta Gur is not religious, at least not in the usual sense. If I detect ancient sounds of legend in his narrative, is that his

fault? If I hear echoes of the Talmud in his tales, is that his fault?" Wiesel, "Motta Gur," 187.

12. Elie Wiesel, "Postwar: /1967," in idem, *One Generation After*, 176–177.

13. Elie Wiesel, *A Beggar in Jerusalem*, trans. Lily Edelman and Elie Wiesel (New York: Schocken, 1985).

14. Elie Wiesel, "At the Western Wall," in idem, *Against Silence: The Voice and Vision of Elie Wiesel*, ed. Irving Abrahamson (New York: Holocaust Library, 1985), 2: 187–88.

15. Quoted from *Yediot Ahronot* (March 1968) in George Baramki Azar, *Palestine: A Photographic Journey* (Berkeley and Los Angeles: University of California Press, 1991), 34. Noam Chomsky later expanded upon Leibowitz's concerns: "As many Israeli doves had expected and feared, the 1967 war led to radical changes within Israel: a growing reliance on force and violence, alliance with 'pariah states' such as South Africa, increased chauvinism, irrationality and religious fanaticism, and grandiose conceptions of Israel's global mission. It has also predictably led to much heavier dependence on the U.S., service to U.S. global interests, and association with some of the most reactionary currents in American society." Noam Chomsky, *Fateful Triangle: The United States, Israel, and the Palestinians*, upd. ed. (Cambridge, MA: South End, 1999), 118.

16. Quoted in Andrew and Leslie Cockburn, *Dangerous Liaison: The Inside Story of the U.S.-Israeli Covert Relationship* (New York: HarperCollins, 1991), 154.

17. Quoted in Finkelstein, *Image and Reality*, 136.

18. Quoted in Quigley, *Palestine and Israel*, 170.

19. "Excerpts from Begin Speech at National Defense College," *New York Times*, 21 August 1982, A6.

20. For background, see Noam Chomsky, *World Orders Old and New*, upd. ed. (New York: Columbia University Press, 1996).

21. Wiesel, "Postwar: / 1967," 172.

22. Ibid., 175.

23. Ibid.

24. Wiesel, "To a Concerned Friend," in idem, *One Generation After*, 191.

25. Ibid.

26. Ibid., 192.

27. Elie Wiesel, "A Moral Victory," in idem, *Against Silence*, 2: 195.

28. Wiesel, "To a Concerned Friend," 195.

29. Ibid., 196.

30. Ibid., 197.

31. Ibid., 198.

32. Elie Wiesel, "Israel Twenty Years Later," in idem, *Against Silence*, 2: 191.

33. Wiesel, "To a Concerned Friend," 198.

34. Ibid.

35. Ibid., 199.

36. In a memorandum two years after his famous declaration, Lord Arthur Balfour stated bluntly, "For in Palestine we do not propose even to go through the form of consulting the wishes of the present inhabitants of the country, though the American [King–Crane] Commission has been going through the form of asking what

they are. The four great powers are committed to Zionism, and Zionism, be it right or wrong, good or bad, is rooted in age-long tradition, in present needs, in future hopes, of far profounder import than the desires and prejudices of the 700,000 Arabs who now inhabit that ancient land." Quoted in Chomsky, *Fateful Triangle*, 90.

37. Wiesel's reaction was far from unique. Neff commented more generally: "a picture had taken shape in the West of Israel the underdog, a triumphant nation more moral than others, holding itself to a higher standard, its occupation a model of civility. There was an almost childish innocence in this adoration bestowed on Israel, especially in the United States, by a Christian world thrilled by decisive action, suddenly shorn of its Holocaust guilt and happy to share in the joy of Jews everywhere." Neff, *Warriors For Jerusalem*, 333.

38. Ibid., 329–333.

39. On the post-1967 settlement policies of the Israeli Labor government, see Chomsky, *Fateful Triangle*, 103–107.

40. In 1995 there were revelations in the Hebrew press about assassinations of Arabs by Israeli soldiers during the 1967 War. Wiesel conceded, "It was only in 1995 that I discovered that the Six-Day War was not as noble as I thought. . . . How I regret today not having known these facts, this horror, when I met with Moshe Dayan. Had he not been minister of defense during the Six-Day War?" Elie Wiesel, *And the Sea Is Never Full: Memoirs, 1969–*, trans. Marion Wiesel (New York: Alfred A. Knopf, 1999), 66.

41. Elie Wiesel, "The Meaning of Munich," in idem, *Against Silence*, 1: 130.

42. Ibid., 131.

43. Ibid., 134.

44. Benjamin Beit-Hallahmi, *Original Sins: Reflections on the History of Zionism and Israel* (New York: Olive Branch, 1993), 178.

45. For background on the diplomacy of this period, see Chomsky, *World Orders Old and New*, 206–221.

46. For an analysis of the 1973 War, see Finkelstein, *Image and Reality*, 150–171.

47. Elie Wiesel, "The Faces of War: *Yom Kippur, 1973*," in idem, *Against Silence*, 2: 198.

48. Ibid.

49. See Chomsky, *Fateful Triangle*, 9–37.

50. Elie Wiesel, "Against Despair," in idem, *A Jew Today*, trans. Marion Wiesel (New York: Vintage, 1979), 189.

51. Ibid., 191.

52. See *Zionism & Racism: Proceedings of an International Symposium* (Tripoli: International Organization for the Elimination of all Forms of Racial Discrimination, 1977). See also Arie Dayan, "The Debate Over Zionism and Racism: An Israeli View," *Journal of Palestine Studies* 22 (Spring 1993): 96–105.

53. Elie Wiesel, "Zionism and Racism," in idem, *A Jew Today*, trans. Marion Wiesel (New York: Vintage, 1979), 41.

54. Ibid.

55. Ibid., 42.

56. Ibid., 42–43.

57. For an analysis of the settler-colonial modus vivendi of Zionism, see Beit-

Hallahmi, *Original Sins*, 82–87 and Edward W. Said, *The Question of Palestine*, upd. ed. (New York: Vintage, 1992), 56–114. For a view that emphasizes Jewish religious requirements over political considerations, see Israel Shahak, *Jewish History, Jewish Religion: The Weight of Three Thousand Years* (London: Pluto, 1994).

58. Quoted in Chomsky, *Fateful Triangle*, 51. For Wiesel's recent commentary on Meir's denial, see Wiesel, *All Rivers Run to the Sea*, 310.

59. As Edward Said put it, "What we will discover is that everything positive from the Zionist standpoint looked absolutely negative from the perspective of the native Arab Palestinians." Said, *The Question of Palestine*, 84.

60. That modest victory was later nullified after the Gulf War by the Bush administration, which put pressure on countries to repeal the resolution, without debate or discussion, in the General Assembly. See Phyllis Bennis, "The United Nations and Palestine: Partition and Its Aftermath" in Haddad, Talhami, and Terry, *The June 1967 War after Three Decades*, 111–113.

61. Elie Wiesel, "To a Young Palestinian Arab," in idem, *A Jew Today*, 121–128.

62. Ibid., 122.

63. Ibid. Emphasis Wiesel's. In a recent study of Israel's founders, Israeli historian Zeev Sternhell pointed out that "neither the Zionist movement abroad nor the pioneers who were beginning to settle the country could frame a policy toward the Palestinian national movement. The real reason for this was not a lack of understanding of the problem but a clear recognition of the insurmountable contradiction between the basic objectives of the two sides. If Zionist intellectuals and leaders ignored the Arab dilemma, it was chiefly because they knew that this problem had no solution within the Zionist way of thinking . . . in general both sides understood each other well and knew that the implementation of Zionism could be only at the expense of the Palestinian Arabs. The leadership of the Yishuv did not conceal its intentions; nor was it able to do so. Similarly, the Arabs, who knew from the beginning that Zionism's aim was the conquest of the land, made perfectly clear their refusal to pay the price for the Jewish catastrophe." Zeev Sternhell, *The Founding Myths of Israel: Nationalism, Socialism, and the Making of the Jewish State*, trans. David Maisel (Princeton, NJ: Princeton University Press, 1998), 43–44.

64. Ibid., 122–123.

65. Ibid., 123.

66. Ibid., 124.

67. Ibid., 125.

68. Ibid., 126.

69. Ibid., 127.

70. Ibid.

71. Edward S. Herman, *The Real Terrorism Network: Terrorism in Fact and Propaganda* (Boston: South End, 1982), 201.

72. See Livia Rokach, *Israel's Sacred Terrorism* (Belmont, MA: Association of Arab-American Graduates, 1980); Noam Chomsky, *Pirates and Emperors: International Terrorism in the Real World* (New York: Claremont Research and Publications, 1986); and Herman, *The Real Terror Network*, 76–79. More broadly, see Alexander George, ed., *Western State Terrorism* (London: Routledge, 1991).

73. Not to mention Israel's support for other state terrorists, as it armed

numerous regimes that committed grievous human rights abuses, such as
Nicaragua (under Somoza), Argentina, and South Africa. For details, see Israel
Shahak, *Israel's Global Role: Weapons for Repression* (Belmont, MA: Association of
Arab-American Graduates, 1982).

74. Elie Wiesel, "A Jew Today," in idem, *Against Silence*, 1: 163.

75. Ibid.

76. See Amir Cheshin, Bill Hutman, and Avi Melamed, *Separate and Unequal:
The Insider Story of Israeli Rule in East Jerusalem* (Cambridge, MA: Harvard University Press, 1999).

77. See Edward Tivnan, *The Lobby: Jewish Political Power and American Foreign
Policy* (New York: Simon and Schuster, 1987).

78. See Benjamin Beit-Hallahmi, *The Israeli Connection: Who Israel Arms and
Why* (New York: Pantheon, 1987) and Paul Findley, *Deliberate Deceptions: Facing the
Facts about the U.S.-Israeli Relationship* (Chicago: Lawrence Hill, 1995).

79. For background, see Michael Jansen, *The Battle of Beirut: Why Israel Invaded
Lebanon* (Boston: South End, 1983); Ze'ev Schiff and Ehud Ya'ari, *Israel's Lebanon
War*, ed. and trans. Ina Friedman (New York: Simon and Schuster, 1984); Robert
Fisk, *Pity the Nation: The Abduction of Lebanon* (New York: Simon and Schuster,
1990); and Chomsky, *Fateful Triangle*. See also the critical report by Israeli Lieu-
tenant Colonel, Dov Yermiya, *My War Diary: Lebanon June 5-July 1, 1982*, trans.
Hillel Schenker (Boston: South End, 1983).

80. The stances of the various Israeli governments amounted to rejectionism
toward the Palestinians, comparable to the rejectionism of some extremist Palestinian groups regarding Israeli Jews. For more on the double standard of the term
rejectionism, see Chomsky, *Fateful Triangle*, 39–88.

81. See Findley, *Deliberate Deceptions*, 60.

82. Quoted in Chomsky, *Fateful Triangle*, 130.

83. Elie Wiesel, "Israel's Dilemmas," in idem, *Against Silence*, 2: 212.

84. Wiesel did not likely have in mind Israel's exporting of arms to regimes that
did not match such humane standards. Political analyst Jane Hunter: "Already
under intentional censure for its oppression of the Palestinians in the territories it
occupies, Israel's dealings with the scum of the world's tyrants—including the white
clique in South Africa, Somoza of Nicaragua, Gen. Pinochet of Chile, Marcos of
the Philippines, Duvalier of Haiti, Mobutu of Zaire, the allegedly cannibalistic
Bokassa of Central African Republic—invariably result in its further exclusion from
more 'respectable' circles." Jane Hunter, *Israeli Foreign Policy: South Africa and Central America* (Boston: South End, 1987), 14.

85. Wiesel, "Israel's Dilemmas," 213.

86. Ibid.

87. Ibid.

88. Ibid.

89. Ibid., 214.

90. Ibid. For Wiesel's further reflections on his experience with this young
Palestinian poet, see Wiesel, *And the Sea Is Never Full*, 305–308.

91. Elie Wiesel, "Voices of Hate," in idem, *Against Silence*, 2: 215.

92. Ibid.

93. One of these was Dr. Shlomo Shmelzman, whose son served during the

Lebanon war. Shmelzman went on a hunger strike to protest the war and in a letter to the press stated: "In my childhood I have suffered fear, hunger and humiliation when I passed from the Warsaw Ghetto, through labor camps, to Buchenwald. Today, as a citizen of Israel, I cannot accept the systematic destruction of cities, towns, and refugee camps. I cannot accept the technocratic cruelty of the bombing, destroying and killing of human beings. I hear too many familiar sounds today, sounds which are being amplified by the war. I hear 'dirty Arabs' and I remember 'dirty Jews.' I hear about 'closed areas' and I remember ghettos and camps. I hear 'two-legged beasts' and I remember 'Untermenschen.' I hear about tightening the siege, clearing the area, pounding the city into submission and I remember suffering, destruction, death, blood and murder. . . . Too many things in Israel remind me of too many other things from my childhood." Quoted in Chomsky, *Fateful Triangle*, 257–258.

94. Wiesel, "Voices of Hate," 216.

95. See the sample of press reports in *The Beirut Massacre: Press Profile: September 1982* (New York: Claremont Research and Publications, 1982).

96. Elie Wiesel, "The Massacre in Lebanon," in idem, *Against Silence*, 2: 218. The statement originally appeared in the *New York Times*, September 22, 1982.

97. Ibid.

98. Quoted in Chomsky, *Fateful Triangle*, 98. On Begin's use of the Holocaust, see Ilan Peleg, *Begin's Foreign Policy, 1977–1983: Israel's Move to the Right* (Westport, CT: Greenwood, 1987), 63–68.

99. Susanne Jonas, *The Battle for Guatemala: Rebels, Death Squads, and U.S. Power* (Boulder, CO: Westview, 1991), 149.

100. Quoted in Noam Chomsky, *Turning the Tide: U.S. Intervention in Central America and the Struggle for Peace* (Boston: South End, 1985), 36. In a recent work, Chomsky identified the Nobel laureate as MIT Biology Professor Salvador Luria. See Noam Chomsky, *The New Military Humanism: Lessons from Kosovo* (Monroe, ME: Common Courage, 1999), 110.

101. Hunter, *Israeli Foreign Policy*, 111.

102. In 1981 journalist Penny Lernoux observed about some of Israel's associates: "Though hard to credit, the same nation that was born of the Holocaust is on excellent terms with the neo-Nazi regime in Argentina. Thus while Jewish newspaper publisher Jacobo Timerman was being tortured by the Argentine military in cells painted with swastikas, three Israeli generals, including the former armed forces chief of staff, were visiting Buenos Aires on a 'friendly mission' to sell arms." Quoted in Shahak, *Israel's Global Role*, 53.

103. See Zachary Lockman and Joel Beinin, eds., *Intifada: The Palestinian Uprising against Israeli Occupation* (Boston: South End, 1989); Al-Haq, *Punishing a Nation: Human Rights Violations during the Palestinian Uprising December 1987-December 1988* (Boston: South End, 1990); Don Peretz, *The Intifada: The Palestinian Uprising* (Boulder, CO: Westview, 1990); Rosemary Radford Ruether and Marc H. Ellis, eds., *Beyond Occupation: American Jewish, Christian, and Palestinian Voices for Peace* (Boston: Beacon, 1990); Joost R. Hiltermann, *Behind the Intifada: Labor and Women's Movements in the Occupied Territories* (Princeton, NJ: Princeton University Press, 1991); and Norman G. Finkelstein, *The Rise and Fall of Palestine: A Personal Account of the Intifada Years* (Minneapolis: University of Minnesota Press, 1996).

104. Wiesel, *And the Sea Is Never Full*, 285.

105. Elie Wiesel, "A Mideast Peace—Is It Impossible?" *The New York Times*, 23 June 1988, A23. All subsequent quotations are taken from this op-ed.

106. For Wiesel's response to a young Palestinian couple who asked him why he seemed to speak out for everybody but the Palestinians, see Wiesel, *And the Sea Is Never Full*, 374.

107. In recent decades, a new generation of Israeli scholars has disputed many of the founding myths of the early years of the State of Israel. See the survey by Avi Shlaim, "The Debate about 1948" in *The Israel/Palestine Question*, ed. Ilan Pappe (New York: Routledge, 1999), 171–192. See also Laurence J. Silberstein, *The Postzionism Debates: Knowledge and Power in Israeli Culture* (New York: Routledge, 1999).

108. Jansen, *The Battle of Beirut*, 119.

109. Contra Wiesel's long-standing characterization of sad and innocent Israeli soldiers, see the powerful selection of testimony about Israeli brutality in Noam Chomsky, *Necessary Illusions: Thought Control in Democratic Societies* (Boston: South End, 1989), 209–214.

110. For Wiesel's subsequent admission about the humiliation of Palestinians that spring, see Wiesel, *And the Sea Is Never Full*, 134–135.

111. For a thorough list of various UN resolutions censuring Israel (and vetoed by the United States), see Findley, *Deliberate Deceptions*, 184–194.

112. Elie Wiesel, "Introduction: Israel under Siege," *Midstream* 34 (December 1988): 21. All subsequent quotations in this section are from this page of the "Introduction."

113. Emphasis Wiesel's. In his 1999 memoir, Wiesel revisits this issue; see Wiesel, *And the Sea Is Never Full*, 134.

114. In one of the rare references I could find to Wiesel's even acknowledging harmful Israeli policies toward Palestinians, he declared, "openly that the collective punishments meted out routinely under both governments leave me aghast. The sight of an Arab house demolished by the army just because a young Palestinian has been caught carrying a weapon does not leave me indifferent. And I consider all fanatical groups dangerous and evil." Wiesel, *And the Sea Is Never Full*, 135.

115. For critical analyses, see Chomsky, *World Orders Old and New*; Edward W. Said, *Peace and Its Discontents: Essays on Palestine in the Middle East Peace Process* (New York: Vintage, 1996); Naseer Aruri, *The Obstruction of Peace: The U.S., Israel and the Palestinians* (Monroe, ME: Common Courage, 1995); Graham Usher, *Palestine in Crisis: The Struggle for Peace and Political Independence after Oslo* (London: Pluto, 1995); and Nicholas Guyatt, *The Absence of Peace: Understanding the Israeli-Palestinian Conflict* (New York: Zed, 1998).

116. For example, after the election of Benjamin Netanyahu in 1996, Wiesel counseled calm about the peace negotiations: "Don't be worried. There is something called the wisdom of the people, and we must have faith in it. A Jewish wise man once said, 'Trust the people, for they may not be prophets, but they are the children of prophets.' History is irreversible. Think about tomorrow. There will be negotiations. During the campaign, Netanyahu spoke like Peres; Peres spoke like Netanyahu. So don't worry. It will be O.K. . . . I am convinced that no leader in Israel can simply stop the peace process; it is irreversible. So many people here were

afraid [last week], because they don't remember that Begin was as hawkish as Netanyahu seems to be. It was after all Begin who signed the first peace agreement with Egypt—he was the one who gave up the entire Sinai. So let's not start coming out with statements of fear; there is no reason to panic. For me, it's not a matter of personalities, it's a matter of principle. I am for the peace process; it will continue because it must continue." Elie Wiesel, quoted in "Across the Spectrum," *Time Magazine* (10 June 1996), at www.time.com/time/magazine/archive/1996/dom/960610/forum.html.

117. In a statement made in early 2000, more than one hundred Palestinian intellectuals expressed their opposition to the peace process: "The historic settlement is becoming a settlement between Israelis themselves, not a settlement with the Palestinians. It is a settlement that suffocates the Palestinians humanly, territorially, security-wise and politically; humanly, because it does not recognize their human and historical rights; territorially, because it isolates them within confined areas in towns and villages while progressively confiscating their land; security-wise because it places Israeli security in principle over and above Palestinian rights, existence and security; politically because it prevents Palestinians from determining their future and controlling their borders." Abdel Rahman Abu Gharbia et al., "Message to the Israeli and Jewish Public," ZNet, www.zmag.org/palmessage.htm.

118. For a strong critique of Arafat, see Edward W. Said, *The End of the Peace Process: Oslo and After* (New York: Pantheon, 2000).

119. Wiesel, *And the Sea Is Never Full*, 73. Later, Wiesel wrote, "For the government of Shimon Peres [Arafat] was the only valid interlocutor. The terrorist of yesterday has become Israel's ally. Fine. I support with all my heart their policy of reconciliation and their aspirations to peace." Ibid., 321.

120. Ibid., 136.

121. Ibid., 273. Wiesel was criticized roundly by various Israelis because, among other reasons, he practiced solidarity from afar and did not pay the price Israeli Jews did in building and protecting their country. See the revealing polemic written in the form of a letter to Wiesel by Israeli journalist, Matti Golan, *With Friends Like You: What Israelis Really Think of American Jews*, trans. Hillel Halkin (New York: Free Press, 1992). Golan's indignant tone is conveyed by the following passage: "You want a Jewish state? Then please be so kind as to stand guard over it yourself. I've been doing it for dozens of years. Now it's your turn. Let's switch lives. You come here, serve in the army, worry about the intifada, deal with the Orthodox, and shell out 50% of your income taxes, and I'll live in America, send you money, and visit you now and then, and criticize. Didn't you say we were partners? Then it seems to me a fair offer. I've given this project called Israel over forty years of my life. Why don't you give forty years of yours now, and I'll support you financially and politically." Ibid., 178. For Wiesel's retort, see Elie Wiesel, . . . *Et La Mer N'est Pas Remplie* (Paris: Seuil, 1996), 150–151. See further selections from the Hebrew press translated in Alexander Cockburn, "Double Your Standard," *The Nation*, 8 November 1986, 478–479 and Beit-Hallahmi, *Original Sins*, 199–200.

122. Wiesel might also have commented on the divisions, conflicts, and fragmentation of American Jewry; see Jack Werthheimer, *A People Divided: Judaism in Contemporary America* (New York: Basic Books, 1993).

123. See Israel Shahak and Norton Mezvinsky, *Jewish Fundamentalism in Israel* (London: Pluto, 1999). Interestingly, Goldstein was an admirer of the Lubavitcher rebbe, Menachem Schneerson, with whom Wiesel had a strong relationship for many years.

124. Wiesel, *And the Sea Is Never Full,* 135.

125. Ibid., 137.

126. Ibid., 125.

127. In fact, in his creative work, Wiesel even imagined Jews putting God on trial for supposed divine indifference to the suffering of the Chosen People; see Elie Wiesel, *The Trial of God,* trans. Marion Wiesel (New York: Schocken, 1986).

128. About this issue, Norman G. Finkelstein, son of Holocaust survivors, and one who has made a strong commitment of solidarity with the Palestinians, stated, "Israel won sympathy and masked its systematic violations of human rights in no small part by exploiting the memory of the Jewish people's martyrdom. To mute criticism, it claimed to be acting in our name and in the name of our tragedy. Many decent people, Jews and non-Jews, deferred to that claim, turning a blind eye to the suffering of the Palestinians. Jews who chose silence therefore passively collaborated in Israel's crimes, for their silence left Israel unchallenged and unimpeached." Finkelstein, *The Rise and Fall of Palestine,* 11.

129. See Edward S. Herman, "Normalizing Israeli Repression," *Z Magazine* (June 1994), www.zmag.org/zmag/articles/june94herman.htm.

Notes to Chapter Five

1. See Peter Novick, *The Holocaust in American Life* (New York: Houghton Mifflin, 1999).

2. I have borrowed the expression "culture industry" in this context from Gillian Rose, *Mourning Becomes the Law: Philosophy and Representation* (Cambridge, U.K.: Cambridge University Press, 1996), 30. For a critical treatment, see Norman G. Finkelstein, *The Holocaust Industry: Reflections on the Exploitation of Jewish Suffering* (London: Verso, 2000).

3. See Hilene Flanzbaum, ed., *The Americanization of the Holocaust* (Baltimore: Johns Hopkins University Press, 1999).

4. I am indebted for this expression to Edward Said, who observed to interviewer David Barsamian, "Of course, in the general political economy of memory and recollection that exists in public culture in the West, there's no room for the Palestinian experience of loss." See Edward W. Said, *The Pen and the Sword: Conversations with David Barsamian* (Monroe, ME: Common Courage, 1994), 95.

5. For a selection of Wiesel's book reviews, forewords, and afterwords, see Elie Wiesel, *Against Silence: The Voice and Vision of Elie Wiesel,* ed. Irving Abrahamson (New York: Holocaust Library, 1985), 3: 267–398.

6. For a critical analysis of this period, see Noam Chomsky, *Towards a New Cold War: Essays on the Current Crisis and How We Got There* (New York: Pantheon, 1982).

7. On Carter's difficult relations with American Jewry, see Edward Tivnan, *The*

Lobby: Jewish Political Power and American Foreign Policy (New York: Simon and Schuster, 1987), 98–104.

8. On the genesis of the U.S. Holocaust Memorial, see Judith Miller, *One, by One, by One: Facing the Holocaust* (New York: Touchstone, 1990); James E. Young, *The Texture of Memory: Holocaust Memorials and Meaning* (New Haven, CT: Yale University Press, 1993); and Edward T. Linenthal, *Preserving Memory: The Struggle to Create America's Holocaust Museum* (New York: Viking, 1995).

9. Quoted in Miller, *One, by One, by One*, 256.

10. Ibid., 257.

11. Linenthal, *Preserving Memory*, 17.

12. Quoted in ibid., 21.

13. Quoted in ibid.

14. Quoted in ibid.

15. Elie Wiesel, *And the Sea Is Never Full: Memoirs, 1969–*, trans. Marion Wiesel (New York: Alfred A. Knopf, 1999), 182.

16. Linenthal, *Preserving Memory*, 21–22. On Wiesel's commitment to a museum rather than a monument, see Harry James Cargas, *Conversations with Elie Wiesel*, 2d rev. enl. ed. (South Bend, IN: Justice, 1992), 148–149.

17. For a selection of Wiesel's pronouncements as the chairman of this commission, see Wiesel, *Against Silence*, 1: 149–167.

18. David Biale reflected on this status: "Consider the success of the American Jewish community in placing the Holocaust on the American political landscape by building a Holocaust museum on the Mall in Washington. It was as if by transferring the *European* genocide to America American Jews might continue their European identity as the chosen minority. Yet the very political influence and economic wherewithal necessary to construct the Holocaust Museum immediately belied this message: only a group securely part of the majority could institutionalize its history in this way. Only the genocide of Europeans by Europeans could find canonical status, while the home-grown mass sufferings of African and Native Americans could not. Almost by definition, the real emblematic minorities are precisely those whose story no one wants to hear." David Biale, "The Melting Pot and Beyond: Jews and the Politics of American Identity" in *Insider/Outsider: American Jews and Multiculturalism*, eds. David Biale, Michael Galchinsky, and Susannah Heschel (Berkeley and Los Angeles: University of California Press, 1998), 28. Emphasis Biale's.

19. Elie Wiesel, "A Quest for Memory and Justice," in idem, *Against Silence*, 3: 149.

20. Ibid., 150.

21. On the conflicts faced by Wiesel and his colleagues, see the detailed account in Linenthal, *Preserving Memory*, 17–56.

22. Quoted in ibid., 27. Carter evidently had gotten this figure from Nazi-hunter Simon Wiesenthal. On Simon Wiesenthal's inventing the figure of eleven million, see Novick, *The Holocaust in American Life*, 215–216.

23. Linenthal, *Preserving Memory*, 41.

24. This issue, too, provoked controversy from the Gypsy or Romani camp of survivors; see Linenthal, *Preserving Memory*, 240–246. For one study of their extermination that contradicts Wiesel's view, see Ian Hancock, "Response to the Porrajamos:

The Romani Holocaust," in *Is The Holocaust Unique? Perspectives on Comparative Genocide*, ed. Alan S. Rosenbaum (Boulder, CO: Westview, 1996), 39–64.

25. Elie Wiesel, "Against Extrapolation," in idem, *Against Silence*, 3: 156.

26. Quoted in Linenthal, *Preserving Memory*, 50.

27. Quoted in ibid., 51. Emphasis mine.

28. Ibid., 54–55.

29. For Wiesel's views on Arthur Goldberg's suspicions about the politics involved in this memorial effort, see Wiesel, *And the Sea Is Never Full*, 209–210.

30. Elie Wiesel, "Presentation of the Report of the President's Commission on the Holocaust to the President of the United States," in idem, *Against Silence*, 3: 166.

31. Miller, *One, by One, by One*, 227.

32. Quoted in Ibid., 228. Wiesel admitted, "the Senate distrusts [the Committee on Conscience] because it fears we might make declarations and take initiatives that might be embarrassing to the executive branch." Wiesel, *And the Sea Is Never Full*, 213. However, the Committee on Conscience got a second life when, in June 1995, it became a project of the U.S. Holocaust Memorial Museum. The goal remained "to alert the national conscience, influence policy makers, and stimulate worldwide action to confront and work to halt acts of genocide or related crimes against humanity." See the website of the U.S. Holocaust Memorial Museum, www.ushmm.org/conc.html.

33. Pierre Bourdieu, *Language and Symbolic Power*, ed. John B. Thompson, trans. Gino Raymond and Matthew Adamson (Cambridge, MA: Harvard University Press, 1991), 239–240. Emphases Bourdieu's.

34. John G. Taylor, *Indonesia's Forgotten War: The Hidden History of East Timor* (London: Zed, 1991), 175.

35. In their study of the Holocaust, Richard L. Rubenstein and John K. Roth offer a sobering comment in light of the Carter administration's support of both Holocaust remembrance and its Indonesian ally: "In particular is there anything that study about the Holocaust can accomplish to make human life less under threat, to keep genocidal tendencies at bay? Many advocates of study about the Holocaust assume that there is. Frequently appealing to George Santayana's pronouncement that 'those who do not remember the past are condemned to repeat it,' they suppose that study of what has happened can safeguard against such massive wasting of life in the future. Evidence in favor of such a new is not overwhelming, however, because population elimination continues at the very time when the Holocaust is studied by more people than ever before." Richard L. Rubenstein and John K. Roth, *Approaches to Auschwitz: The Holocaust and Its Legacy* (Atlanta, GA: John Knox, 1987), 19. The 1995 approved Committee on Conscience (see note 32 above) did send a letter to President Bill Clinton in September 1999 regarding the vicious rampage by Indonesian militias in East Timor. See www.ushmm.org/conc/etimor.htm.

36. Noam Chomsky made the following grim commentary on the U.S. penchant for blaming its Vietnamese victims: "Things have reached the point where an American President [Jimmy Carter] can appear on national television and state that we owe 'no debt' to the Vietnamese, because 'the destruction was mutual.' And there is not a whisper of protest when this monstrous statement, worthy of Hitler or Stalin, is blandly produced in the midst of a discourse on human rights. Not only

do we owe them no debt for having murdered and destroyed and ravaged their land, but we may now stand back and sanctimoniously blame them for dying of disease and malnutrition, deploring their cruelty when hundreds die trying to clear unexploded ordnance by hand from fields laid waste by the violence of the American state, wringing our hands in mock horror when those who were able to survive the American assault—predictably, the toughest and harshest elements—resort to oppression and sometimes massive violence, or fail to find solutions to material problems that have no analogue in Western history perhaps since the Black Death." Noam Chomsky, "Intellectuals and the State," in idem, *Towards a New Cold War*, 74–75. For Carter's remarks, see "Transcript of President's News Conference on Foreign and Domestic Issues," *New York Times*, 25 March 1977, A10.

37. Novick, *The Holocaust in American Life*, 15.

38. Quoted in Young, *The Texture of Memory*, 336.

39. Wiesel, *And the Sea Is Never Full*, 212.

40. All quotations are taken from Wiesel's statement in Senate, Elie Wiesel Testifying on the Genocide Treaty to the Senate Foreign Relations Committee, 99th Congress, 1st sess., *Congressional Record* (7 March 1985), S2856–S2858.

41. Ibid., S2856.

42. Ibid., S2857.

43. Ibid.

44. See, for example, Elie Wiesel, Introduction to *The Abandonment of the Jews: America and the Holocaust, 1941–1945*, by David S. Wyman (New York: Pantheon, 1985), vii–ix.

45. Wiesel, "Genocide Treaty," S2857. Former Air Force pilot during World War II, historian Howard Zinn offered this critical perspective: "The evidence was powerful: the Allied powers—the United States, England, the Soviet Union—had not gone to war out of compassion for the victims of fascism. The United States and its allies did not make war on Japan when Japan was slaughtering the Chinese in Nanking, did not make war on Franco when he was destroying democracy in Spain, did not make war on Hitler when he was sending Jews and dissidents to concentration camps, did not even take steps *during* the war to save Jews from certain death. They went to war when their national power was threatened." Howard Zinn, *You Can't Be Neutral on a Moving Train: A Personal History of Our Times* (Boston: Beacon, 1994), 99. Emphasis Zinn's.

46. Ibid.

47. Ibid.

48. Ibid.

49. Ibid. For Wiesel's personal reaction to Helms, see Wiesel, *And the Sea Is Never Full*, 96–97.

50. Leo Kuper, "The United States Ratifies the Genocide Convention," in *The History and Sociology of Genocide: Analyses and Case Studies*, eds. Frank Chalk and Kurt Jonassohn (New Haven, CT: Yale University Press, 1990), 422–423.

51. Wiesel, "Genocide Treaty," S2857.

52. See Holly Sklar, *Washington's War on Nicaragua* (Boston: South End, 1988).

53. The U.S. Senate ratified the Genocide Treaty in 1986, the same year that the World Court held the U.S. guilty of violating international law against

Nicaragua, a ruling the United States dismissed. For a thorough criticism of the U.S. amendments to the Genocide Treaty, see Ward Churchill, *A Little Matter of Genocide: Holocaust Denial in the Americas 1492 to the Present* (San Francisco: City Lights, 1998), 363–398.

54. For the relevant documents and helpful chronologies, see the following collections: Ilya Levkov, ed., *Bitburg and Beyond: Encounters in American, German and Jewish History* (New York: Shapolsky, 1987) and Geoffrey Hartman, ed., *Bitburg in Moral and Political Perspective* (Bloomington: Indiana University Press, 1986).

55. Wiesel, *And the Sea Is Never Full*, 231.

56. Quoted in Levkov, *"Bitburg on Reagan's West German Agenda,"* 39.

57. Quoted in Wiesel, *And the Sea Is Never Full*, 241. In his memoirs, Wiesel placed this outrage of Reagan's (on April 18) after his own treatment of receiving the Gold Medal (on April 19), as if Reagan's equation of victims and victimizers came after his receiving the medal instead of the day before. Wiesel also noted that at the council meeting on April 18, with this "shameful vote against collective resignation," he decided at the "first opportunity" to turn in his resignation to the president.

58. Ibid., 237.

59. In Wiesel's words, the medal "represents a rare and prestigious distinction—it has been awarded to no more than one hundred or so individuals in all of American history." Wiesel, *And the Sea Is Never Full*, 229–230.

60. Pierre Bourdieu and Loïc J. D. Wacquant, *An Invitation to Reflexive Sociology* (Chicago: The University of Chicago Press, 1992), 210.

61. Quoted in Levkov, "Reagan Awards Holocaust Writer Elie Wiesel Congressional Gold Medal," 41.

62. Quoted in Levkov, " 'Your Place Is with the Victims,' Wiesel Tells Reagan," 42.

63. On this theme, see Douglas V. Porpora, *How Holocausts Happen: The United States in Central America* (Philadelphia: Temple University Press, 1990).

64. Quoted in Levkov, " 'Your Place Is with the Victims,' Wiesel Tells Reagan," 42.

65. Ibid., 43.

66. Ibid., 44.

67. Wiesel recognized the public power of this encounter: "Never before and only rarely afterward did I receive so much mail, extraordinary not only by its volume but by its content. By standing up to the most powerful man in the world, the former refugee in me had in just a few minutes touched a thousand times more people than I had with all my previous writings and speeches." Wiesel, *And the Sea Is Never Full*, 240.

68. For example, journalist M. J. Rosenberg stated: "Think of the cabinet members over the decades who—after resigning over a policy dispute—have stood before the cameras and announced that they were leaving government because of their health or their desire to practice law. . . . Think of all the people who, determined to address the president on a moral issue, backed off as the aura of the White House stifled their protest." Quoted in Charles Silberman, *A Certain People: American Jews and Their Lives Today* (New York: Summit, 1985), 361. Silberman agreed that Wiesel's "speaking truth to power" was a phenomenal moment in American

Jewish history. Wiesel speech also elicited a few highly critical responses for not showing enough deference to Reagan; see, for instance, Jacob Neusner's reprimand of Wiesel in his "Reagan Did Better than Wiesel," in Levkov, *Bitburg and Beyond,* 386–387. For his strong criticism of those Jews who feared confrontation, see Wiesel, *And the Sea Is Never Full,* 235.

69. Wiesel, *And the Sea Is Never Full,* 239.

70. In his study of Guatemalan Nobel Peace Laureate Rigoberta Menchú, David Stoll noted the dynamics around such icons: "Whether an icon is good or bad depends on your opinion of how it is used, that is, the practical result of its aura of unchallengeability. . . . The aura of unchallengeability around an icon plays both ways: Although it brings people together in a common cause, it can also discourage questions that need to be asked, prevent lessons from being learned, and redound against the movement it represents." David Stoll, *Rigoberta Menchú and the Story of All Poor Guatemalans* (Boulder, CO: Westview, 1998), 246.

71. Bob Costas, "A Wound that Will Never Be Healed: An Interview with Elie Wiesel," in *Telling the Tale: A Tribute to Elie Wiesel: On the Occasion of His 65th Birthday—Essays, Reflections, and Poems,* ed. Harry James Cargas (St. Louis, MO: Time Being, 1993), 152–153.

72. For more on this theme, see Edward S. Herman's essay, "Politically Correct Holocausts," in idem, *The Triumph of the Market: Essays in Economics, Politics, and the Media* (Boston: South End, 1995), 103–110.

73. See his self-criticism as chairman in Wiesel, *And the Sea Is Never Full,* 247.

74. Miller, *One, by One, by One,* 227–228.

75. Quoted in Linenthal, *Preserving Memory,* 136.

76. For a critical review of how Wiesel's supporters "lobbied" for him to receive the prize, including the drive to secure greater social recognition from, among other political bodies, the U.S. Senate, see Jacob Weisberg, "Pop Goes Elie Wiesel," *The New Republic,* 10 November 1986, 12–13. For a more general appraisal of the Nobel Committee's selections in the field of literature (for which Wiesel also had been nominated several times), see George Steiner, "The Scandal of the Nobel Prize," *The New York Times Book Review,* 30 September 1984, 1.

77. Weisberg, "Pop Goes Elie Wiesel," 13.

78. One example is the awarding of the 1996 Nobel Peace Prize to Bishop Carlos Belo and José Ramos-Horta of East Timor for their work on behalf of peace and justice for the East Timorese people. Invariably, Indonesian officials were miffed, given that such attendant publicity would only be negative in light of their twenty-one year occupation of the former Portuguese colony.

79. Quoted in Carol Rittner, R.S.M., "Foreword," in *Elie Wiesel: Between Memory and Hope,* ed. Carol Rittner, R.S.M. (New York: New York University Press, 1990), x.

80. Elie Wiesel, "The Nobel Address," in idem, *From the Kingdom of Memory: Reminiscences* (New York: Summit, 1990), 233.

81. Ibid., 234.

82. Ibid., 234–235. Emphasis Wiesel's.

83. See Jane Hunter, *Israeli's Foreign Policy: South Africa and Central America* (Boston: South End, 1987).

84. Wiesel on the Nobel's influence: "There is prestige in having a movie star to dinner, or a Nobel Prize winner on one's roster of speakers. It is both chic and serious. You are asked to name your terms. You travel first-class or on the Concorde. You stay in luxury hotels. Rewarded for your activities or your work, you no longer have the time to pursue them." Wiesel, *And the Sea Is Never Full*, 288.

85. Quoted in John Rockwell, "2 New Citadels of Lofty Thoughts," *New York Times*, 30 January 1993, A13.

86. See Elie Wiesel and John Cardinal O'Connor, *A Journey of Faith* (New York: Donald I. Fine, Inc., 1990) and François Mitterand and Elie Wiesel, *Memoir in Two Voices*, trans. Richard Seaver and Timothy Bent (New York: Arcade, 1996).

87. See Carde Samdep, "An Open Letter from Nobel Peace Laureates on the Fifth Anniversary of Aung San Suu Kyi's Arrest," *New York Review of Books*, 22 September 1994, 76.

88. Wiesel, *And the Sea Is Never Full*, 388. Wiesel's self-criticism on Bosnia could also be applied to Palestine in the 1990s or much earlier. In this light, consider Edward Said's remarks from 1979: "Precisely those liberals who discover causes and outrages everywhere simply have nothing to say about [Menachem] Begin, about torture in Israel, or about the literally unstoppable annexationist policies of the Israeli state." Edward W. Said, *The Question of Palestine*, upd. ed. (New York: Vintage, 1992), 44.

89. See Rabia Ali and Lawrence Lifschultz, eds., *Why Bosnia? Writings on the Balkan War* (Stony Creek, CT: Pamphleteer's, 1993); Roy Gutman, *A Witness to Genocide* (New York: Lisa Drew, 1993); and David Rieff, *Slaughterhouse: Bosnia and the Failure of the West* (New York: Simon and Schuster, 1995).

90. Wiesel, *And the Sea Is Never Full*, 388. On the importance of print and television images of the camps and emaciated prisoners in triggering Holocaust analogies, see Jeffrey Shandler, *While America Watches: Televising the Holocaust* (New York: Oxford University Press, 1999), 240–245.

91. Ibid., 390.

92. Ibid., 392.

93. Ibid., 393.

94. Ibid., 395.

95. Elie Wiesel "Shadows in the Camps," *New York Times*, 25 February 1993, A19.

96. Ibid.

97. Quoted in Linenthal, *Preserving Memory*, 263.

98. Wiesel, *And the Sea Is Never Full*, 395. See also Elie Wiesel, foreword to *The Tenth Circle of Hell: A Memoir of Life in the Death Camps of Bosnia*, by Rezak Hukanovic, trans. Colleen London and Midhat Ridjanovic (New York: Basic Books, 1996), v–ix.

99. Rieff, *Slaughterhouse*, 27.

100. Thomas Cushman and Stjepan G. Mestrovic, eds., *This Time We Knew: Western Responses to Genocide in Bosnia* (New York: New York University Press, 1996).

101. See "Remarks by the President and Elie Wiesel in a Statement from the Oval Office," 13 December 1995, www.pub.whitehouse.gov/uri-res/I2R?urn:pdi://

oma.eop.gov.us/1995/12/14/5.text.1. All subsequent quotations from Wiesel and Clinton in this section come from this source.

102. Wiesel, *And the Sea Is Never Full*, 199–200.

103. See Stephen Rosskamm Shalom, *Imperial Alibis: Rationalizing U.S. Intervention after the Cold War* (Boston: South End, 1993) and William Blum, *Killing Hope: U.S. Military and CIA Intervention since World War II* (Monroe, ME: Common Courage, 1995).

104. Quoted in Elli Wohlgelernter, "Fears for the Future," *The Jerusalem Post Internet Edition*, 26 May 1997, www.jpost.com/com/Archive/26.May.1997/Features/Article-9.html.

105. Diego Ibarguen, "Hundreds Pack Anti-Impeachment Rally at NYU," *Nando Times News*, 15 December 1998, www.nando.net/nt/special/nyu1214.html.

106. Elie Wiesel, "The Perils of Indifference: Lessons Learned from a Violent Century," 12 April 1999, www.whitehouse.gov./WH/New/html/19990413-850.html. Subsequent quotations from Mrs. Clinton and Wiesel come from this source.

107. See Tariq Ali, ed., *Masters of the Universe? NATO'S Balkan Crusade* (London: Verso, 2000), and Noam Chomsky, *The New Military Humanism: Lessons from Kosovo* (Monroe, ME: Common Courage, 1999).

108. "An Interview with Elie Wiesel," *Tikkun* 14:4 (May–June 1999), 33–34.

109. On Turkey, see Stephen R. Shalom, "Reflections on NATO and Kosovo," www.zmag.org, Crisis Sections: Kosovo. For background, see John Tirman, *Spoils of War: The Human Cost of America's Arms Trade* (New York: Free Press, 1997).

110. "An Interview with Elie Wiesel," 33–34. Despite Wiesel's insistence on seeing the NATO war as indisputably moral, President Clinton also articulated other motives for engagement on March 23, that the United States had a strong interest in "a Europe that is safe, secure, free, united, a good partner with us for trading; . . . and someone who will share the burdens of taking care of the problems of the world. . . . Now . . . that's what this Kosovo thing is all about." Quoted in Alex Callinicos, "The Ideology of Humanitarian Intervention" in Ali, *Masters of the Universe?*, 176.

111. "Text of a Report from Elie Wiesel to the President of the United States," www.fas.org/man/dod-101/ops/docs99/990609-kosovo-wh3.htm.

112. See Chomsky, *The New Military Humanism*, 20–21.

113. Alvin Gouldner described this discourse as follows: "The culture of critical discourse is characterized by speech that is *relatively* more *situation-free*, more context or field 'independent.'. . . The culture of critical speech requires that the validity of claims be justified without reference to the speaker's *societal position or authority.* . . . Most importantly, the culture of critical speech forbids reliance upon the speaker's person, authority, or status in society to justify his claims. As a result, [the culture of critical discourse] de-authorizes all speech grounded in traditional societal authority, while it authorizes itself, the elaborated speech variant of the culture of critical discourse, as the standard of *all* 'serious speech.' " See Alvin W. Gouldner, *The Future of Intellectuals and the Rise of the New Class* (New York: Seabury, 1979), 28–29. Emphases Gouldner's.

114. Walter Benjamin, "Theses on the Philosophy of History," in idem, *Illuminations: Essays and Reflections*, ed. Hannah Arendt, trans. Harry Zohn (New York:

Schocken, 1969), 256. Consider Edward Said who offered a similar view in that "the role of the intellectual is that of testifying: he/she testifies against the misuses of history or against the injustices that befall the oppressed. I should add that he/she must be a rebel against power and against prevailing ideas. The intellectual must raise doubts about the illusions of the status quo, all that is tyrannical in society, especially for the sake of the deprived and the oppressed." See "Interview with Edward Said by Abdullah al-Sinnawi" in Edward W. Said, *Peace and Its Discontents: Essays on Palestine in the Middle East Peace Process* (New York: Vintage, 1996), 184. For further elaboration, see Edward W. Said, *Representations of the Intellectual: The 1993 Reith Lectures* (New York: Pantheon, 1994).

115. In his memoirs, Wiesel told the story of one General Palmer organizing a special honorary parade for him at West Point: "I am astounded: This whole parade is mine? What am I to do with it? Four thousand cadets, their sparkling uniforms and banners flapping in the wind, salute me as if I were a head of state. The Jewish child in me thinks he is dreaming. Never in my life have I been a soldier. And suddenly these future officers—perhaps generals—looking grave and solemn, do me the honors reserved for a president." Wiesel, *And the Sea Is Never Full*, 147.

Notes to Chapter Six

1. Elie Wiesel, *Zalmen, or The Madness of God*, trans. Nathan Edelman (New York: Schocken, 1985) and Elie Wiesel, "The Story of Zalmen," in idem, *Against Silence: The Voice and Vision of Elie Wiesel*, ed. Irving Abrahamson (New York: Holocaust Library, 1985), 3: 97.

2. See Peter Dews, ed., *Autonomy and Solidarity: Interviews with Jürgen Habermas*, rev. enl. ed. (London: Verso, 1992), 225–227.

3. See Johann Baptist Metz, "Christians and Jews after Auschwitz," in idem, *The Emergent Church: The Future of Christianity in a Postbourgeois World*, trans. Peter Mann (New York: Crossroad, 1986), 17–33 and idem, "Facing the Jews: Christian Theology after Auschwitz" in idem and Jürgen Moltmann, *Faith and the Future: Essays on Theology, Solidarity, and Modernity* (Maryknoll, NY: Orbis, 1995), 38–48.

4. Johann-Baptist Metz, "The Future in the Memory of Suffering," in Metz and Moltmann, *Faith and the Future*, 15–16. For a juxtaposition of Metz and Wiesel's views, see Ekkehard Schuster and Reinhold Boschert-Kimming, *Hope against Hope: Johann-Baptist Metz & Elie Wiesel Speak Out on the Holocaust*, trans. J. Matthew Ashley (Mahwah, NJ: Paulist, 1999). German philosopher Jürgen Habermas also addressed this need for exacting remembrance: "First, there is the obligation incumbent upon us in Germany—even if no one else were to feel it any longer—to keep alive, without distortion and not only in an intellectual form, the memory of the suffering of those who were murdered by German hands. It is especially these dead who have a claim to the weak anamnestic power of a solidarity that later generations can continue to practice only in the medium of a remembrance that is repeatedly renewed, often desperate, and continually on one's mind. If we were to brush aside this Benjaminian legacy, our fellow Jewish citizens and the sons, daughters, and grandchildren of all those who were murdered would feel themselves unable to

breathe in our country. . . . The current debate, however, concerns not an indebted memory but the more narcissistic question of the attitude we are to take—for our own sakes—toward our own traditions. If we do not resolve this question without illusions, remembrance of the victims will also become a farce." Jürgen Habermas, "On the Public Use of History" in idem, *The New Conservatism: Cultural Criticism and the Historian's Debate*, ed. and trans. Shierry Weber Nicholsen (Cambridge, MA: MIT Press, 1989), 233–234.

5. Elie Wiesel, "The Nobel Lecture," in idem, *From the Kingdom of Memory: Reminiscences* (New York: Summit, 1990), 249.

6. Elie Wiesel, *And the Sea Is Never Full: Memoirs 1969–*, trans. Marion Wiesel (New York: Alfred A. Knopf, 1999), 96.

7. Daniel McGowan and Marc H. Ellis, eds., *Remembering Deir Yassin: The Future of Israel and Palestine* (New York: Olive Branch, 1998).

8. See Daniel A. McGowan, "Elie Wiesel and the Sound of Silence," *The Link* 29: 4 (September–October 1996), 8–9. However, in a 1975 exchange of letters in the *New York Times Book Review* with Paul Good, Wiesel did make a reference to the Deir Yassin massacre: "Mr. Good seems to be sad that only 11 Jews were killed in Munich—while 254 Arabs were slain by Irgun and Stern members in 1948. He should learn that there are certain analogies that must not be made. No Jewish fighter—no Jewish terrorist—ever massacred children, any children, in cold blood, as Arafat's guerrillas did in Maalot." Elie Wiesel, "Blood of Israel," *New York Times Book Review*, 13 July 1975, 40. Consider, though, Edward Said's recollection: "My aunt and her daughter in particular had been in Jerusalem (about four kilometers away from Deir Yassin) at the time [9 April 1948], but had heard only the desperate and horrified accounts of the ordeal of those 250 men, women, and children—innocents all of them—ruthlessly murdered in cold blood by 'the Jew,' as everyone called them. More than any single occurrence in my memory of that difficult period it was Deir Yassin that stood out in all its awful and intentional fearsomeness—the stories of rape, of children with throats slit, mothers disemboweled, and the like." Edward W. Said, "Deir Yassin Recalled," in idem, *The End of the Peace Process: Oslo and After* (New York: Pantheon, 2000), 157.

9. "An Interview with Elie Wiesel," *Tikkun* 14: 4 (May–June 1999), 34.

10. A contrary, recent example in Israel was the showing of "'Tkuma'" on Israeli television, which took a much more critical look at Israeli history. In the Israeli newspaper *Haaretz*, Aryeh Caspi observed, "Showing 'Tkuma' forces us to deal with the moral dimension of the conflict and to remember facts that we would like to forget. The anger at 'Tkuma' is because we don't want to know and we can't bear the sense of guilt. The establishment of the State of Israel was justice for the Jews, but it was accompanied by a terrible injustice for the Palestinians." Quoted in Joel Greenberg, "Israel's History, Viewed Candidly, Starts a Storm," *New York Times*, 10 April 1998, A8.

11. Alice Eckardt, "We Are Called to Remember in Worship: Creating Christian Yom HaShoah Liturgies" in *Liturgies on the Holocaust: An Interfaith Anthology*, ed. Marcia Sachs Littell (Lewiston, NY: Edwin Mellen, 1986). For further reflections suitable for incorporating into such liturgies, see also Elie Wiesel and Albert H. Friedlander, *The Six Days of Destruction: Meditations toward Hope* (Mahwah, NJ: Paulist, 1988).

12. Harry James Cargas, "A Holocaust Commemoration for Days of Remembrance for Communities, Churches, Centers and for Home Use" in Sachs Littell, *Liturgies on the Holocaust*, 19.

13. Franklin H. Littell, "The Language of Liturgy," in Sachs Littell, *Liturgies on the Holocaust*, 10.

14. The Religious Task Force on Central America and Mexico offers resources on these annual events. See their website, www.igc.apc.org/rtfcam/. See also Joseph E. Mulligan, S.J., *The Jesuit Martyrs of El Salvador: Celebrating the Anniversaries* (Baltimore: Fortkamp, 1994).

15. Margaret Swedish, *Oscar Arnulfo Romero: Prophet to the Americas* (Washington, D.C.: Religious Task Force on Central America and Mexico, 1995). The quotation above is taken from the task force's website at www.igc.apc.org/rtfcam/romero.htm.

16. Quoted in Noam Chomsky, *Letters from Lexington: Reflections on Propaganda* (Monroe, ME: Common Courage, 1993), 71.

17. REMHI, *Guatemala: Never Again!* (Maryknoll, NY: Orbis, 1999). This is an abridged English translation of the four-volume Spanish report, *Guatemala: Nunca Más*.

18. See Thomas Quigley, "Foreword to the English Edition," in REMHI, *Guatemala: Never Again!*, xvi.

19. Monsenor Juan Gerardi, "On the Occasion of the Presentation of the REMHI Report," in REMHI, *Guatemala: Never Again!*, xxv.

20. REMHI, *Guatemala: Never Again!*, xxxiii.

21. Quoted in Marc H. Ellis, *Toward a Jewish Theology of Liberation: The Uprising and Beyond*, upd. ed. (Maryknoll, NY: Orbis, 1989), 35.

22. Ibid., 45.

23. See the essays in Noam Chomsky, *Deterring Democracy*, upd. ed. (New York: Hill and Wang, 1992).

24. See Paul Ricoeur, *Freud and Philosophy: An Essay in Interpretation*, trans. Denis Savage (New Haven, CT: Yale University Press, 1970), 32.

25. Elie Wiesel, "To Be a Jew," in idem, *A Jew Today*, trans. Marion Wiesel (New York: Vintage, 1979), 13–14.

26. Richard Falk, *Explorations at the Edge of Time: The Prospects for World Order* (Philadelphia: Temple University Press, 1992), 16.

27. Quoted in Ishai Menuchin, "Occupation, Protest, and Selective Refusal" in *Walking the Red Line: Israelis in Search of Justice for Palestine*, ed. Deena Hurwitz (Philadelphia: New Society, 1992), 81.

28. In what follows, I am indebted to the gripping study by James Cone, *Martin & Malcolm & America: A Dream or a Nightmare* (Maryknoll, NY: Orbis, 1991), 235–243.

29. Quoted in ibid., 237.

30. Quoted in ibid., 239.

31. Jack Nelson-Pallmeyer, *School of Assassins: The Case for Closing the School of the Americas and for Fundamentally Changing U.S. Foreign Policy* (Maryknoll, NY: Orbis, 1997).

32. See the School of the Americas Watch website at www.soaw.org.

33. Václav Havel, "The Power of the Powerless," in idem et al., *The Power of the Powerless: Citizens against the State in Central-Eastern Europe*, ed. John Keane (Armonk, NY: M.E. Sharpe, 1985), 23.

34. See Havel's essays and enthusiastic testimonies from his admirers in Václav Havel, *Living in Truth*, ed. Jan Vladislav (London: Faber and Faber, 1989).

35. Havel, "The Power of the Powerless," 31.

36. Ibid., 40.

37. Václav Havel, "An Anatomy of Reticence," in idem, *Living in Truth*, 192–193.

38. Havel, "The Power of the Powerless," 78–81.

39. One should note that there is plenty that can be done to help people struggling for life without going so far as to engage in civil disobedience and risk jail sentences. Historian Peter Novick points how ten million children die every year from preventable diseases. These children do not die at the hands of ethnic cleansing fanatics; they die because the world community—governments and citizens alike— do not trouble themselves to respond. Novick offers one simple and straightforward alternative to being bystander before such unnecessary mass death: "As concerns the children dying today, each of us individually (via OXFAM, UNICEF, or other agencies) can save not just one life but many, not in some one-time crisis, but every year. And doing so does not involve, as it did in occupied Europe, risking our own lives and the lives of others; at most it's a matter of forgoing some luxury we'd hardly miss." Novick, *The Holocaust in American Life*, 256–257. In 1989 Wiesel and dozens of other Nobel Laureates signed a "Manifesto against Extermination by War and Hunger," which decries the social arrangements that allow millions to die from starvation and underdevelopment. The manifesto observed: "An unprecedented holocaust, whose horror includes in a single year all the horror of the exterminations which our generations saw in the first half of the century, is still happening today and continuing to widen, every moment that passes, the perimeter of barbarities and death in the world, no less than in our consciences." See the full text and signers at www.riformatori.st.it/english/tnrs/npwinapp.htm.

40. See essays collected in Nathan A. Scott, Jr., and Ronald A. Sharp, eds., *Reading George Steiner* (Baltimore: Johns Hopkins University Press, 1994).

41. George Steiner, *Language and Silence: Essays on Language, Literature, and the Inhuman* (New York: Atheneum, 1967), ix.

42. See George Steiner, "A Kind of Survivor," in idem, *Language and Silence*, 140–154. Steiner dedicated the essay to Elie Wiesel.

43. George Steiner, "Jewish Values in the Post-Holocaust Future: A Symposium," *Judaism* 16 (Spring 1967): 285–286. Emphasis Steiner's.

44. See Berel Lang, *Heidegger's Silence* (Ithaca, NY: Cornell University Press, 1996).

45. Walter Benjamin, *Illuminations: Essays and Reflections*, ed. Hannah Arendt, trans. Harry Zohn (New York: Schocken, 1969), 255.

46. "Unworthy prophets," those who resist state power (for example, Havel), can expect neither honor nor praise from the agents of the state or, very likely, the mainstream media. One example of such an "unworthy prophet" in the United States is the Jesuit priest Daniel Berrigan, a committed peace activist who threw his

lot in with the victims of U.S. power and has resisted the violence of U.S. nuclear policy and intervention abroad. See, among many works, Daniel Berrigan, S.J., *Steadfastness of the Saints: A Journal of Peace and War in Central and North America* (Maryknoll, NY: Orbis, 1985). See also the testimonies to Berrigan's practice of peacemaking and solidarity in John Dear, S.J., ed., *Apostle of Peace: Essays in Honor of Daniel Berrigan* (Maryknoll, NY: Orbis, 1996).

47. See Arthur Hertzberg, "An Open Letter to Elie Wiesel," reprinted in *Beyond Occupation: American Jewish, Christian, and Palestinian Voices for Peace*, eds. Rosemary Radford Ruether and Marc H. Ellis (Boston: Beacon, 1990), 125–131.

48. Ibid., 126.

49. Ibid., 130. Israeli novelist A. B. Yehoshua was also critical of Wiesel in an interview with Michael Lerner: "I watched with amazement how the world honored Elie Wiesel as somehow a prophet of morality, and how simultaneously Wiesel managed to fail to criticize Israeli policy in the territories. Elie Wiesel, after winning the Nobel Prize, had a moral responsibility to speak out against the policies of the State of Israel while Israel is trying to impose on 1,700,000 Palestinians a permanent position of noncitizenship. . . . I'm a friend of Wiesel's and I like him, and I know the important work he once did to promote an awareness of the Holocaust two decades ago; but I cannot accept his silence. He speaks about 'The Jews of Silence.' But *he* is now a Jew of silence. He cannot ask others to speak up about other situations of oppression and then remain silent when he can clearly see what is happening on the West Bank. If he were a right-winger who thought that Israel should hold onto the West Bank, at least I could understand his position. But he is a dove at heart, so he should be speaking clearly. You cannot be ambiguous in this kind of situation at this kind of historical moment." Michael Lerner, "Jewish Neurosis in Israel and the Diaspora: A Conversation with A. B. Yehoshua," *Tikkun* 5: 5 (1990), 34. Emphasis Yehoshua's.

50. Ibid. In reflecting on a critical speech he had planned to give in Israel but did not, Wiesel took a different view toward such prophetic criticism: "I still don't understand my inability to criticize Israel. Perhaps I am guided by the readings of the biblical and talmudic commentaries. Is it not said that even our teacher Moses was punished for having been too harsh with our people?" Wiesel, *And the Sea Is Never Full*, 65. See the prophet Jeremiah for a different perspective on harshness.

51. Wiesel, *And The Sea Is Never Full*, 361.

52. See Ramsey Clark, *The Fire This Time: U.S. War Crimes in the Gulf* (New York: Thunder's Mouth, 1994).

53. See the collection of essays by Anthony Arnove, ed., *Iraq under Siege: The Deadly Impact of Sanctions and War* (Cambridge, MA: South End, 2000).

54. Quoted in Noam Chomsky, *The New Military Humanism: Lessons from Kosovo* (Monroe, ME: Common Courage, 1999), 67.

55. See the website of Voices in the Wilderness for resources and updates, www.nonviolence.org/vitw/.

56. Phyllis Bennis and Denis J. Halliday, interviewed by David Barsamian, "Iraq: The Impact of Sanctions and US Policy," in Arnove, *Iraq under Siege*, 45.

57. For background, see Kevin Danaher, ed., *50 Years Is Enough: The Case against the World Bank and the International Monetary Fund* (Boston: South End, 1994); Jerry Mander and Edward Goldsmith, eds., *The Case against the Global Economy: And for a*

Turn toward the Local (San Francisco: Sierra Club, 1996); and Michel Chossudovsky, *The Globalisation of Poverty: Impacts of IMF and World Bank Reforms* (London: Zed, 1997).

58. For a visionary ecofeminist perspective from Brazil, see Ivone Gebara, *Longing for Running Water: Ecofeminism and Liberation*, trans. David Molineaux (Minneapolis: Fortress, 1999).

59. Edward W. Said, *Representations of the Intellectual: The 1993 Reith Lectures* (New York: Pantheon, 1994), 35. On Said, see Michael Sprinker, ed., *Edward Said: A Critical Reader* (Cambridge, MA: Blackwell, 1992).

60. For critical perspectives on modernity from liberation philosophy, see Enrique Dussel, *The Invention of the Americas: Eclipse of "the Other" and the Myth of Modernity*, trans. Michael D. Barber (New York: Continuum, 1995) and idem, *The Underside of Modernity: Apel, Ricoeur, Rorty, Taylor, and the Philosophy of Liberation*, trans. and ed. Eduardo Mendieta (Atlantic Highlands, NJ: Humanities Press International, 1996). For detailed analyses, see Noam Chomsky, *Year 501: The Conquest Continues* (Boston: South End, 1993); idem, *World Orders Old and New*, 2d ed. (New York: Columbia University Press, 1996); and idem, *Profit over People: Neoliberalism and Global Order* (New York: Seven Stories, 1999).

61. Falk, *Explorations at the Edge of Time*, 33. On the controversy over the Smithsonian exhibit pertaining to Hiroshima and Nagasaki in 1995 on the fiftieth anniversary of the attack, see Edward T. Linenthal and Tom Engelhardt, eds., *History Wars: The Enola Gay and Other Battles for the American Past* (New York: Metropolitan Books/Henry Holt, 1996).

62. See Robert S. McNamara, *In Retrospect: The Tragedy and Lessons of Vietnam* (New York: Times, 1995).

63. James E. Young, *The Texture of Memory: Holocaust Memorials and Meaning* (New Haven, CT: Yale University Press, 1993), 21, 353.

64. See the website devoted to remembering the twenty-fifth anniversary of the end of the Vietnam War, www.vietnam25.org.

65. Quoted in Edward T. Linenthal, *Preserving Memory: The Struggle to Create America's Holocaust Museum* (New York: Viking, 1995), 266.

66. One can gain a different perspective from that easily available in the mainstream by attending to such testimonies as Jean-Bertrand Aristide, *In the Parish of the Poor: Writings from Haiti* (Maryknoll, NY: Orbis, 1990); Jennifer Harbury, *Bridge of Courage: Life Stories of the Guatemalan Compañeros and Compañeras* (Monroe, ME: Common Courage, 1994); Constâncio Pinto and Matthew Jardine, *East Timor's Unfinished Struggle: Inside the Timorese Resistance* (Boston: South End, 1997); Mev Puleo, *The Struggle Is One: Voices and Visions of Liberation* (Albany: State University of New York Press, 1994); Mitri Raheb, *I Am a Palestinian Christian*, trans. Ruth C. L. Gritsch (Minneapolis: Fortress, 1995); Maria Teresa Tula, *Hear My Testimony: Maria Teresa Tula, Human Rights Activist of El Salvador*, ed. and trans. Lynn Stephen (Boston: South End, 1994); and Michele Turner, *Telling: East Timor, Personal Testimonies 1942–1992* (Kensington, Australia: New South Wales University Press, Ltd., 1992).

67. Elie Wiesel, *All Rivers Run to the Sea: Memoirs*, trans. Marion Wiesel (New York: Alfred A. Knopf, 1995), 320.

Index